Learning Latin

Third Edition

by Natalie Harwood

ALPHA

A member of Penguin Group (USA) Inc.

To my mother, who always believed I would write a book.
To my children and grandchildren, who continually shape my life in wonderful ways.
To my sister, who called me from New York.
To my brother and sister-in-law, for their great sense of humor.
To Miss Dorothy Rounds, who would have wanted to be known for publishing An Index to Festschriften. *For me, however, she will always be the dedicated Arlington High School Latin teacher who had a dress with sleeves like bat wings and who fell into the wastebasket while reading from* Apollonius Rhodius.

ALPHA BOOKS

Published by the Penguin Group

Penguin Group (USA) Inc., 375 Hudson Street, New York, New York 10014, USA

Penguin Group (Canada), 90 Eglinton Avenue East, Suite 700, Toronto, Ontario M4P 2Y3, Canada (a division of Pearson Penguin Canada Inc.)

Penguin Books Ltd., 80 Strand, London WC2R 0RL, England

Penguin Ireland, 25 St. Stephen's Green, Dublin 2, Ireland (a division of Penguin Books Ltd.)

Penguin Group (Australia), 250 Camberwell Road, Camberwell, Victoria 3124, Australia (a division of Pearson Australia Group Pty. Ltd.)

Penguin Books India Pvt. Ltd., 11 Community Centre, Panchsheel Park, New Delhi—110 017, India

Penguin Group (NZ), 67 Apollo Drive, Rosedale, North Shore, Auckland 1311, New Zealand (a division of Pearson New Zealand Ltd.)

Penguin Books (South Africa) (Pty.) Ltd., 24 Sturdee Avenue, Rosebank, Johannesburg 2196, South Africa

Penguin Books Ltd., Registered Offices: 80 Strand, London WC2R 0RL, England

Publisher: *Marie Butler-Knight*
Editorial Director: *Mike Sanders*
Managing Editor: *Billy Fields*
Acquisitions Editor: *Michele Wells*
Senior Production Editor: *Janette Lynn*
Copy Editor: *Keith Cline*

Cartoonist: *Richard King*
Book Designers: *Kurt Owens and Trina Wurst*
Cover Designer: *Bill Thomas*
Indexer: *Tonya Heard*
Layout: *Ayanna Lacey*
Proofreader: *Aaron Black*

Contents at a Glance

Contents

Foreword

The Complete Idiot's Guide to Learning Latin, now in its third edition, is a new and fresh approach to a subject of practically unlimited possibilities. While producing a substantial survey of grammar and vocabulary in an amusing and attractive format, Natalie Harwood has liberated Latin from its narrow focus on a handful of ancient authors and texts. This guide introduces the reader to the whole range Latin has occupied in Western civilization—from antique myths to modern medicine and law, from generals and emperors to comebacks and mottoes, from love poetry and drinking songs to hymns and Christmas carols. Natalie Harwood shows the pervasiveness of Latin in the Western world, a pervasiveness that continues in the twenty-first century in the numerous professional vocabularies that depend on Latin.

Although all the major components of Latin syntax and morphology are included, they are usually followed by a *"But hey, forget all that!* All you really need to remember is ..." Ms. Harwood's many years of experience teaching Latin show in her deft presentation, in an accessible and fun manner, of one of the most feared topics in the curriculum. Various sidebars give clever mnemonics for vocabulary, brief historical and cultural sketches, study tips, and "Hysteria's Herstory"—accounts of famous Roman women to balance the picture of the mostly male history. All this supplementary material has been chosen carefully to integrate the grammar and vocabulary with the study of Roman and medieval culture. From the beginning to the end, Natalie Harwood's exuberant sense of humor makes the whole enterprise a delight.

Answers to all exercises and Latin translations are given in a key so readers can work through the text by themselves and check their own work. A complete glossary of the 2,400 Latin words introduced in the text is complemented by an English–Latin glossary to help readers write their own compositions. There is something here for everyone—those who studied Latin years ago and would like to revisit the old friend, those who never studied Latin and thought they had missed their chance, and even Latin teachers who are looking for fresh ideas and approaches to this rich subject.

The presentation moves sensibly from words to phrases to sentences to interesting selections from ancient and medieval authors that show how very modern the issues and problems that puzzled generations of Latin writers are. Authors of selections include Terence, Caesar, Cicero, Vitruvius, Pliny, the Vulgate, Augustine, and many more.

If you thought Latin was a dead language that required more effort than it could be worth—*Tolle! Lege!* (Take! Read!). *The Complete Idiot's Guide to Learning Latin* was written for you!

Stephen A. Nimis
Professor of Classics
Miami University
Oxford, Ohio

Introduction

Latin, a dead language? Doctors use Latin—*vertebra, fibula, humerus, patella.* Lawyers use Latin—*nolo contendere, habeas corpus, res iudicata, subpoena.* Architects use Latin—*tympanum, basilica, post, lintel.* You use Latin when you buy a car—*Aurora, Saturn, Maxima*—when you write a research paper—*ibid, idem, et al.*—when you exchange money—*annuit coeptis, e pluribus unum*—when you go to church—*mea culpa, pater noster*—or when you're just sitting around the house watching old movies such as *Spartacus* or *Julius Caesar.*

Perhaps you want to know what the Latin actually means. Perhaps you want to read the words of Caesar, Cicero, and other writers from 2,000 years ago. Perhaps you're in Latin I class and are wondering how to ace it. Perhaps you're an advanced Latin student but were sleeping when everyone else learned the relative pronouns.

In any case, reading this book will help you review or learn from scratch the language that is basic to all the Romance languages. In the process you will learn history, improve your vocabulary, freshen up your English grammar, and maybe even have a little fun!

This Is Not (*Shudder*) a Latin Textbook!

This book is based on the premise that you can learn a language as an adult by imitating how you learned a language as a child. If you were a fairly normal child, you began speaking English (or your native language) one word at a time. Like most children, you did not come out with complete sentences at the age of 12 months. And you certainly didn't learn English by reciting grammar rules or memorizing lists of words.

So you approach learning Latin the same way. You start with single words; then combinations; then phrases, clauses, sentences; and finally paragraphs. I have tried to include words that have useful derivatives, words you can use at work, in the boardroom, or at a boxing match (*quite a pugilist!*).

I've tried to group words in interesting ways, rather than simply alphabetically. Nouns are listed as living things, places, and inanimate things. Verbs are grouped into very physical, slightly active, and couch potato states of being.

In broad strokes, here's what you'll find in this book:

Part 1, "Frequently Asked Questions," gives you useful rationalizations for not knowing Latin. The history of Latin is explained, and simple pronunciation guides help you speak Latin correctly. Finally, I give you plenty of reasons for learning Latin, just in case you have a dimwitted friend who laughs at you for reading this book. Remember, *stulti Latinam linguam rident* (fools laugh at the Latin language).

Part 2, "What's in a Word?" starts you off with handy nouns you can use every day. You learn about number, gender, and case (only the nominative and genitive), and you get lots of practice. Then you learn verbs (so your nouns can do something), objects, and adjectives so you can describe your nouns. After a few more necessities such as pronouns and time and place words—and lots of practice—you are ready to move on.

Part 3, "Expressing Yourself in Latin," expands your capabilities with infinitive phrases, prepositional phrases, and the notorious ablative absolute. Then we jump into relative clauses, purpose, and result clauses. The last two chapters of this part put to work all the previous lessons and give you a chance to review your English grammar. Remember complex, compound, and simple sentences?

Part 4, "Reading Latin—Selections from Ancient Authors," gives you, at last, some original Latin. Selections from Pliny, Cicero, Julius Caesar, Terence, and Vitruvius get you started reading authentic Latin and learning something about people who lived 2,000 years ago.

Part 5, "Coping With Latin in the Modern World," explores the Latin words and expressions that people working in the everyday world today experience. The historical background is explained and the actual meaning of some of the Latin words will leave you saying, "I always wondered what that really meant!" Lawyers, scientists, doctors, and even stay-at-home moms will find this section relevant.

Part 6, "Grammar Workbook," gives you more opportunity to work with what you've learned. The exercises in vocabulary, grammar, and translations in this final part help you hone your Latin skills.

Finally, the appendixes include vocabulary lists, grammatical summaries, selections from favorite authors, and answer keys.

How to Use This Book

If you're learning Latin from scratch, start with Chapter 1 and work through Parts 1 through 3. You can refer to Part 5 at your leisure, for those chapters do not require much grammatical know-how. You'll need to do Parts 1 through 3, however, before tackling the real Latin in Part 4.

Perhaps you know some Latin—you got through Latin II and then wimped out for French or Spanish in high school—and just want to freshen up your memory. Start at the beginning. However, because people have different amounts of Latin expertise, you may be able to skip the first declension nouns, for example, or just skim over the present tense. Most students begin to bog down in the third declension, and many leave the arena when faced with relative clauses and the subjunctive mood. This book should guide you through the rough spots with ease. Use the grammatical index to look up those irregular adjectives or the subjunctive mood that stumped you 30 years ago.

Extras (a Latin Word That Means "Outside the Usual")

In addition to Latin vocabulary, grammatical explanations, impressive polysyllabic additions to your vocabulary, practice exercises, and Latin selections, you will find even more information by reading the sidebars sprinkled throughout the text:

Tene Memoria

This sidebar reminds you to memorize a few important details. It also refreshes your memory of important points from previous chapters.

Cave!

This sidebar describes ambiguities, pitfalls, and fraudulent cognates. It warns you of common mistakes many Latin students make and gives you tips on ways to avoid them.

Grammar Guru

This sidebar explains basic grammatical facts and gives mnemonic devices to help you remember.

Latin Today!

Here you'll find easy Latin words to take out into the world, whether it be on campus or in the workplace. Here you also find Latin words and expressions we use in our daily life perhaps without even realizing they are Latin. (The English pronunciation is included if it's different from the Latin.)

Hysteria's Herstory

Read this sidebar to learn more about gender-specific historical tidbits. Hitherto unknown facts and deeds of famous and not-so-famous women of the Roman world are highlighted in these boxes.

And if this weren't enough, you'll also find plenty of exercises throughout the book to help you evaluate your knowledge each step along the way. You won't be composing Ciceronian orations or Vergilian epic poetry by the time you're finished with this book, but you can expect to be able to read simple, real Latin and understand much more of the Latin you'll encounter in the modern world.

Special Thanks to the Technical Reviewer

The Complete Idiot's Guide to Learning Latin, Third Edition, was reviewed by an expert who double-checked the accuracy of what you'll learn here, to help us ensure that this book gives you everything you need to know about learning Latin. Special thanks are extended to Andrew Hagerty.

Andrew learned Latin at the Summer Latin Institute at the City University of New York (C.U.N.Y.) and continued his studies at New York University and the C.U.N.Y. Graduate School and University Center. He now teaches at Townsend Harris High School in Flushing, New York.

Trademarks

All terms mentioned in this book that are known to be or are suspected of being trademarks or service marks have been appropriately capitalized. Alpha Books and Penguin Group (USA) Inc. cannot attest to the accuracy of this information. Use of a term in this book should not be regarded as affecting the validity of any trademark or service mark.

Part  Frequently Asked Questions

When you carry this book in public, three things will happen to you. First, people will look at you quizzically as if you were an idiot.

"Latin?" they will say. "Don't you know it's a dead language?"

Second, they'll then try to show their erudition by spouting forth the little Latin they know, probably mangled irreparably from misuse since their high school days. Then they'll say, "It's Greek to me."

Finally, they'll launch into their favorite story about their Latin teacher and how she fell into the wastebasket or stood on a chair imitating Cicero.

Be prepared! *Semper Paratus!*

Why Learn Latin?

In This Chapter

- ◆ Latin—not the favorite of foreign languages
- ◆ Latin increases your English vocabulary
- ◆ Latin helps you learn about history
- ◆ Tips on pronouncing Latin
- ◆ You already know some Latin!

> Latin is a language
> Dead as it can be.
> First it killed the Romans
> And now it's killing me!

This age-old witticism is a good example of Latin's bad press. Why does everyone roll his or her eyes, groan, and grimace when you mention that you want to learn Latin? Inevitably, such nonfans of Latin will repeat the word in disbelief and peer at you as if you have lost your mind. *Latin?* Why on Earth?

Latin—the Bad Boy of Foreign Languages

Latin is so hard! Take French or Spanish instead! High school students perpetuate the myth that Latin is difficult to learn. But the truth is that learning Latin doesn't have to be arduous. Look at these words: *elephantus, dictator, navigator, Europa, Italia, intellegentia, gloria.* Are you having trouble translating those?

Latin is much easier than Japanese or Chinese. It has cultural and historical foundations that easily transfer to English. *Senator? Architectus?* What's so hard about that?

The first step in learning Latin is to rid yourself of the mindset that Latin will be difficult. Attitude is everything. Latin will be a breeze.

> ### Latin Today!
>
> *Words to take to class:* While sitting in class, casually jot down this easy Latin in English:
>
> professor (*proh-FESS-ohr*)
>
> doctor (*DOHK-tor*)
>
> classis (*KLAS-is*)
>
> atrium (*AH-tree-um*)

Dead but Not Forgotten

Languages, like people, have lives. Languages are born, grow, change, and exist to help people communicate. They live useful lives, spreading culture, making distinctions, and expressing emotions. Sometimes, like people, the language dies; and if nothing has been written, it becomes extinct. When the culture disappears, as with the Romans, but the language has been preserved, then the language is simply dead—gone, but not forgotten.

So why learn a dead language? English, still alive and kicking, changes all the time. Compare, for example, the language of Chaucer—*forsworn, hath*—with today's language—*Internet, rap.* Latin, the dead language, will not change because no one is using it every day to communicate. This is why science uses Latin. A genus name will be internationally understood and won't change over time.

Latin is old and classic, so people use it to give prestige to a name—Super Bowl XIX, the Nissan Maxima.

But the most important reason for learning Latin is so anyone from the twentieth century can read the words and, therefore, the minds and hearts of men and women who lived in the first century. Reading Latin authors brings history to life and perpetuates the miracle of a civilization that started on the shores of the Mediterranean Sea. Best of all, reading Latin reminds us that for 2,000 years—and we hope for 2,000 more to come—women get mad at their husbands, people keep fish as pets, and human beings are still trying to catch an elephant.

It's true that Latin is an inflected language. Different endings serve different purposes. German is inflected, too, and you don't see people crying about German being so difficult. The problem is that Latin textbooks give you all the endings at once. Memorize the first declension. Learn the perfect personal endings. In this book, I let the endings fend for themselves or just worm their way into your consciousness. And the ones that are hardly ever used, I just ignore.

Alumneye or *Alumnee?*

How do teachers know how to pronounce Latin? Obviously, they have no direct recordings of Romans hanging out in the Forum discussing the latest model of chariots. But scholars have extrapolated from written evidence—poetry, prose, and dialogue from plays—and they do have a reasonable idea of how Latin sounded. Luckily for you, most of the letters are pronounced exactly as in English. The exceptions include the following:

> *a* as in *ago;* with long mark ā as in *father*
>
> *e* as in *bed;* with long mark ē as in *late*
>
> *i* as in *bit;* with long mark ī as in *knee*
>
> *o* as in *often;* with long mark ō as in *dope*
>
> *u* as in u*s;* with long mark ū as in *you*

Grammar Guru

In many Latin textbooks, you'll find a diacritical mark, the macron (¯), used frequently over vowels. The long mark, as it is also called, alters the pronunciation and can affect the quantity of the syllable in poetry. There are also many texts, however, in which the macron is not used, and then you are left without your crutch. This book is not using the macron, and you will be better off in the long run. Learn to stand on your own two feet, diacritically speaking.

Sometimes two vowels are used together and have one sound. These are called diphthongs:

> *ae* as in *bye*
>
> *au* as in *now*
>
> *ei* as in *hey*
>
> *oe* as in *oil*

The consonants are pronounced as in English except the following:

   v as in *wine*

   c and *g* are always hard as in *car* and *game*

   j as in *yes*

There are more rules, of course, but these will get you started. Phonetic spelling (*foe-NET-ik SPEL-leeng*) is included for the first few chapters and for difficult words throughout the book. For the pronunciation of Ecclesiastical Latin, or the Latin you used to hear in church, see Chapter 22. Look for pronunciation guides in the front of any Latin dictionary if you're really into this sort of thing.

Two final questions: Who cares if I'm pronouncing correctly? And what about *alumni* (pronounced *ah-LUM-nee*) and *alumnae* (pronounced *ah-LUM-neye*)?

No Roman is around to give you a dirty look if you mispronounce a Latin word. But consistency is the key here. When you read, you often say the word, if not aloud, then mentally. Good readers hear as well as see the words. Beginning readers often move their lips as they read, perhaps sounding out the words. As you're learning Latin, you'll want to say as well as read the words, and consistency of the sounds makes the remembering easier.

One of the biggest problems facing Latin students today is that many words have become English: *senator, dictator, alumnus, alumna*. Do you use the English or the Latin pronunciation? My solution is to use the anglicized pronunciation when the word has become an English word. To put it another way, if the word is in the English dictionary, follow the dictionary phonetic spelling. So *alumni* becomes *alumneye* and *alumnae*, *alumnee*, using the English pronunciation. (See Chapter 23 for more Latin expressions in English and how to pronounce them.)

If, on the other hand, you're standing around with a bunch of Latin students and you're all speaking Latin, then, of course, you would say, *Alumnee bonee sunt* (Men who have graduated from this university are good).

> **Tene Memoria**
>
> It's a good idea to have a paperback Latin dictionary on hand when you're beginning to learn Latin. Latin words are notorious for having many different meanings, and you can check for the length of vowels, too.

Latin Words You Know Already

Because so many of the words in the English language came to us from Greek or Latin, you'll see the resemblance of many Latin words to their English counterparts.

Except for pronouncing *v*'s like *w*'s and *c*'s like *k*'s, Latin even sounds like the English. However, Romans tended to place the accent toward the end of the word, whereas English speakers, always eager and impetuous, tend to accent the first syllable they come to: we say *INdustry*, while the Latin is *inDUStria*; we say *VICtory* as opposed to *vicTORia*.

> **Cave!**
>
> Watch out for small changes in spelling. *Intelligence* is a good example. Knowing the Latin *inteLEGentia* might cause you to misspell *intelLIGence*. For the most part, Latin helps you remember your English spelling—but sometimes it can lead you astray.

Romans had three simple rules for determining when to stress the syllable. In a word of two syllables, the accent is on the first. In a word of three or more syllables, the accent falls on the next-to-last syllable if that syllable is long. Otherwise, the accent falls on the syllable before that.

How do you know when a syllable is long? The syllable is long if the vowel is long and if the vowel is a diphthong (two vowels, one sound, as in *inaures* [*ihn-OW-rays*]).

The following table lists some Latin words you know already.

Latin	English	Pronunciation
calamitas	calamity	*kah-LAH-mih-tahs*
causa	cause	*COW-sah*
clamor	clamor, noise	*KLAH-more*
cura	cure, care	*COO-rah*
discordia	discord	*dis-COR-dee-ah*
elephantus	elephant	*ell-eh-FAHN-toos*
est	is	*ehst*
Europa	Europe	*yoor-OH-pah*
forma	form	*FOR-mah*
fungus	mushroom	*FUN-gus*
gloria	glory	*GLOH-ree-ah*
hippopotamus	hippopotamus	*hip-poh-POT-ah-moos*
industria	industry	*in-DUS-tree-ah*
intellegentia	intelligence	*ihn-tehl-leh-GEN-tee-ah*

continues

continued

Latin	English	Pronunciation
Italia	Italy	*ee-TAHL-ee-ah*
nobilis	noble	*NOH-bihl-is*
non	not	*nohn*
palma	palm	*PAHL-mah*
populus	people	*POP-yoo-lus*
professor	teacher	*proh-FESS-or*
Roma	Rome	*ROH-mah*
senator	senator	*SEN-ah-tor*
tuba	tuba	*TOO-bah*
victoria	victory	*wick-TOR-ee-ah*
villa	villa, house	*WEEL-ah*
violentia	violence	*wee-oh-LENS-ee-ah*

The Latin language does not have definite and indefinite articles, so Romans didn't have to worry about whether to say *a* or *an*, and they never had to bother about that silly little word that clutters up our English sentences: *the*. When you translate, you have to put them in wherever you feel comfortable. For example, *Elephantus nobilis est* is not "Elephant is noble," but "An elephant is noble" or "The elephant is noble." Either one is correct and true.

The other huge difference about Latin is that more often than not the word order differs from English. In Latin, the verb is usually near the end of the sentence. For example, if you want to say "Rome is in Italy" in Latin, you'd say, *Roma in Italia est*, not *Roma est in Italia*.

Hysteria's Herstory

The word *hysteria* is from the Greek *hystera*, meaning "womb." An illness that manifests itself in violent movements of the arms and legs and wild, exaggerated facial expressions was thought to be caused by movements of the womb and, therefore, affected women only. This unfortunate fallacy persists to this day when it is said that women become hysterical, whereas men are merely excited.

Practice Makes Perfect

Practice reading the following sentences aloud. Then decide when, where, or whether ever to use *a/an* or *the* as you translate into English. The answers to this and all exercises are in Appendix D.

1. Senator hippopotamus non est.

2. Fungus nobilis est.

3. Roma in Europa est.

4. Roma in America non est.

5. Discordia calamitas est.

6. Victoria gloria est.

The Least You Need to Know

- Latin has an unjustified bad reputation.

- You won't have to memorize long lists of incomprehensible endings when learning Latin using this book.

- Many Latin words look exactly like English.

What Exactly Is Latin?

In This Chapter

- ◆ An examination of Indo-European roots
- ◆ The rise and fall of Rome in one paragraph
- ◆ A look at Late Latin
- ◆ You already know some Latin!

Latin has its roots in the Proto-Indo-European language spoken by the inhabitants of Latium (the central part of what is now Italy) from at least the eighth century B.C.E.

Latin became the language of Roman literature, which started with translations from the Greek and swiftly became the vehicle of original Roman poetry, prose, and drama. Livius Andronicus was the first to translate the *Odyssey* into Latin, around 200 B.C.E. Plautus was an early playwright, famous for *Aulularia, The Pot of Gold,* and other comedies. Cicero has left us many speeches, letters, and essays, among which are his famous *On Friendship* and *Old Age.* Julius Caesar wrote *The Gallic Wars,* a classic in every second-year Latin class. Vergil, of course, wrote *The Aeneid,* an oft-quoted epic poem on the glories of Rome. Horace and Juvenal wrote poetry and satires, and Ovid and Catullus are famous for their works on the art of love. The influence of these authors survived the Dark Ages and

Middle Ages and flourished during the Renaissance, and their ideas and works are found in every aspect of Western civilization.

Digging Up Your Indo-European Roots

Isn't English a Germanic language? Father—*Vater?* Mother—*Mutter?* Book—*Buch?* Why is it that so many words come from Latin?

Latin and German spring from the same parent language, Indo-European. Scholars believe that many thousands of years ago there was one language, probably in Eastern Europe, called Proto-Indo-European. Based on linguistic evidence, this language is the mother of Sanskrit, Hindi, Persian, Pashto, Lithuanian, Latvian, Russian, Polish, Serbo-Croatian, Armenian, Albanian, Greek, all Celtic languages, Latin, Italian, French, Spanish, Portuguese, Romanian, German, English, Dutch, and the Scandinavian languages. The earliest written Indo-European language is Hittite, from the seventeenth century B.C.E. Samples from other early languages such as Sanskrit and Greek show that all Indo-European languages were highly inflected (having different endings for different grammatical purposes).

> **Grammar Guru**
>
> Don't be put off by the grammatical concept of inflection. Remember that Indo-European speakers never heard of them, and they managed to learn their language just fine.

Romance Languages

When the Romans occupied Europe, including parts of Germany and the British Isles, much of Roman culture, including language, was assimilated by the native population. These languages were derived from Latin and became known as Romance languages.

Romance Languages

Latin	Italian	Spanish	French	English
liber	libro	libra	livre	book
tempus	tempo	tiempo	temps	time
bene	bene	bien	bien	well
facere	fare	hacer	faire	make, do
dicere	dire	decir	dire	say

Derivatives are listed throughout the book. These are words that have come down from Latin and have the same basic root and, thus, a related meaning. For example, the Latin *pono*, *ponere*, *posui*, *positus*, meaning "to put," gives us English words such as *deposit* (to put down), *composite* (to put together), *juxtapose* (to put next to), *interpose* (to put in between), and *predispose* (to put away before).

A Brief History of Rome

Latin is the language of the Latins, whose king, Latinus, welcomed Aeneas, the mythical hero and partly divine refugee from the Trojan War. With the help of Lavinia, Latinus's daughter, the Latins founded the Latin family. Romulus, one of their descendants, established a city and named it Rome after himself. Rome added suburbs, cities, and countries and eventually deposed its king and became a republic lasting roughly 500 years. Augustus took over, and Rome became an empire for another 500 years. Then it got so fat that it burst into two sections and self-destructed.

Hysteria's Herstory

Although there were many Roman women poets, the name of only one has survived to us, Sulpicia, circa 15 B.C.E. She wrote love poetry, of which 40 lines from 6 poems are extant. She probably remained single all her life and lived with her patron, Messalla. Her poetry, addressed to her lover, Cerinthus, is remarkably open and fervid. Here is an excerpt:

Tandem venit amor, qualem texisse pudori quam nudasse alicui sit mihi, Fama, magis.

At last love has come, of such quality that to cover it would be more shameful than to lay it bare.

Late Latin

Even after the fall of Rome in the sixth century, Latin continued to be spoken. In the Dark Ages, when the Christian church rose in stature, its adoption of Latin as the official language ensured the language's eternal life. Late Latin, also known as Medieval Latin or Church Latin, is the language of the European monasteries, cathedrals, and schools of the sixth to the sixteenth centuries. Late Latin includes all the new vocabulary necessary for the functioning of the church. Late Latin has also come down to us in the drinking songs of the Goliards, the wandering scholar-poets of the twelfth and thirteenth centuries. I've included some examples of these in Chapter 23.

More Latin Words You Already Know

The following words vary in grammatical type from nouns to adjectives to proper nouns; the English derivative comes to us almost untouched.

Remember that *v*'s are pronounced like *w*'s and all *a*'s are ah.

Latin	English	Pronunciation
architectus	architect	*ahr-kee-TEC-tus*
consul	consul	*KOHN-sool*
Ephesus	Ephesus	*EH-fee-soos*
humanus	human	*hoo-MAH-noos*
inferior	inferior	*een-FEER-ee-or*
magistratus	magistrate	*mah-gees-TRA-toos*
orator	orator	*OH-rah-tor*
privatus	private	*pree-WAH-toos*
publicus	public	*POO-bli-coos*
senatus	senate	*sehn-AH-toos*
silentium	silence	*sih-LEHN-tee-um*
superior	superior	*soo-PEER-ee-or*
toga	toga	*TOW-gah*
troglodyta	troglodyte	*troh-glow-DIH-tah*
universitas	university	*oon-ih-WEHR-sih-tahs*
vasum	vase	*WAH-sum*

Practice Makes Perfect 1

Match the opposites:

1. inferior
   (*in-FEH-ree-ohr*)

2. humanus
   (*hoo-MAH-nus*)

3. victoria
   (*wihk-TOH-ree-ah*)

4. publicus
   (*POO-blih-kus*)

5. clamor
   (*CLAH-mohr*)

calamitas
(*cah-LAH-mih-tahs*)

silentium
(*sih-LEHN-tee-um*)

superior
(*soo-PEH-ree-or*)

divinus
(*dih-WEE-nus*)

privatus
(*pree-WAH-tus*)

Some words that are identical in Latin and English have acquired connotations that would be quite foreign to a Roman. *Toga*, for example, a very short word for a very long garment, has come to be associated with wild fraternity parties. However, the original toga represented a personality just the opposite of the party animal. Beginning as a rectangular blanket wrapped around the body for warmth, it developed a certain style all its own.

Cave!

Ladies! Don't go to a toga party in a toga! Only men wore togas. Women wore a dress, a *stola*, and over it a plain length of material, draped as a stole, a *palla*.

Hysteria's Herstory

There are many Latin words used for work men do—*consul, senator, dictator, architectus*—but the work of women has been largely ignored in both language textbooks and history. Women of all classes worked at varied occupations. Lower-class women were handmaidens, attendants, hairdressers, fishmongers, and bath attendants. Upper-class women usually oversaw the household activities. They were also businesswomen, weavers, and poets.

Practice Makes Perfect 2

Read the following sentences aloud and then use the pattern to ask questions to a friend or your boss:

Esne consul? *(ess-nay KOHN-sul)*	Are you a consul?
Esne hippopotamus? *(ess-nay hih-poh-POH-tah-mus)*	Are you a hippopotamus?
Esne troglodyta? *(ess-nay troh-glow-DIH-tah)*	_____
Esne orator? *(ess-nay OH-rah-tor)*	_____
Esne senator? *(ess-nay SEH-nah-tor)*	_____

Latin Today!

Words to take to history class: Only your history professor may know about these:
lingua franca (*LIN-gwah FRAHN-kah; FRANK-ah* in English)
pax Augusta (*PAHKS aw-GUST-ah*)
pax Britannica (*PAHKS brih-TAN-ih-kah*)

The Least You Need to Know

♦ Latin, German, and English are Indo-European languages.

♦ The word *Latin* comes from a tribe, an area, and a king from central Italy, all of which begin with *Lat-*.

♦ Rome grew from a one-horse town to an empire and then collapsed.

♦ Latin used in the Middle Ages is called Late Latin.

Part 2

What's in a Word?

A single word can smile, laugh, cry, yell, and shout. It can sneer, humiliate, or praise. We start learning Latin in the following pages with single words, many of which you know already. *Superior.*

Some Latin words will be very similar to another language such as *mater* (*Mutter*, German), *bonus* (*bon*, French), or *aqua* (*agua*, Spanish). Single words can denote more than single subjects, such as men, women, or ideas. Finally, derivatives from these single words add color and excitement to your vocabulary—your mashed potatoes are *margaritaceous!*

3

People, Places, and Things

In This Chapter

- Declensions, word order, and conjugations
- First declension feminine nouns
- The nominative and genitive cases
- Second declension masculine and neuter nouns
- Fun with plurals

Words are powerful communicators. Edgar Allen Poe's raven drove a man to insanity with one word—*Nevermore!* Single words can command (*jump*), describe (*beautiful*), exclaim (*wow!*), or make a statement (*cool*). Put two words together, and you compound the meaning—*bulldog* and *feather-brain*. Words can also bore you to death—*antidisestablishmentarianism*.

The Romans used single words to make a point, many of which are still with us. Cicero said, "*O tempora, o mores,*" bewailing the lack of morals in then-modern times (65 B.C.E.). Julius Caesar's immortal words, "*Veni, vidi, vici,*" recall his world-famous military victories.

So let's start learning Latin with single words, many of which will ultimately appear in the Latin selections in Part 4 when you begin to read longer selections of real Latin. This first list names people, places, or things.

I include simple and not-so-simple derivatives to help you remember the Latin word and its meaning.

First-Declension Feminine Nouns

The first grammarians back in ancient times started out so logically: group together all the nouns ending in *a* and call them feminine, and because it's always ladies first, call these nouns the first declension. So far, so good.

Living Things and Their Parts

All nouns first appear in the nominative case ending in vocabulary lists. The nominative case shows the subject of a sentence. It is also used for the predicate noun, placed after a linking verb in English. The genitive case is always second and is translated *of* or *'s*.

Living Things and Their Parts

Nominative	Genitive	Meaning	Derivative
beta (*BEH-tah*)	betae (*BEH-teye*)	beet	betaine
cerevisia (*keh-reh-WHI-see-ah*)	cerevisiae	beer	cereal
cauda (*KOW-dah*)	caudae (*KOW-deye*)	tail	caudal
herba (*HEHR-bah*)	herbae (*HEHR-beye*)	grass	herbicide
hora (*HOH-rah*)	horae (*HOH-reye*)	hour	hour
hospita (*HOHS-pih-tah*)	hospitae (*HOHS-pih-teye*)	guest	hospice
malva (*MAHL-wah*)	malvae (*MAHL-weye*)	mallow	marshmallow
muraena (*moor-EYE-nah*)	muraenae (*moor-EYE-neye*)	eel	moray eel
ostrea (*OHS-treh-ah*)	ostreae (*OHS-treh-eye*)	oyster	oyster

Nominative	Genitive	Meaning	Derivative
perna (*PEHR-nah*)	pernae (*PEHR-neye*)	ham, thigh	pernio
turba (*TUR-bah*)	turbae (*TUR-beye*)	crowd	turbulent
vinea (*WHIN-ee-ah*)	vineae (*WHIN-ee-eye*)	vine	vine

When you come to the *coda* in your musical composition, remember it comes from the Latin *cauda*. And while you are standing in line at the bakery waiting to buy that last loaf of marble rye, you can entertain the people in the queue by reminding them that *queue* comes from *cauda*.

Remember your grandmother complaining about having chilblains? Another name for that redness of toes and pains in the legs associated with chilly weather is *pernio*, derived from the Latin word that means "leg, thigh, especially of a hog used for food." A bit of a stretch there, I'll admit.

Betaine refers to a salt contained in beet juice. It's edible, unlike a beta ray or radiation particle.

The *mallow* is a pinkish, purplish plant. The roots produce a sticky substance used in—of all things—the marshmallow!

Finally, beware the *moray*, described as brightly colored, often savage, voracious eel with narrow jaws and strong, knifelike teeth. Nice aquarium pet.

The good news is that all words designating females are feminine.

Nominative	Genitive	Meaning	Derivative
amica (*ah-MEE-kah*)	amicae (*ah-MEE-keye*)	girlfriend	amicable
capella (*kah-PEL-lah*)	capellae (*kah-PEL-leye*)	nanny goat	caper
dea (*DEH-ah*)	deae (*DEH-eye*)	goddess	deify
femina (*FEM-in-ah*)	feminae (*FEM-in-eye*)	woman	feminine

continues

continued

Nominative	Genitive	Meaning	Derivative
filia (*FEE-lee-ah*)	filiae (*FEE-lee-eye*)	daughter	filicide
hecyra (*heh-KEH-rah*)	hecyrae (*heh-KEH-reye*)	mother-in-law	—
puella (*poo-EHL-ah*)	puellae (*poo-EHL-eye*)	girl	—
serva (*SEHR-wah*)	servae (*SEHR-weye*)	female slave	servant

Places and Inanimate Things

Remember that even though these are places and things, in Latin they are considered grammatically feminine.

Nominative	Genitive	Meaning	Derivative
aqua (*AH-kwah*)	aquae (*AH-kweye*)	water	aquatic
barba (*BAHR-bah*)	barbae (*BAHR-beye*)	beard	barber
cena (*KAY-nah*)	cenae (*KAY-neye*)	dinner	cenacle
concha (*KOHN-kah*)	conchae (*KOHN-keye*)	shell	conch
epistula (*eh-PISS-too-lah*)	epistulae (*eh-PISS-too-leye*)	letter	epistle
impensa (*im-PEHN-sah*)	impensae (*im-PEHN-seye*)	cost	impending
insula (*EEN-soo-lah*)	insulae (*EEN-soo-leye*)	island	insulate
margarita (*mahr-gahr-EE-tah*)	margaritae (*mahr-gahr-EE-teye*)	pearl	margaritaceous
mensa (*MEHN-sah*)	mensae (*MEHN-seye*)	table	mensa

Nominative	Genitive	Meaning	Derivative
pecunia (*peh-KOON-ee-ah*)	pecuniae (*peh-KOON-ee-eye*)	money	pecuniary
pila (*PEE-lah*)	pilae (*PEE-leye*)	ball	——
piscina (*piss-KEE-nah*)	piscinae (*piss-KEE-neye*)	fishpond	piscine
poena (*POI-nah*)	poenae (*POI-neye*)	penalty	penal
solea (*SOH-le-ah*)	soleae (*SOH-le-eye*)	sandal	sole
terra (*TEHR-rah*)	terrae (*TEHR-reye*)	land	terrarium
vita (*WEE-tah*)	vitae (*WEE-teye*)	life	vital

A *cenacle*, by the way, is from the Latin *cena* and denotes the room where the Last Supper took place. It has also come to mean a religious retreat house. Feel free to use *margaritaceous* (*mahr-geh-reh-TAY-shuss*) at your next dinner party. You can apply it to the boiled onions or your dinner partner's teeth. It means "pearly white."

And it's not all right to call your Aunt Martha *piscene* (*PEYE-seen*) even though she breathes through her mouth and tends to roll her eyes like a tuna.

Hysteria's Herstory

Cornelia, wife of Sempronius Gracchus and mother of two political reformers, was famous for her virtuous conduct and devotion to her family. Once she was visiting with another Roman matron who was showing off her pearls and precious gems. "Where are your jewels?" asked the woman curiously. Proudly, Cornelia brought forth her two small sons and in a statement about as old as Eve said, "These are my jewels."

The Case of the Life of an Oyster

To review, Latin nouns are always listed with the first word in the nominative case, *ostrea*, and the second form in the genitive case, *ostreae*. The nominative case is used for the subject of a sentence, and the genitive case is used to show possession. In English, we use the 's or the preposition *of*. So *ostrea, ostreae,* would translate, "the oyster, of the oyster." Latin has no words for *the* or *a* or *an*, so you can throw them in wherever English would need them.

Practice Makes Perfect 1

Say aloud and translate. Remember that many of these expressions will show up in the Latin selections later on.

1. Vita ostreae
   (*WHEE-tah OHS-treh-eye*)   _____

2. Solea puellae
   (*SOH-leh-ah poo-EHL-eye*)   _____

3. Aqua Romae
   (*AH-kwah ROH-mah*)   _____

4. Cena herbae
   (*KAY-nah HEHR-beye*)   _____

5. Filia deae
   (*FEE-lee-ah DEH-eye*)   _____

Now try translating into Latin:

1. The grass of Rome   _____

2. Life of the girl   _____

3. The table of the caveman   _____

4. The pearl of the oyster   _____

5. A woman of the fishpond   _____

Second Declension Masculine and Neuter Nouns

The letter after the genitive case in the vocabulary list designates the gender. Most words for women are feminine; most words for men are masculine. The *n.* designates neuter, which is the Latin word for *neither*. So why in the world is *world* masculine? No one knows for sure. You can be sure, however, that all Latin words have gender, sensible or not.

Living Things and Their Parts—Masculine Nouns

The following list consists of masculine nouns. Bring them to your next party and be the *vita convivii* with such witticisms as "I have been otiose all week" or "The verbosity of a funambulist is elephantine."

Nominative	Genitive	Meaning	Derivative
amicus (*ah-MEE-kuhs*)	amici (*ah-MEE-kee*)	friend	amicable
coquus (*KOH-kwuhs*)	coqui (*KOH-kwee*)	cook	cook
deus (*DEH-uhs*)	dei (*DEH-ee*)	god	deify
discipulus (*dihs-KIH-pu-luhs*)	discipuli (*dihs-KIH-pu-lee*)	student	disciple
filius (*FEE-lee-uhs*)	filii (*FEE-lee-ee*)	son	filial
funambulus (*foo-NAM-boo-luhs*)	funambuli (*foo-NAM-boo-lee*)	tightrope walker	funambulist
Graecus (*GREYE-koos*)	Graeci (*GREYE-kee*)	a Greek	Greek
hircus (*HIHR-cus*)	hirci (*HIHR-kee*)	a billy goat	hircine
lautus (*LOW-tuhs*)	lauti (*LOW-tee*)	gourmet, gentleman	lavish
nasus (*NAH-suhs*)	nasi (*NAH-see*)	nose	nasal
nervus (*NEHR-wuhs*)	nervi (*NEHR-wee*)	nerve	nerve
populus (*POHP-yoo-luhs*)	populi (*POHP-yoo-lee*)	people	popular
pullus (*PUHL-luhs*)	pulli (*PUHL-lee*)	young animal, chicken	poultry
servus (*SEHR-wuhs*)	servi (*SEHR-wee*)	slave	servant
vir (*WHEER*)	viri (*WHEER-ee*)	man	virile

Lautus comes from the Latin *lavo*, "to wash." Additional meanings are "nicely turned out" and "sumptuous." So *gourmet*, in this context, means more of someone enjoying life to the fullest, rather than one who is an Epicurean expert.

Hircine means "smelling like a goat." Try to use this one only in reference to goats.

Of course, it may be difficult to enjoy life if you are *nasicorn*, that is, bearing a horn on the nose. The rhinoceros is a nasicorn animal. Unfortunately, so is Uncle Edwin.

Places and Things—Masculine Nouns

These places and things are grammatically masculine in Latin and, therefore, end in *-r* or *-us* in the nominative and *-i* in the genitive singular.

Nominative	Genitive	Meaning	Derivative
animus (*AHN-ee-muhs*)	animi (*AHN-ee-mee*)	mind	animated
fundus (*FOON-duhs*)	fundi (*FOON-dee*)	farm	fundamental
lectus (*LEHK-toos*)	lecti (*LEHK-tee*)	bed	lectisternium
liber (*LIH-behr*)	libri (*LIH-bree*)	book	library
locus (*LOH-kuhs*)	loci (*LOH-kee*)	place	local
modus (*MOH-duhs*)	modi (*MOH-dee*)	way	mode
mundus (*MOON-duhs*)	mundi (*MOON-dee*)	world	mundane
nodus (*NOH-duhs*)	nodi (*NOH-dee*)	knot	node
nucleus (*NOO-kleh-us*)	nuclei (*NOO-kleh-ee*)	kernel	nucleus
versiculus (*wehr-SIK-coo-luhs*)	versiculi (*wehr-SIK-coo-lee*)	single line	versicule

A *lectisternium* is a special celebration, mostly in Greek and Roman times, during which couches are laid out for the gods and food is spread for their enjoyment. I suppose if they fail to show up for the party, you are entitled to eat till you drop. While dining on the food of the gods, you might recite a *versicule*, a short poem.

Places and Things—Neuter Nouns

Finally, let's look at things that are neuter in both English and Latin. Note that neuter nouns end in *-um* in the nominative and *-i* in the genitive singular.

Nominative	Genitive	Meaning	Derivative
aedificium (*eye-dih-FIHC-ee-uhm*)	aedifici (*eye-dih-FIHC-ee*)	building	edifice
aurum (*OW-ruhm*)	auri (*OW-ree*)	gold	aureate
balineum (*bah-LIH-nee-um*)	balinei (*bah-LIH-neh-ee*)	bath	—
consilium (*kohn-SIHL-ee-uhm*)	consili (*kohn-SIHL-ee-ee*)	plan	counsel
convivium (*kohn-WEE-wee-uhm*)	convivi (*kohn-WEE-wee-ee*)	party	convivial
decretum (*deh-KREH-tuhm*)	decreti (*deh-KREH-tee*)	judgment	decree
dictum (*DIK-tuhm*)	dicti (*DIK-tee*)	contract	dictum
ferrum (*FEHR-ruhm*)	ferri (*FEHR-ee*)	iron, steel	ferrous
otium (*OH-tee-uhm*)	otii (*OH-tee-ee*)	leisure	otiose
poculum (*POH-coo-lum*)	poculi (*POH-coo-lee*)	cup	poculiform
prandium (*PRAHN-dee-uhm*)	prandi (*PRAHN-dee*)	dinner	prandial
pretium (*PREH-tee-uhm*)	preti (*PREH-tee*)	price	—
vasum (*WAH-suhm*)	vasi (*WAH-see*)	vase	vase
verbum (*WEHR-buhm*)	verbi (*WEHR-bee*)	word	verbosity
vinum (*WHEE-num*)	vini (*WHEE-nee*)	wine	vineyard

A *postprandial* belch used to be a good thing, a compliment to the chef.

Practice Makes Perfect 2

Be sure to read the Latin aloud and then translate.

1. Poculum discipuli
    (*POH-koo-lum dihs-KIHP-pu-lee*)   _____

2. Vir silentii
    (*WIHR sih-LEHN-tee-ee*)   _____

3. Nasus elephanti
    (*NAH-sus eh-leh-FAHN-tee*)   _____

4. Otium populi
    (*OH-tee-um POH-poo-lee*)   _____

5. Vasum ferri
    (*WAH-sum FEH-ree*)   _____

6. Modus mundi
    (*MOH-dus MUHN-dee*)   _____

7. Cerevisia feminae
    (*keh-reh-WHI-see-ah FEH-mihn-eye*)   _____

Now into Latin:

1. The price of land   _____

2. Word of the penalty   _____

3. The son of the gourmet   _____

4. Single line of the letter   _____

5. A guest of the Greek   _____

A Quick Summary

By now you can see that feminine nouns end in *-a* in the nominative and *-ae* in the genitive. Masculine nouns end in *-us* or *-r* in the nominative and *-i* in the genitive. Neuter nouns end in *-um* in the nominative and *-i* in the genitive. Remember, the genitive can be translated *'s* or *of*.

Mouse, Mice; House, Hice? Plurals

In English, we have separate forms for plurals—*boy* and *boys*, *man* and *men*—so it really isn't any inconvenience to do the same in Latin. We can't keep talking about just one elephant and one tail, supposing you see one elephant with *two* tails. If you haven't been drinking, you might want to write it in Latin.

Here are some plurals you will see and their translations.

Latin	English	Latin	English
aedificia (*eye-dih-FIH-kee-ah*)	buildings	loci (*LOW-keye*)	places
betae (*BEH-teye*)	beets	nervi (*NEHR-wee*)	nerves
caudae (*KOW-deye*)	tails	poenae (*PWAY-neye*)	punishments
dei (*DEH-ee*)	gods	vasa (*WAH-sah*)	vases
filii (*FEE-lee-ee*)	sons	verba (*WEHR-bah*)	words

Here are the plural endings for the first and second declension nouns, masculine, feminine, and neuter.

	Masculine	**Feminine**	**Neuter**
Nominative	i	ae	a
Genitive	orum	arum	orum

Latin Today!

Words to take to the party: Fraternity night out? Impress your friends with the Latin words for wine, cup, beer, and bar! And don't forget to toss out *aqua vitae* (*AH-kwa WHI-teye; AH-kwa vih-tee* in English).

vinum (*WHEE-num*)   cerevisia (*keh-reh-WHIH-see-ah*)

poculum (*POH-koo-lum*)   taberna (*tah-BEHR-nah*)

Practice Makes Perfect 3

Translate the following expressions:

1. Villae Graecorum
   (*WHEE-leye greye-KOH-rum*) _____

2. Nervi ferri
   (*NEHR-wee FEHR-ree*) _____

3. Nuclei ostrearum
   (*NOO-kleh-ee ohs-treh-AH-rum*) _____

4. Pocula cerevisiae
   (*POH-koo-lah keh-reh-WHI-see-eye*) _____

5. Balinea discipulorum
   (*bah-LIH-nee-ah dihs-kip-yoo-LOH-rum*) _____

Here's the ultimate test! Translate these into Latin:

1. Vases of the goddess _____

2. Dinners of men _____

3. The places of sons _____

4. The life of the party _____

5. The couch of the guest _____

Declensions—It's All Downhill from Here!

Try filling in the blanks with all the endings you've learned so far.

	Masculine Singular/Plural	Feminine Singular/Plural	Neuter Singular/Plural
Nominative	_____/_____	_____/_____	_____/_____
Genitive	_____/_____	_____/_____	_____/_____

Notice the patterns. Nouns with the genitive ending in -*ae* are usually feminine. They are said to be in the first declension. Nouns with the genitive ending in -*i* are masculine or neuter and in the second declension.

Don't be put off by the word *declension*. Somebody in the distant past thought of all these pesky endings as falling down from the nominative—hence *declining* and, therefore, *declension*. It's really just a way of bunching certain words together that have certain similar characteristics. Just think of declension as family. So nouns with -*ae* in the genitive belong to the Smith family, and the nouns with -*i* in the genitive belong to the Gotti family.

> **Tene Memoria**
>
> Remember to learn the nominative, genitive, and gender for each noun. Be sure to pronounce them correctly as you memorize—*ostre-ah, ostre-eye, mod-us, mod-ee.*

Word Order—the Oyster Elephant's or the Elephant's Oyster?

The Romans were famous for their sense of order. They organized and recorded their legal code. They arranged their legions in admirably straight lines and could set up a camp for 6,000 legionaries in a different place every night. They had a strict order of political offices so one could rise to power according to protocol.

But when it came to language, the Romans lost it. They depended on case endings to designate how a word was used in a sentence, not word order, and if you forgot your second declension genitive plural, you didn't know who belonged to what! English, of course, counts on word order to give meaning to a phrase or sentence. There's a mountain of difference between "The man ate the oyster" and "The oyster ate the man."

So watch out for those endings—*ostrea viri* and *viri ostrea* mean the same thing in Latin: "the man's oyster."

Speaking of oysters (you will be reading about them in Part 4), the Roman cook Apicius once had fresh oysters trucked (so to speak) from Rome to the Emperor Trajan in Parthia, a journey of many days. His gourmet recipe?

> **Cave!**
>
> The nominative plural and the genitive singular of some words appear to have the same ending. Compare *viri* (men) with *viri* (of the man). How can you tell the difference? Use your common sense, and make an educated guess. For example, *Viae Romae* wouldn't make sense translated as "Romes of the Road."

Combine in a big pot chopped oysters, ovaries of sea urchins, almonds, and shellfish liquid. Boil and enjoy!

And ... Conjunctions!

Conjunctions are used to join words (see Chapter 5 for a full explanation of conjunctions) and come in two varieties. *Coordinating* conjunctions are used to join words and phrases of equal importance. The other type, *subordinating* conjunctions, are used for joining clauses and phrases and are covered in Part 3. For now let's use the following conjunctions.

Latin	Meaning	Latin	Meaning
at (*aht*)	but, and	-que (*kway*)	and
aut (*owt*)	or	sed (*sehd*)	but
autem (*OW-tem*)	moreover, on the other hand	sicut (*SEE-kut*)	just as, as
et (*eht*)	and	et ... et	both ... and
etiam (*EH-tee-ahm*)	also	aut ... aut	either ... or
non modo ... sed etiam	not only ... but also		

Practice Makes Perfect 4

Say these aloud and then translate:

1. Perna et ova   _____

2. Feminae virique   _____

3. Publicus et privatus   _____

4. Ostreae sed non elephanti   _____

5. Elephanti sed etiam hippopotami _____

The Least You Need to Know

- ◆ A noun is a person, place, or thing.
- ◆ Latin nouns are presented in two forms, nominative and genitive.
- ◆ Latin nouns have gender: masculine, feminine, or neuter.
- ◆ Latin nouns have separate forms for singular and plural.
- ◆ The genitive form is translated *of* or *'s*.
- ◆ Conjunctions join words, phrases, and parts of sentences.

Chapter 4

What's in a Name?
More Nouns

In This Chapter

- ◆ Third declension words
- ◆ Fourth and fifth declension words
- ◆ Roman names for men and those other people

After finishing this chapter, you will have more than enough nouns to read the Latin selections in Part 4. Try to get comfortable with declensions: the third, the fourth, and fifth are added here. You should be familiar with the nominative and genitive cases by now. They are basic to vocabulary skills, and you'll be using them for the rest of your Latin reading life.

However, don't get the idea that Romans spoke only one or two words naming people, places, or things. We'll get to the other parts of speech soon.

Third Declension Nouns

If you think of declensions as families, the first declension is a group of mostly girls and all blondes—feminine nouns with nominative case ending -*a*. The second declension is a group of all boys and a few oddballs, and they all have crew cuts—masculine and neuter nouns with nominative case endings –*us*, -*r*, or -*um*. The third declension is as different as the crowd at Macy's parade. The nouns, unfortunately, have all three genders and many different nominative forms. What makes them related is the genitive singular, *is*.

As in previous vocabulary lists, we start with living things and their parts. Note that the entire family is here, as well as ancestors and family pets.

Nominative	Genitive	Gender	Meaning	Derivative
arbor (*AHR-bohr*)	arboris (*ahr-BOHR-is*)	f.	tree	arboretum
Caesar (*KEYE-sahr*)	Caesaris (*keye-SAHR-is*)	m.	Caesar	czar
caro (*KAH-roh*)	carnis/caronis (*KAHR-nis*)/ (*kah-ROH-nis*)	f.	meat	carnal
clunis (*KLOO-nis*)	clunis (*KLOO-nis*)	f.	buttock	—
comes (*KOH-mayss*)	comitis (*KOH-mih-tihs*)	m./f.	companion	comity
crus (*KROOS*)	cruris (*KROO-ris*)	n.	leg	crural
dens (*DEHNS*)	dentis (*DEHN-tis*)	m.	tooth	dental
dictator (*DIK-tah-tor*)	dictatoris (*dik-tah-TOR-ris*)	m.	dictator	dictator
dux (*DOOKS*)	ducis (*DOO-kis*)	m.	leader	ducal
femur (*FEH-moor*)	femoris (*feh-MOH-ris*)	n.	thigh	femoral
frater (*FRAH-tehr*)	fratris (*FRAHT-ris*)	m.	brother	fraternity

Nominative	Genitive	Gender	Meaning	Derivative
gladiator (*glah-dee-AH-tor*)	gladiatoris (*glah-dee-ah-TOH-ris*)	m.	gladiator	gladiator
homo (*HOH-moh*)	hominis (*HOH-mih-nis*)	m.	man	hominoid
maiores (*may-YOHR-ayss*)	maiorum (*may-YOHR-um*)	m. pl.	ancestors	major
pater (*PAH-tehr*)	patris (*PAH-tris*)	m.	father	patricide
pes (*PAYSS*)	pedis (*PEH-dis*)	m.	foot	pedal
pisces (*PIHS-kayss*)	piscis (*PIHS-kiss*)	m./f.	fish	pisciculture
poples (*POHP-lays*)	poplitis (*POP-lih-tis*)	m.	behind the knee, hamstring	popliteal
pugil (*POO-gihl*)	pugilis (*POO-gih-lis*)	m.	fighter	pugilist
urinator (*oo-rihn-AH-tor*)	urinatoris (*oo-rin-ah-TOH-ris*)	m.	diver	urinant
vox (*WOHKS*)	vocis (*WOH-kiss*)	f.	voice	vocal

You will remember some third declension words from previous chapters. *Caesar*, for example, is a third declension noun with the genitive *Caesaris*. Most nouns ending in *-tor*, such as *navigator*, *dictator*, and *gladiator*, have the genitive *oris* and are masculine, third declension.

As in the first declension, all nouns referring to females are feminine.

Nominative	Genitive	Gender	Meaning	Derivative
adiutrix (*ahd-JOO-triks*)	adiutricis (*ahd-joo-TRIK-is*)	f.	helper	adjutant
anser (*AHN-sehr*)	anseris (*ahn-SEHR-is*)	m./f.	goose	anserine

continues

continued

Nominative	Genitive	Gender	Meaning	Derivative
apis (*AH-pis*)	apis (*AH-pis*)	m./f.	bee	apiary
mater (*MAH-tehr*)	matris (*MAH-tris*)	f.	mother	maternal
mulier (*MOO-lee-yehr*)	mulieris (*moo-lee-YEHR-iss*)	f.	woman	muliebral
soror (*SOH-ror*)	sororis (*soh-ROH-ris*)	f.	sister	sorority
uxor (*OOK-sohr*)	uxoris (*ook-SOH-ris*)	f.	wife	uxoricide

Some of these words will be easy to remember; most people know when they have stumbled into an *apiary* (buzzing noises?) as opposed to an *arboretum* (leaves falling?).

Comity means "civility" or "mutual courtesy," often used in a phrase such as "There was comity between nations." This word is not seen much, however, because of its proximity to *comedy*, "causing ridicule," or *committee*, which might result in endless meetings going nowhere.

There isn't much point in complaining to your spouse, "Ow! I'm having crural pain!" because she will think you said "cruel" or "rural." It will impress your masseuse, however.

Hysteria's Herstory

Mulier comes from *mollis*? Whose cockamamie idea was that? In truth, *female* and the Latin *femina* may originally come from an earlier word meaning "to suck." *Feminine* might also relate to *fecundus*, meaning "productive and fertile," and ultimately Felix, the lucky, productive feline.

Hominoid means "manlike," which is the old-fashioned way of saying "humanlike," which includes women.

Muliebral, relating to women, is probably related to the Latin *mollis*, meaning "soft, malleable."

The following table shows more third declension nouns. As with the first and second declensions, many of what we would consider neuter things have masculine or feminine gender and as such are referred to with the appropriate pronoun. So in Latin we would say, "The axe is large and she is embedded in the tree." More on this later when we get to pronouns.

Nominative	Genitive	Gender	Meaning	Derivative
aestas (*EYE-stahs*)	aestatis (*eye-STAH-tis*)	f.	summer	aestivate
aestimatio (*eyes-tim-AH-tee-oh*)	aestimationis (*eyes-tim-ah-tee-OH-nis*)	f.	estimate	estimate
agmen (*AHG-mehn*)	agminis (*ahg-MIH-nis*)	n.	line of battle	agminate
bipennis (*bih-PEHN-nis*)	bipennis (*bih-PEHN-nis*)	f.	axe	bipenniform
civitas (*KEE-wih-tahs*)	civitatis (*kee-wih-TAH-tis*)	f.	city, state	civic
condicio (*kohn-DIK-ee-oh*)	condicionis (*kohn-dik-ee-OH-nis*)	f.	condition	condition
fraus (*FROWS*)	fraudis (*FROW-dis*)	f.	mischief	fraud
hiems (*HEE-ehms*)	hiemis (*HEE-eh-mis*)	f.	winter	hiemal
honor (*HOH-nor*)	honoris (*hoh-NOH-ris*)	m.	honor	honor
inaures (*ihn-OW-rays*)	inaurium (*ihn-OW-ree-um*)	f. pl.	earrings	—
ius (*YOOS*)	iuris (*YOO-ris*)	n.	right	justice
lex (*LEHKS*)	legis (*LEH-gis*)	f.	law	legal
magnitudo (*mahg-nih-TOO-dih-noh*)	magnitudinis (*mahg-nih-TOO-dih-nis*)	f.	size	magnitude
merx (*MEHRKS*)	mercis (*MEHR-kis*)	f.	merchandise	merchant
mors (*MOHRS*)	mortis (*MOHR-tis*)	f.	death	mortal
opus (*OH-pus*)	operis (*OH-peh-ris*)	n.	work	opera
pars (*PAHRS*)	partis (*PAHR-tis*)	f.	part	part

continues

continued

Nominative	Genitive	Gender	Meaning	Derivative
pax (*PAHKS*)	pacis (*PAH-kis*)	f.	peace	pacify
pernicitas (*pehr-NIHK-ih-tahs*)	pernicitatis (*pehr-nih-kih-TAH-tis*)	f.	agility	pernicity
rete (*RAY-teh*)	retis (*RAY-tis*)	n.	net	reticule
rumor (*ROO-mohr*)	rumoris (*roo-MOH-ris*)	m.	rumor	rumor
sal (*SAHL*)	salis (*SAH-lis*)	m./n.	salt	saline
tempus (*TEM-pus*)	temporis (*tem-POH-ris*)	n.	time	temporal
varietas (*wahr-ee-AY-tahs*)	varietatis (*wahr-ee-ay-TAH-tis*)	f.	variety	variety
vetustas (*weh-TUS-tahs*)	vetustatis (*weh-tus-TAH-tis*)	f.	old age	veteran

Agminate comes from the Latin *ago*, "to do or drive," and the suffix *-ate*, meaning things that do something. So *agminate*, like a *congregate*, is a group of people who do something together. It is also a line of an army or a marching column. So impress your listeners with statements like "Why are those sheep agminated?" or "The stockbrokers are all agminated!" (not to be confused with *agitated*).

Bipenniform means "having the shape of a double-edged axe" and is also related to *bipinnate*, the shape of a leaf.

Your popliteal (pronounced *pop-LIT-e-al*) space is the lozenge-shape space at the back of the knee joint. This word will go far, as in the classic pickup line, "I couldn't help but admire your outstandingly beautiful popliteal space!" It may also get your face slapped.

> **Grammar Guru**
>
> Did you know the Latin words for *fork* and *thief* are related? *Fur* (*FOOR*) means "thief," and *furca* (*FOOR-kah*) is the forked frame put on a man's neck as punishment for a crime. His arms were fastened to the projecting ends.

Finally, you are thinking there has been a typo. *Urinator* means "diver"? Although there is a Latin word, *urina*, meaning "urine," the verb *urino* and the noun *urinator* mean "to plunge into water." In heraldry, a fish or water animal that is placed head down on a shield is called a *urinant*.

The Third Declension—the *I* of the Storm

Remember that this declension, which has more words than the others, is characterized by *i*. The genitive singular is always *is*, and the genitive plural is *um* and sometimes *ium*. The nominative plural is *es*. The third declension is famous for its familial relations—ma, pa, bro, sis—and body parts—foot, mouth, buns, thigh, head, tooth, and others.

Fourth and Fifth Declension and "That's All, Folks"

The last two declensions are like your long-lost cousins from Alaska. There is a family resemblance, but they're not people you see very often. The fourth declension has *u*'s all over the place. The genitive is *-us* and *-uum*; the nominative plural is *-us*. The fifth declension has about three words that are used often and is characterized by the only vowel left, *e*. The genitive singular is *-ei*, the plural is *-erum*, and the nominative plural is *-es*.

Nominative	Genitive	Gender	Meaning	Derivative
actus (*AHK-tus*)	actus (*AHK-toos*)	m.	act	act
conventus (*kohn-WHEN-tus*)	conventus (*kohn-WHEN-toos*)	m.	coming together	convention
dies (*DEE-ayss*)	diei (*dee-EH-ee*)	m.	day	diurnal
res (*RAYSS*)	rei (*REH-ee*)	f.	thing, matter	reify
strepitus (*STREH-pih-tus*)	strepitus (*STREH-pih-toos*)	m.	noise	strepitous
sumptus (*SUMP-tus*)	sumptus (*SUMP-toos*)	m.	cost	sumptuary
venatus (*when-AH-tus*)	venatus (*when-AH-toos*)	m.	hunting	venatic
vultus (*wul-TUS*)	vultus (*wul-toos*)	m.	face, countenance	—

To *reify* is to make a concept or abstraction into a concrete thing. So if you're in a bar having a heated argument about existentialism and you hear, "Would you like to step outside and reify this?" unless you are a renowned pugilist, head for the back door.

And beware of your spouse laying down the *sumptuary* law. It probably means your credit card balance is out of sight.

Here is a summary of the endings you've learned so far. A complete table of all noun endings is found in Appendix B.

Declension	Nominative		Genitive	
	Singular	*Plural*	*Singular*	*Plural*
First	a	ae	ae	arum
Second	us/r	i	i	orum
Third	—	es	is	um
Fourth	us	us	us	uum
Fifth	es	es	ei	erum

Practice Makes Perfect 1

Read aloud and translate the following:

1. Conventus fratrum   _____

2. Agmen elephantorum   _____

3. Calamitas civitatis   _____

4. Vetustas dictatoris   _____

5. Comes feminae   _____

Now try into Latin:

1. The cost of the university   _____

2. The estimates of the architect   _____

3. The time of life   _____

4. The trees of Rome   _____

5. Buns of steel   _____

Names for Men and Those Other People

Some people have long names, like John Jacob Jingle Heimer Schmitt, and others, short, like Cher. Some names describe what you do—Baker, Smith, or Farmer—whereas others describe where you live—Hill, Fields, or Woods—or whose child you are—Johnson, Jackson, or Peterson.

The Roman upper-class male had three names. The first name, the *praenomen* (*PREYE-noh-mehn*), was his personal name. The second, the *nomen* (*NOH-men*), was the name of his clan. The third, the *cognomen* (*COG-noh-men*), was originally a nickname but came to denote the particular family within the clan. So Marcus Tullius Cicero was called Marcus and belonged to the Tullian clan and the Cicero family, the originator of which probably had a nose like a chickpea. The famed Julius Caesar was called Gaius and belonged to the Julian clan and the Caesar side of the family, whose progenitor may have had a huge head of hair (not passed on to the notoriously balding Julius).

The word *spurious*, meaning "not genuine, counterfeit," comes from a Latin name. The members of the Spurius (*SPOO-ree-us*) family were aristocrats who lived in the first century B.C.E. They were darn proud of their name … until a cloud came over it.

It happened this way: when a mother had a child out of wedlock—a no-no even then—she had to record the child as *Sine Patre*, "without a father." This came to be abbreviated as *Sp*, which was also the abbreviation for the Spurious family. Uh oh. The Spurius family name just quietly disappeared in the first century C.E.

Latin Today!

Words to take to the art museum: Be sure to mutter quietly:

ars gratia artis (*AHRS GRAH-tee-ah AHR-tis; AHRS GRAY-shee-ah AHR-tis* in English)

Roman boys were always named for their father or adopted father, as was the case with Pliny. Gaius Plinius Secundus (*GEYE-yus PLIH-nee-us se-KUN-dus*), known as Pliny the Elder, was the scholar and natural historian who died while investigating the eruption of Mt. Vesuvius. His adopted son, Gaius Plinius Caecilius Secundus (*GEYE-yus PLIH-nee-us keye-KIH-lee-us se-KUN-dus*), known as Pliny the Younger, was actually the son of L. Caecilius, Pliny the Elder's wife's brother. The younger Pliny declined an invitation to go near the eruption on that fateful day in 79 C.E., saying that he preferred to stay home and read. See? It pays to study!

Very often a second cognomen was added to a man's name to commemorate a special event or victory in his life. Publius (*POO-blee-us*) Cornelius (*Kor-NAY-lee-us*) Scipio (*SKIH-pee-oh*) Africanus (*ahf-rih-KAH-nus*) was so named for his triumph over Hannibal in Africa.

A girl was named for her father. So Julia is the daughter of Julius, Marcia of Marcus, Lucia of Lucius, and Antonia of Antonius. If ill fortune plagued her house and another girl was born, she would be named Julia Secunda or, heaven forbid, Julia Tertia. Sometimes sisters were called Julia Major and Julia Minor. Her formal name would include the father's name in the genitive case: Julia (*YOO-lee-ah*), filia Gaii (*GEYE-ee*) Julii (*YOO-lee-ee*) Caesaris (*keye-SAHR-is*).

Slaves had only one name, often denoting their place of origin. So Syrus (*SIH-rus*) was from Syria, Germanicus (*ger-MAHN-ih-kus*) from Germany, and Phrygia (*Frih-gee-ah*) from Phrygia. They, too, took the name of their master in the genitive case.

So what name did the Romans use to call each other? For women and slaves with only one name, no problem. For men and boys, practice varied. If you stood on a Roman street corner and yelled "Hey, Marcus!" probably half the male population would turn around and say "What?" That's because there were only about a dozen first names at that time. Traditionally, Gaius Julius Caesar was known by his third name; Publius Vergilius Maro, by his second. We know Marcus Tullius Cicero by his third name, Cicero, and well as Cato from Marcus Porcius Cato.

Key to Roman *Praenomina*, First Names

Abbreviation	Full Name	Abbreviation	Full Name
A.	Aulus (*OW-lus*)	M'.	Manius (*MAH-nee-uhs*)
C. or G.	Gaius (*GEYE-uhs*)	P.	Publius (*POO-blee-uhs*)
Cn.	Gnaeus (*NEYE-uhs*)	Q.	Quintus (*KWIHN-tuhs*)
D.	Decimus (*DEH-kih-muhs*)	Ser.	Servius (*SEHR-wee-uhs*)
L.	Lucius (*LOO-kee-uhs*)	Sex.	Sextus (*SEHKS-tuhs*)
M.	Marcus (*MAHR-kuhs*)	T.	Titus (*TIH-tus*)

Many men's names were often written without the praenomen. The C. abbreviation for Gaius was used for monuments and inscriptions. Gaius was never pronounced *KEYE-uhs*. (Tell that to Elizabeth Taylor, a.k.a. Cleopatra, who speaks to Caesar, a.k.a. Rex Harrison, calling him *KEYE-uhs* in the 1963 movie.)

And then we have the Roman names Manius Manilius in the first century C.E., reminiscent of our modern Johnny Johnsons and Robin Robbins!

Practice Makes Perfect 2

Fill in the table with the correct endings.

	Nominative		Genitive	
Declension	**Singular**	**Plural**	**Singular**	**Plural**
First	_____	_____	_____	_____
Second	_____	_____	_____	_____
Third	_____	_____	_____	_____
Fourth	_____	_____	_____	_____
Fifth	_____	_____	_____	_____

Now see how you do reading aloud and translating the following:

1. Res vitae   _____

2. Pedes pugilium   _____

3. Rete gladiatoris   _____

4. Vasum salis   _____

5. Silentium agnorum   _____

Now, into Latin:

1. Women of the house   _____

2. The noise of the streets   _____

3. A convention of companions _____

4. Leg of lamb   _____

5. Leaders of the world   _____

By now you have figured out that some words have similar endings (*i, ae*) yet are in different cases (nominative, genitive). Let's see how much you remember. Check the appropriate box or boxes.

Latin Word	Nominative Singular	Nominative Plural	Genitive Singular	Genitive Plural
gloriae	❑	❑	❑	❑
Caesaris	❑	❑	❑	❑
alumni	❑	❑	❑	❑
alumna	❑	❑	❑	❑
ostreae	❑	❑	❑	❑
pacis	❑	❑	❑	❑
res	❑	❑	❑	❑
rete	❑	❑	❑	❑
uxor	❑	❑	❑	❑
ferri	❑	❑	❑	❑
strepitus	❑	❑	❑	❑
sumptuum	❑	❑	❑	❑
comitium	❑	❑	❑	❑
viri	❑	❑	❑	❑
silentii	❑	❑	❑	❑
pacum	❑	❑	❑	❑

Remember that the second declension neuter nominative ending is *-um*, not to be confused with *-arum* and *-orum*, the genitive plural endings.

The Least You Need to Know

♦ The third declension has many different endings in the nominative forms.

♦ The most important third declension ending is the genitive singular, *-is*.

♦ Roman men had three names. Roman women had no name of their own.

♦ The fourth and fifth declensions have *u*'s and *e*'s.

5

Let's Have Some Action

In This Chapter

♦ Active, sedentary, and couch potato verbs

♦ Conjugations

♦ The present tense

♦ To be or not to be able

♦ Your goose is cooked … or is it doing the cooking?

It's time for some action. Nouns—people, places, and things—must do something to make a sentence come to life. Verbs make your world exciting. So in this chapter, our cavemen jump, and the oysters swim. We also learn passive verbs, where something is done to the subject. Elephants are jumped on by the cavemen, oysters are captured by the divers, and your goose is cooked.

Words to Be Memorized

The following lists consist of verbs—action words or words describing a state of being. Latin verbs are universally listed in dictionaries beginning with the first person singular, present tense active form, then the present active infinitive, the first person singular, perfect tense active form, and finally the perfect passive participle.

But hey, forget all that! In these lists, the third person singular follows the first person present and then the third person plural. For example, the first listing translates, "I knock down; he, she, or it knocks down; they knock down." The traditional forms can be found in the vocabulary list in Appendix A.

Notice that if the first word ends in *-io*, the third person plural form is *-iunt* rather than *-unt*.

Really Active Verbs

This list of verbs describes all physical actions, ranging from mild (grab a beer) to violent (knock down a tree). These are all found in the readings in Part 4.

First Singular (I)	Third Singular (he)	Third Plural (they)	Meaning	Derivative
accido (*ah-KIH-doh*)	accidit	accidunt	cut down	accident
affligo (*ah-FLIH-goh*)	affligit	affligunt	knock down, damage	afflict
apprehendo (*ah-preh-HEN-doh*)	apprehendit	apprehendunt	grab	apprehend
cado (*KAH-doh*)	cadit	cadunt	fall	cadence
caedo (*KEYE-doh*)	caedit	caedunt	kill, cut	matricide
capio (*KAH-pee-oh*)	capit	capiunt	take, capture	captive
clamo (*KLAH-moh*)	clamat	clamant	shout	clamor
concido (*kohn-KIH-doh*)	concidit	concidunt	fall	coincidence
convolo (*kohn-WOH-loh*)	convolat	convolant	fly about	volatile
coquo (*KOH-kwo*)	coquit	coquunt	cook	cook

First Singular (I)	Third Singular (he)	Third Plural (they)	Meaning	Derivative
decido (*day-KIH-doh*)	decidit	decidunt	fall down	deciduous
desilio (*day-SIH-lee-oh*)	desilit	desiliunt	jump down	saltate
exerceo (*ehks-ehr-KAY-reh*)	exercet	exercent	exercise	exercise
procumbo (*proh-KOOM-boh*)	procumbit	procumbunt	fall down	recumbent
pugno (*PUG-noh*)	pugnat	pugnant	fight	pugnacious
stipo (*STIH-poh*)	stipat	stipant	press, plant	stipe
sudo (*SOO-doh*)	sudat	sudant	sweat	sudoriferous
subruo (*sub-ROO-oh*)	subruit	subruunt	uproot	rush

Just a few explanations. *Desilio* comes from the Latin *salto*, which means "to jump or dance." So you can yell at your kids, "Don't saltate on the bed!" and by the time you have explained what it means, they will have stopped.

From *stipo* comes *stiff* and *stipe*, which is a short stalk or stem.

Cubo means "to lie down or recline," and for a Roman this meant climbing on your couch and planting your arm in a pillow and leaning on it. So *cubitum* came to mean "elbow." From there it came to mean a sharp bend resembling the elbow, and after adding a few sides and sticking them all together, we get—*voilà!*—a cube.

There are two potentially confusing verbs. *Cado* means "to fall," whereas *caedo* means "to cut." The confusion comes when the verb forms are compounds, the base word with a prefix. Both *cado* and *caedo* change to *cido* in compounds. So *accido* can mean "fall toward" and "cut toward." Same problem with *decido*, which can mean "fall down or cut down." So how do you tell the difference? Well, if your sentence includes a woodsman with an axe and a tree, *decido* is probably "cut down." If, on the other hand, your sentence is about a person chewing gum and walking at the same time, *decido* will probably be "fall down."

Practice Makes Perfect 1

Fill in the blank with an appropriate verb form:

1. I go to the football game and _____.

2. At the boxing match _____.

3. In the kitchen the cook _____.

4. I _____ my roses in the garden.

5. The president is chewing gum and walking and _____.

Slightly More Sedentary Verbs

The following verbs describe actions to be done with minimal effort. Burying a body might be the exception, requiring some time and strength. However, burying your head in the sand is minimal, especially if you're an ostrich.

First Singular	Third Singular	Third Plural	Meaning	Derivative
abhorreo (*ahb-HOH-reh-oh*)	abhorret	abhorrent	shrink back	abhor
admoneo (*ahd-MOH-neh-oh*)	admonet	admonent	warn	admonish
antecedo (*ahn-teh-KAY-doh*)	antecedit	antecedunt	surpass	antecedent
appello (*ah-PEHL-loh*)	appellat	appellant	call, name	appellation
applico (*ahp-PLIH-koh*)	applicat	applicant	apply, attach	applicable
condio (*KOHN-dee-oh*)	condit	condiunt	season	condiment
consumo (*kohn-SOO-moh*)	consumit	consumunt	use up	consume
diffundo (*dih-FUN-doh*)	diffundit	diffundunt	pour out	diffuse

First Singular	Third Singular	Third Plural	Meaning	Derivative
exigo (*ehks-IH-goh*)	exigit	exigunt	take out, demand	exigency
obruo (*ohb-ROO-oh*)	obruit	obruunt	bury, hide	rush
orno (*ohr-NOH*)	ornat	ornant	decorate	ornate
peto (*PEH-toh*)	petit	petunt	beg, attack	petition
refero (*reh-FEH-roh*)	refert	referunt	bring back	refer
relinquo (*reh-LINK-woh*)	relinquit	relinquunt	leave	relic

Didn't you always wonder why ketchup was called a *condiment?* Well, now you know.

Be sure to use *exigencies*, accent on the first syllable, as a synonym for *needs*, *demands*, and *requirements*. Somehow it sounds more urgent. "The exigencies of my job require longer vacations" will certainly impress your boss and result in another week at the beach.

Practice Makes Perfect 2

Change the singular form to plural or the plural to singular. Then translate.

1. condit _____

2. exigunt _____

3. abhorret _____

4. relinquit _____

5. obruunt _____

Couch Potato Verbs

Here's my favorite list—words describing actions from the couch. I don't think the average Roman was much of a couch potato, or Latin would include words for clicking the remote or ordering in.

First Singular	Third Singular	Third Plural	Meaning	Derivative
dico (*DEE-koh*)	dicit	dicunt	speak, say	dictate
exsisto (*ehk-SIS-toh*)	exsistit	exsistunt	stand out, appear	exist
includo (*ihn-KLOO-doh*)	includit	includunt	include	include
—	inquit	inquiunt	he/she says	—
obligo (*OHB-lih-goh*)	obligat	obligant	obligate, earmark	obligate
placeo (*PLAH-keh-oh*)	placet	placent	please	placid
possum (*POH-soom*)	potest	possunt	be able	potent
praesto (*PREYE-stoh*)	praestat	praestant	be responsible	presto
quaeso (*KWEYE-soh*)	quaesit	quaesunt	ask for	question
sum (*SOOM*)	est	sunt	be, is, are	is
volo (*WOH-loh*)	vult	volunt	want	voluntary

Conjugations or the Perfect Marriage

Conjugation is related to the Latin word *iugum*, meaning "a yoke by which a plough or chariot is drawn." A device of the same shape was used to carry baskets or buckets of water. An *iugum* was used to humiliate conquered prisoners of war by forcing them to bend low and walk under the yoke.

So being yoked together with someone (forget the subjection and humiliation part) is a conjugation, and thus we talk about conjugal rights.

A conjugation joins the stem of the verb with the personal ending. In English, we use the personal pronouns *I, you, he, she* or *it, we, you,* and *they* to show who is doing the action. Although Latin also has personal pronouns, they are used mostly to show emphasis. Instead, the personal ending is added directly to the verb. These endings are *-o, -s, -t, -mus, -tis,* and *-nt.*

Grammar Guru

The prefix *con* means "with"— *condominium* (ownership with), *confide* (trust with), *conform* (shape with), *conjugal* (yoked with ... in the good sense, of course).

Singular	English	Plural	English
coquo (*KOH-kwoh*)	I cook	coquimus (*KOH-kwih-mus*)	we cook
coquis (*KOH-kwis*)	you cook	coquitis (*KOH-kwih-tis*)	you (pl.) cook
coquit (*KOH-kwit*)	he, she cooks	coquunt (*KOH-kwunt*)	they cook

More often than not you will have a subject—the goose, the elephant, love, marriage, agility—whatever. In that case, remember to have the verb ending agree with the subject in number (singular or plural) and person (first, second, or third). So if the subject is *I, you, he, or she,* you must use the first. If the subject is *we the people,* you must use the first person plural ending. If it's *you all,* you need ....

But hey, forget all that! Just remember *-o* means "I," *-t* means "he, she, or it," and *-nt* means "they." We'll worry about agreeing with the other people later.

Tene Memoria

Remember declensions? The first declension also featured an *-a.*

It's Happening Now!

So verbs show action or a state of being. Now that you can show *who* is doing the action, the next step is to show *when.* The present tense in English has three different forms:

- Simple present (*I cook*)

- Progressive present (*I am cooking*)

- Emphatic present (*I do cook*)

Latin Today!

Words to take to the gym: Put these in your gym bag:

gymnasium (*gihm-NAH-zee-um*)   pila (*PEE-lah*)

exercere (*ehks-ehr-KAY-reh*)   sudare (*soo-DAH-reh*)

And on reaching the top of the climbing wall:

Excelsior! (*eks-KEL-see-or; eks-SELL-see-or* in English)

In Latin it's a little simpler. There's only one form of the present tense, and it's formed by adding the personal endings to the present stem of the verb. Verbs of the first conjugation have present stem *a*—*amat* (he loves), *appellant* (they call), *convolat* (it flies about).

How do you know if the verb is in the first conjugation? You can look in the dictionary and look at the second word listed, the present infinitive. It should end in *-re*, and if it's a first conjugation verb it will end in *-are*. So you will find *amo* and *amare*, *appello* and *appellare*, *volo* and *volare*.

The second conjugation verb ends in *-eo*, and the infinitive ends in long *-ere*—*habeo* and *habere*, *respondeo* and *respondere*, *admoneo* and *admonere*—and has an *e* before the personal ending.

The third and fourth conjugations (there is no fifth, thank goodness!) end in *-o* or *-io* and have the infinitives of *ere* and *ire*. In the present tense they both have the same stem, *i* in the singular and *u or iu* in the plural.

But hey, forget all that! I promised no long and complicated rules. Just look at the following words and I'll bet you can translate them. Just remember the *-o*, *-t*, and *-nt* thing.

Practice Makes Perfect 3

Translate and remember, if there is no subject noun, you have to provide a personal pronoun:

1. Stipant   _____

2. Coquo   _____

3. Funambuli antecedunt   _____

4. Mensa concidit   _____

5. Frater relinquit   _____

To Be or Not To Be Able

The verb *esse*, "to be," is irregular and, therefore, special. The complete present tense conjugation is given in the following table.

Singular	English	Plural	English
sum (*soom*)	I am	sumus (*SOO-mus*)	we are
es (*ehs*)	you are	estis (*EHS-tis*)	you are
est (*ehst*)	he, she it is	sunt (*soont*)	they are

Memorize these, because these forms are used as helping verbs for other tenses. The infinitive, *esse*, gives you the English *essence*, *essential*, *absence*, and *presence*.

Although the verb *to be* is often at the end of the sentence, sometimes it's found at the beginning, and then it's translated as "there is" or "there are." So *Sunt ostreae* could be translated as "They are oysters," "There are oysters," or "Oysters are."

A predicate noun is a word that follows a linking verb, most often the verb *to be*. In Latin, the predicate noun is in the nominative case because it renames the subject. In English, we also use the nominative or subjective case after a linking verb. That's why you should say "It is I," not "It is me."

Because the verb usually comes near the end of the sentence in Latin, you cannot count on word order to indicate a predicate noun. Often the predicate noun is before the verb:

Vir pugil est.   The man is a boxer.

Meus frater urinator est.   My brother is a diver.

Finally, the verb *possum*, "to be able," is conjugated very much like *sum*, as shown in the following table.

Singular	English	Plural	English
possum (*POH-soom*)	I am able	possumus (*POH-soo-mus*)	we are able
potes (*POH-tehs*)	you are able	potestis (*poh-TEHS-tihs*)	you are able
potest (*POH-tehst*)	he is able	possunt (*POH-sunt*)	they are able

Practice Makes Perfect 4

Fill in the blanks with words from the following pool. You should only have to use a word once, but it may not work out and, hey, it's an imperfect world.

1. _____ dux est.   6. _____ desiliunt.

2. Est _____ apium.   7. _____ affligunt.

3. _____ est elephantus.   8. _____ petit.

4. _____ sunt urinantes.   9. _____ cadit.

5. _____ cadunt.   10. _____ obruunt.

Word pool: graecus, coquus, muraenae, dictatores, trogodytae, arbores, dux, ostreae, apis, funambulus.

Now try writing some Latin verbs. Remember that the personal pronoun is the ending of the verb. The first one is done for you.

1. I ask.   Peto.

2. He comes.   _____

3. They fall down.   _____

4. He attaches.   _____

5. They uproot.   _____

Hysteria's Herstory

The youngest son of Tarquinius Superbus, the last king of Rome, was named Sextus Tarquinius and was enamoured of Lucretia, the lovely wife of his cousin, Tarquinius Collatinus. Unable to control himself, he raped her one night, saying that if she did not submit, he would kill her and then place the body of a slain slave next to her in the bed and everyone would think that …. So the next day Lucretia, a most noble and virtuous woman, called her husband and father to her, related the whole ugly story, took a knife, and stabbed herself to death rather than live as a dishonored woman. Of course, this led to a general revolt among the friends of Collatinus and eventually Brutus, an ancestor of the "*Et tu, Brute*" Brutus, assassinated the hated king, and thus began the republic.

The Goose Is Cooked

We might as well tackle the active/passive voice problem right away, as the passive voice appears much more frequently in Latin than in English.

The passive voice is used when the subject is acted on as opposed to doing the action. It is formed in English by using the verb *to be* and the *-ed* form of the verb. The present passive uses the present tense of the verb *to be*—"I am loved," "the goose is cooked," "we are hunted."

Cave!

Remember that the passive voice has a subject of the verb, but the subject is passive and not acting. So the goose is being cooked as opposed to a very active goose that has gone to cooking school and is now doing the cooking.

In Latin, it's much easier. You simply add an *r* to the *o* in the first person, and an *-ur* to the *-t* and *-nt* of the third singular and plural.

But hey, forget all that! Just look for the *r*'s. So it's *capior*, "I am captured"; *appellantur*, "they are called"; and *coquitur*, "it is cooked."

Practice Makes Perfect 5

Translate the following:

1. Fungi diffunduntur. _____

2. Caesar dictator appellatur. _____

3. Relinquitur. _____

4. Dicitur. _____

5. Pecunia obligatur. _____

Now try translating these short sentences into Latin:

1. The meat is consumed. _____

2. The work is included. _____

3. The oyster is held. _____

4. Feet are planted. _____

5. Gold is buried. _____

The Least You Need to Know

♦ Latin verbs show who or what is the subject by the personal endings: *-o = I*, *-t = he*, *-nt = they*.

♦ The present tense is formed by conjugating the present stem with the personal endings.

♦ The essential words are *sum, es, est, sumus, estis,* and *sunt.*

♦ Predicate nouns are in the nominative case.

♦ Verbs can also be in the passive voice by using the endings *-or, -tur,* and *-ntur.*

♦ If you're a goose, it's better to be active than passive.

6

Action Without an Ending— Verbals

In This Chapter

- ◆ Infinitives: to be or not to be
- ◆ Present participles: seeing is believing
- ◆ Passive periphrastic: things that must be seen
- ◆ A verbal review

A verbal is a verb form that is not used as a verb but as some other part of speech. So instead of being an action word, it can function either as an adjective and describe, or as a noun and be a person, place, or thing. Think of it as being similar to when you use a pencil, not to write with, but to prop up a window. It is no longer a pencil, even though it looks like a pencil. The pencil has become a window propper and functions as one.

Verbal adjectives are participles. Verbal nouns are gerunds and infinitives.

To Be or Not To Be: Infinitives

Has your annoying neighbor ever got your ear at the annual barbecue and gone on and on, *ad infinitum* or *yadda, yadda, yadda*, about how to grow a better tomato?

Infinitive literally means "without an ending" and is the verb form as translated in English with *to*. Also known as the second principle part, the infinitive form is always listed second in dictionaries and vocabulary lists. As mentioned in Chapter 5, the infinitive is an accurate way of classifying verbs in their conjugations: *-are*, first; *-ere*, third; and *-ire*, fourth.

The infinitive can be used as a noun: "To see is to believe." The first infinitive is the subject of the sentence and, therefore, used as a noun. In the sentence, "I like to eat," the infinitive is used as the direct object.

The infinitive is also used to complement or complete the meaning of another verb. *Dicitur* (it is said), *videtur* (it seems), *licet* (it is allowed), *necesse est* (it is necessary), *potest* (he is able), and *vult* (he wants) all can take a complementary infinitive.

When the verbal is the subject of a sentence, it is usually in the infinitive form. For example, "diving is good" translates as *urinare bonum est*.

First Conjugation Verbs

The easiest group of verbs to remember and deal with are those whose infinitive ends in *-are* and have an *a* before the personal ending. Here are some examples.

First Person Singular	Infinitive	Meaning	Derivative
amo (*AH-moh*)	amare	to love	amour
do (*DOH*)	dare	to give	donate
mando (*MAHN-doh*)	mandare	to command	mandate
mangonico (*mahn-GOH-nih-koh*)	mangonicare	to improve appearance	mangonism
permuto (*pehr-MOO-toh*)	permutare	to exchange	permutation
supero (*SOO-pehr-oh*)	superare	to surpass	superior

First Person Singular	Infinitive	Meaning	Derivative
sublevo (*sub-LEH-woh*)	sublevare	to get up	levade
urino (*yoo-RIH-noh*)	urinare	to dive	urinant

Mangonism, believe it or not, is an English word, derived from the Greek word for "to deceive" and the Sanskrit word for "to beautify." It describes the practice of training plants contrary to natural conditions, not too far from beautifying property for the purpose of making a sale. Wait a second! Are we talking Wall Street here?

Second Conjugation Infinitives

Second conjugation verbs have the first person singular, the first word in the dictionary listing, ending in *-eo*. The infinitive ends in long *-ere* and is pronounced *AY-reh*. The personal endings are preceded by an *e*, as you might expect—*doleo* (*DOH-leh-oh*; I am sad), *dolere* (*doh-LAY-reh*; to be sad), *dolet* (he is sad), *dolent* (they are sad).

First Person Singular	Infinitive	Meaning	Derivative
abstineo (*ahb-STIH-neh-oh*)	abstinere	to abstain	abstention
caveo (*KAH-weh-oh*)	cavere	to be careful	caution
deleo (*DEH-leh-oh*)	delere	to destroy	delete
doleo (*DOH-leh-oh*)	dolere	to be sad	dolente
maneo (*MAH-neh-oh*)	manere	to remain	mansion

Third Conjugation Infinitives

The third conjugation infinitive ends in *-ere* and is pronounced *eh-reh*—*agere* (*AH-geh-reh*), *mandere* (*MAHN-deh-reh*). The vowel before the personal endings is *i* or *u* in the third person plural—*agit* (he does), *agunt* (they do).

First Person Singular	Infinitive	Meaning	Derivative
ago (*AH-goh*)	agere	to do	agent
consisto (*kohn-SIS-toh*)	consistere	to stop	consist
duco (*DOO-koh*)	ducere	to lead	ducal
erigo (*AY-rih-goh*)	erigere	to straighten	rigid
ludo (*LOO-doh*)	ludere	to play	ludicrous
mando (*MAHN-doh*)	mandere	to chew	mandible
pendo (*PEHN-doh*)	pendere	to hang	pendant
perago (*pehr-AH-goh*)	peragere	to complete	act
vendo (*WEHN-doh*)	vendere	to sell	vendor

Third *-io* and Fourth Conjugation Infinitives

This last category of verbs has the first word ending in *-io*. Whereas the third conjugation verbs keep the infinitive *-ere*, the fourth conjugation infinitive is *-ire*. However, the formation of the personal endings are similar: *-it* for the third singular and *-iunt* for the third plural—*audit* (he hears), *capit* (he captures), *audiunt* (they hear), *dormiunt* (they sleep).

First Person Singular	Infinitive	Meaning	Derivative
accipio (*ah-KIH-pee-oh*)	accipere	to receive	accept
audio (*OW-dee-oh*)	audire	to hear	audio
dormio (*dohr-mee-oh*)	dormire	to sleep	dormitory
fero (irreg.) (*FEH-roh*)	ferre	to carry	ferry

Dolente is used in music to denote a sorrowful tone. The next time you're watching a movie and all those around you are dabbing their eyes and sniffling, you can impress your friends by saying, "*Sotto voce, multo dolente!*"

When your boss loses 10 pounds, score a few points by saying, "Quite a *permutation!*"

And remember Roy Rogers and his wonder horse Trigger? When Trigger passed on, he was preserved in his famous forefeet-in-the-air stance and now stands in the Roy Rogers Museum in a permanent and eternal *levade*.

Cave!

Don't confuse the root *ferr*, meaning "iron," with the root *fer*, meaning "to bear or carry." Also *mandare* (to command) is quite different from *mandere* (to chew). Remember, the first conjugation has an *a* before the personal ending, and the third conjugation has an *i*. So it's *mandat* (he entrusts) and *mandit* (he chews).

Practice Makes Perfect 1

Say out loud and then translate:

1. Dormire   _____

2. Ferre   _____

3. Permutare   _____

4. Agere   _____

5. Superare   _____

Translate these into Latin:

1. To bring   _____

2. To straighten out   _____

3. To be   _____

4. To demand   _____

5. To get up   _____

continues

continued

Ready to translate into Latin?

1. He is able to command. _____

2. To change _____

3. To sleep is to overcome. _____

4. She seems to be _____

5. It is necessary to straighten up. _____

The present passive infinitive is formed by changing the final *e* of the active infinitive to an *i*, except for the third conjugation, which drops the entire infinitive ending *-ere* and adds an *i*. For example:

Tene Memoria	

Remember that *per-* is a Latin prefix meaning "perfection" or "completion." So the perfect tense shows completion, a *permutation* is a complete change, and a *permanent* is completely yours until it grows out … at least when it comes to hair.

amare (to love)   amari (to be loved)
(*ah-MAH-reh*)   (*ah-MAH-ree*)

tenere (to hold)   teneri (to be held)
(*teh-NAY-reh*)   (*teh-NAY-ree*)

ducere (to lead)   duci (to be lead)
(*DOO-keh-reh*)   (*DOO-kee*)

punire (to punish)   puniri (to be punished)
(*poo-NEE-reh*)   (*poo-NEE-ree*)

These infinitives are often seen complementing or in use with another verb, for example, *Bonum est amari*, "It is good to be loved." Ovid says that people go to the races *videre et videri*, "to see and to be seen."

The Miami University motto includes a present passive infinitive: *Prodesse quam conspici* (To be productive rather than to be looked at).

Seeing Is Believing

In English, the *-ing* form of the verb can be used as a noun, as in "seeing is believing," or as an adjective, as in "seeing-eye dog." When it functions as a noun, it is the gerund. When it functions as an adjective, it is the present participle.

Because it's used as a noun or adjective, the present participle has to belong to a declension and the third declension adopted this hybrid into its family. Here are the present participle forms.

 Grammar Guru

An adjective describes, delimits, or specifies a quantity.

	Masculine/Feminine		Neuter	
	Singular	Plural	Singular	Plural
Nominative	-ns	-ntes	-ns	-ntia
Genitive	-ntis	-ntium	-ntis	-ntium
Dative	-nti	-ntibus	-nti	-ntibus
Accusative	-ntem	-ntes	-ns	-ntia
Ablative	-nti	-ntibus	-nti	-ntibus

But hey, forget all that! Just translate any verb with *-ns* or *-nt* in it as *-ing*. Here's a short list of present participles you might encounter in the readings.

First Person Singular	Infinitive	Present Participle	Meaning
audio	audire	audientes, audientibus	listening
doleo	dolere	dolens	suffering
perago	peragere	peragens	completing
pendo	pendere	pendens	hanging
urino	urinare	urinantes	diving

Especially in the plural, the present participle, while describing people, sometimes actually becomes the people and, therefore, sounds and acts like a noun. *Urinantes* (divers) is really the present participle, "the diving ones." *Audientes* (the listeners) translates as "those listening," *spectantes* (the spectators) be-comes "those watching," and *delentes* (the destroyers) means "the destroying ones." Note that the ending *-es* is for both men and women.

Latin Today!

Words to take shopping: Words to remember, especially if you're buying a car on eBay:

Caveat emptor (*KAH-way-aht EMP-tor; KAH-vee-aht* in English)

Practice Makes Perfect 2

Practice by translating the following expressions:

1. Urinantes pueri _____

2. Dolens femina _____

3. Pendens hortus _____

4. Peragentes _____

5. Audientibus _____

And now translate the following into Latin nominative case:

1. The listeners _____

2. The active man _____

3. The suffering women _____

4. The diver _____

5. Those hanging _____

Things That Must Be Seen—the Passive Periphrastic

Webster's unabridged dictionary has a 50-page *addenda*, things that must be added. Other words that come from the Latin are *corrigenda*, things that must be corrected, and *agenda*, things that must be done.

This wonderful Latin grammatical device, the passive periphrastic construction, consists of the future passive participle and some form of the verb "to be" and implies obligation. The endings for this participle are the same as the second and first declension.

But hey, forget all that! Just remember *-nd* and *-est* means *must be ———ed.*

The same *-nd* form, the future passive participle, can be used as a noun and be translated like the present participle, *-ing.* This is called a gerund in English. It has only four forms—genitive (*-ndi*), dative (*-ndo*), accusative (*-ndum*), and ablative (*-ndo*). So *amando* means "loving," *videndum* means "seeing," and *petendum* means "seeking."

Practice Makes Perfect 3

Translate the following expressions into English:

1. Permutandum est. _____

2. Agendum est. _____

I'm sure you've got the idea. Now try some gerunds:

1. Vendendo _____

2. Ducenda _____

3. Cavendum _____

4. Sublevandi _____

Translate English into Latin:

1. Of suffering _____

2. Sleeping _____

3. It is the time for acting. (use genitive) _____

4. He changes completely for the purpose of selling. (use *ad* with accusative) _____

Reviewing Verbals

Find the verbals in the following sentences and identify them as either gerund, infinitive, passive, or periphrastic participle. As a hint, there are three gerunds, four infinitives, two passives, and one periphrastic participle.

Practice Makes Perfect 4

1. Ea sola dormire vult.

2. Hodie nivis consistere videtur.

3. Villas vendendo mangonicat.

4. Cum primum eam agere coepi, pugiles clamorem fecerunt.

5. Tempus agendi nunc mihi est.

6. Erat officium magistratuum auxilium semper dare.

7. Recipit opus quod curandum est.

8. Ad aestimationem adicienda est.

9. Ad perficiendum pecunia exigitur ex eius bonis.

10. Species arborum stantium reliquit.

The Least You Need to Know

◆ Infinitives end in -*re* and are translated "to."

◆ Present participles end in -*ns* or -*nt* and are translated "ing."

◆ Gerunds and gerundives end in -*nd* and are translated "ing."

◆ The gerund and -*est* implies obligation.

◆ This whole verbal thing is needlessly complicated and has no ending.

The Good and the Bad—
Adjectives and Accusatives

In This Chapter

- ◆ You already know some Latin adjectives
- ◆ Making words agree
- ◆ Adjectives as nouns
- ◆ Degrees of comparison
- ◆ The accusative case
- ◆ Asking questions

Adjectives are words that describe a noun. Adjectives are the writer's palette, used to fill in color, size, shape, texture, or sound. Adjectives make good writing come alive and give depth and dimension to the written picture. A beautiful woman is *curvaceous;* the sound of the saxophone is *mellifluous.*

Classical Latin authors, at least those whose works have survived and remain with us, were not as enamored with the adjective as we are today. Romans were practical, down-to-earth people, and we can thank them for the most clean-lined architecture and a system of codification of laws, but we can't thank them for exciting, vivid writing. Nevertheless, there are many Latin adjectives, used mostly to clarify, enumerate, or describe factually.

More Words You Know Already

The meanings of the following adjectives are fairly obvious. Notice that some end in -*us*, whereas others end in -*is*. Remember declensions in Chapters 3 and 4? Nouns such as *mundus, i,* m., are second declension; and others such as *clunis, clunis,* m., are third declension. Adjectives also come in two varieties. The first and second declension adjectives have those endings, the third declension endings are for …

But hey, forget all that! You'll recognize the endings in due time.

No-Brainer Adjectives

Romans created some adjectives from nouns by adding the suffix -*osus*, meaning "full of." It doesn't take an Einstein to figure out *verbosus* means "full of words." Other adjectives are simply the present participle of verbs—*adulescens, adulescentis* (growing up), *potens, potentis* (powerful), *sapiens, sapientis* (wise), and *flagrans, flagrantis* (burning), just to name a few. These will all be third declension adjectives.

Nominative (Masculine)	Genitive	Meaning	Derivative
absurdus (*ahb-SUR-dus*)	absurdi	absurd	absurd
alienus (*ah-lee-AY-nus*)	alieni	foreign	alien
communis (*KOHM-moon-ihs*)	communis	common	common
credulus (*KREH-doo-lus*)	creduli	gullible	credulous
fungosus (*fuhn-GOH-sus*)	fungosi	spongy	fungous
furiosus (*fuhr-ee-OH-sus*)	furiosi	furious	furious
gloriosus (*gloh-ree-OH-sus*)	gloriosi	glorious	glorious

Nominative (Masculine)	Genitive	Meaning	Derivative
Graecus (*GREYE-kus*)	Graeci	Greek	Greek
herbosus (*her-BOH-sus*)	herbosi	grassy	herbaceous
industriosus (*in-dus-tree-OH-sus*)	industriosi	industrious	industrious
infirmus (*in-FIR-mus*)	infirmi	weak	infirm
immortalis (*im-mor-TAH-lis*)	immortalis	immortal	immortal
medius (*MEH-dee-us*)	medii	middle of	median
mutilus (*MOO-tih-lus*)	mutili	broken	mutilate
nervosus (*ner-WOH-sus*)	nervosi	nervous	nervous
otiosus (*oh-tee-OH-sus*)	otiosi	at leisure	otiose
Romanus (*roh-MAH-nus*)	Romani	Roman	Roman
singulus (*SIN-gu-lus*)	singuli	one at a time	single
summus (*SOO-mus*)	summi	top of	summit
triumphalis (*tree-um-FAH-lis*)	triumphalis	triumphant	triumphal
verbosus (*wehr-BOH-sus*)	verbosi	wordy	verbosity

If you are *otiose*, you are on vacation or just a bum.

Practice Makes Perfect 1

Match the adjective with the meaning:

volens	prudent	clamans	flying about
volitans	shouting	providens	falling
florens	drooping	languens	flourishing
cadens	wanting		

Harder-to-Remember Adjectives

Note that in the following list, some adjectives end in *-er*, like some second declension nouns (such as *puer*, *ager*, *vir*). Like their noun counterparts, you need to know the genitive to find the base and the declension.

Nominative (m., s.)	Genitive	Meaning	Derivative
amplus (*AHM-plus*)	ampli	full, large, wide	ample
asper (*AHS-per*)	asperi	bitter, sharp	asperity
ceterus (*KEH-ter-us*)	ceteri	the rest	et cetera
dexter (*DEKS-ter*)	dextri	right	dexterity
durus (*DOO-rus*)	duri	harsh	endurable
facilis (*FAH-kil-is*)	facilis	easy	facile
latus (*LAH-tus*)	lati	wide	latitude
liber (*LEE-ber*)	liberi	free	liberty
nasutus (*nah-SOO-tus*)	nasuti	long-nosed	nasute
notus (*NOH-tus*)	noti	known	notable

Nominative (m., s.)	Genitive	Meaning	Derivative
omnis (*OHM-nis*)	omnis	all	omniscient
pensilis (*PEHN-sih-lis*)	pensilis	hanging	pensile
praeacutus (*preye-ah-KOO-tus*)	praeacuti	very sharp	acute
propinquus (*proh-PIN-kwus*)	propinqui	neighboring	propinquity
reliquus (*REH-lin-kwus*)	reliqui	remaining	relic
sinister (*SIH-nihs-ter*)	sinistri	left	sinister
suavis (*SWAH-wis*)	suavis	polite, polished	suave
sumptuarius (*sump-too-AH-ree-us*)	sumptuarii	excessive spending	sumptuary

Pensile is used to describe something that hangs, like a bird's nest, not what happened to Great Uncle Obadiah when convicted of murder.

The Romans had *sumptuary* laws, which regulated the amount of money one could spend on a banquet. The American sumptuary law is called credit card limit.

Remember poor *nasicorn* Uncle Edwin? He's also *nasute*.

Irregular Adjectives

The following adjectives are found in forms different from the regular adjectives. These are often irregular in English, too, such as *good, better, best* and *much, more, most*. As indicated, there are a group of adjectives whose forms resemble more the pronoun *hic, haec, hoc* (for more details, see Chapter 8). These adjectives sound exactly as they look. Remember the rule: two-syllable words accent the first syllable; with more than two syllables, accent is usually on the second to last.

Nominative (m., s.)	Genitive (m., s.)	Meaning	English Derivative
alter	alterius	the other	alter ego
bonus	boni	good	bonus
exterus	exteri	the last outward extreme	exterior
extremus	extremi	last	extreme
inferus	inferi	below	inferior
magnus	magni	large	magnify
multus	multi	much, many	multiply
nullus	nullius	none	nullify
similis (*SIH-mi-lis*)	similis	similar	similar
solus	solius	alone	sole
superus	superi	above	superior
totus	totius	all, total	total
ullus	ullius	any	

A *teetotum* is a small top, used in games of chance and inscribed with the letter *T* for "take all"—not to be confused with *teetotaler*, one who abstains completely from alcoholic drink.

Practice Makes Perfect 2

Translate the following expressions into English:

1. Nobilis femina   _____

2. Triumphalis cena   _____

3. In media cauda   _____

4. Infirmum aedificium   _____

5. Populus Romanus   _____

The Most Agreeable Words

The big grammatical rule is that adjectives must agree with the noun they modify in number, gender, and case. So if the noun is *puella* and the adjective *bonus*, the ending on *bonus* must be nominative, singular, and feminine: *bona*.

Easy, you would think. Just use the same letter. Unfortunately, there are five declensions of nouns and two declensions of adjectives, and here come all those endings that send students to loony town.

But hey, forget all that! Just look at the front of the word and we'll let the hard-core grammarians worry about agreement. Of course, if you *are* a hard-core grammarian, just look at the forms in Appendix B.

If you want to try to be agreeable, match the nouns in Column A with the adjectives in Column B:

Column A	Column B
senatoris	bonus
vasis	suavem
coquus	Graecis
denti	nervosi
hospitam	longo
hippopotamus	absurdus

Tene Memoria
Remember that the *-a* ending is a popular one with the Romans. It can be the nominative singular feminine, nominative plural neuter, or accusative plural neuter. Use the context of the sentence to help you decide.

The Goods on Adjectives as Nouns

The English language often uses adjectives as nouns—the goods, evils, the blues. In Latin, also, adjectives can be used alone as nouns. Most frequently these noun/adjectives appear in the neuter nominative or accusative plural, ending in *-a*. They should be translated "things"—*multa* (many things), *bona* (good things), *altera* (the other things).

Adjective	Meaning	English Derivative
alter	the other	alter
bona	goods	bonbon
cetera	other things	et cetera
dextra	the right hand	dexterity
maiores (*meye-yohr-ays*)	ancestors	major
multa	many things	multitude
nota	known facts	notable
nullum	nothing	nullification, null and void
omnes	all, everybody	omnipotent, omniscient
sinistra	the left hand	sinister

If you are *ambidextrous*, you have in effect two right hands—*ambi*. It also means you are unusually skillful in two areas, such as T. S. Eliot in both prose and poetry. Of course, ambidextrous can have a more sinister meaning of being a double dealer, a shyster. On top of that, you might be *sinistral*, a rather sinister-sounding synonym for *left-handed*.

Hysteria's Herstory

Roman women, although treated in some ways as second-class citizens, did enjoy certain modern privileges. By a law, *Bonorum possessio* (the possession of goods), a widow was entitled to her deceased husband's property. If there were children, then she had to divide it equally.

Good, Gooder, Goodest—Degrees of Comparison

Not only do adjectives describe the noun they modify, they can also make comparisons. If your father is wise, your mother may be wiser, and, of course, you are the wisest of all. These suffixes, *-er* and *-est*, come from the Latin comparative and superlative forms, as we see in *longus, longior, longissimus*. These forms are also seen in music when you want to be the loudest, *fortissime*.

Perhaps you are *omnilegent* (*ohm-NIL-eh-jent*). You might know someone who reads everything more than you, but it is awkward to say *omnilegenter.* So another form of the comparative is *more omnilegent* and the superlative, *most omnilegent.* In Latin, we use *magis* and *maxime*, as in *magis intelligens* (more intelligent) and *maxime intelligens* (most intelligent).

Here are some examples of the degrees of an adjective.

Positive	Comparative	Superlative
praeacutus	praeacutior	praeacutissimus
suavis	suavior	suavissimus
nobilis	nobilior	nobilissimus

When you compare something with something else, you can use *quam* followed by the nominative. The ablative case is also used (for more details, see Chapter 9). For example:

> The pig is happier than the man.

Translates as:

> Porcus est laetior quam vir.

Or:

> Porcus est laetior viro.

Remember that every syllable is pronounced in Latin. So it's *ahs-PEHR-ee-us* and *gloh-ree-OH-see-us.*

Cave!

Note that the comparative neuter form ends in *-ius* and can easily be confused with the *us* of the nominative, singular ending, as in *domus, tempus,* or *multus.* The comparative *-ius* is only on adjectives modifying neuter nouns.

Comparative Neuter	Meaning	Derivative
asperius	more bitter	asperity
gloriosius	more glorious	glorious
iucundius	more pleasing	jocund
latius	more wide	lateral
suavius	more charming	suave

If you're the life of the party (the one with the lampshade on your head), you can be *jocund*, *jocose*, or filled with *jocundity*. At any rate, you will probably be making jokes.

On the other hand, if you are trying to impress your boss, remove the lampshade, take out your cell phone, and try to be *suave*.

Practice Makes Perfect 3

Translate the following into English:

1. Nobilior   _____

2. Longior   _____

3. Iratissimus   _____

4. Infirmissimus   _____

5. Communior   _____

A final note on comparison of adjectives and adverbs: the irregular adjectives have irregular comparisons, just as in English. Only 2-year-olds say "This is gooder than that." So in Latin "gooder"—oh sorry, "better"—is *melior*, not *bonior*. For a complete list, see Appendix B.

Latin Today!

Words to take home: Your real home—family, friends, and sleep.

amicae (*ah-MEE-keye*)

amici (*ah-MEE-kee*)

familia (*fah-MIH-lee-ah*)

mater (*MAH-tehr; MAY-tehr* in English)

dormire (*dohr-MEE-reh*)

I Object! The Accusative Case

The accusative case sounds very negative. "*J'accuse!*" exclaims Emile Zola, implying guilt. It is speculated that this case is so named because the attention is focused on the object you accuse. So the accusative case is used as the direct object of a verb as well as the object of a preposition.

The singular endings usually end with *-m*, the plural with *-s*. You find similar endings in *him*, the objective form of *he*, and *us*, the objective form of *we*. So is it that easy? Let's try.

Nominative	Accusative (Singular)	Accusative (Plural)	Meaning
vita	vitam	vitas	life, lives
cibus	cibum	cibos	food, foods
lex	legem	leges	law, laws
actus	actum	actus	act, acts
res	rem	res	thing, things

What could be easier? Of course, it's highly unlikely you'll need the form for plural of right hand unless you're talking about the traditional wedding ceremony in which the bride and groom are asked to join their right hands (*dextras iungere*).

The problem is with the neuter nouns. Look at these examples.

Nominative	Accusative (Singular)	Accusative (Plural)	Meaning
aurum	aurum	aura	gold, gold pieces
mare	mare	maria	sea, seas
tempus	tempus	tempora	time, times
vasum	vasum	vasa	vase, vases

There's a pattern here. The nominative and accusative of neuter nouns are always the same. The plural neuter forms always end in -*a*.

The accusative case endings are used on the direct object of verbs. The direct object is that which receives the action of the verb. If you're looking at something, that something is in the accusative case. If you send something, bite something, peel something, wash something, run over something, paint something, or twist something, all the somethings must be in the accusative case.

Grammar Guru

In English, the direct object almost always comes after the verb—"People eat potatoes." *Potatoes* is the direct object. If the sentence were "Potatoes eat people," then *people* would be the direct object and running for their lives from the *giant killer potatoes!*

Practice Makes Perfect 4

Try translating these phrases. The first one is done for you. Remember, in Latin word order does not indicate direct objects, as in English.

1. Capio vexillum.   I capture the flag.

2. Apprehendo anserem.   _____

3. Elephantum capio.   _____

4. Arbores subruo   _____

5. Coquus cenam coquit.   _____

6. Labor tempus consumit.   _____

7. Caesarem peto.   _____

How's That? Questions

In English, we form questions by using an interrogative word—*Why? How? When? Where?* We also ask questions by inverting the word order—*Can I learn Latin?* Sometimes we indicate written questions by using the question mark—*The movie is over?* In speaking, sometimes we raise our voice at the end of the question—*Is the movie over?* and sometimes we don't—*Where did you put my sandwich?*

Because we have never heard a Roman ask a question, we don't know whether he raised his voice at the end of a sentence. We do know he used body language extensively and there is a word for "shrug"—*umeros allevare* (*OO-meh-rohs ah-lay-WAH-reh*). Because the Romans did not use a lot of punctuation marks, a question was indicated at the beginning of the sentence by ...

♦ Using an interrogative word such as *quis* (who), *quid* (what), *ubi* (where), *quando* (when), *cur* (why), *quo modo* (how), *quantum* (how much), *quot* (how many), or *qualis* (what kind of).

♦ Adding *-ne* to the first word to show that a question was coming; for example, *Esne dictator?* (Are you a dictator?) or *Ambulatne in horto?* (Is she walking in the garden?)

◆ Beginning the sentence with either *num* or *nonne*. *Num* indicates a sentence is coming that needs a *no* answer, and *nonne* indicates a sentence that needs a *yes* answer. These are fine distinctions not ever found on inscriptions, legal terms, or medical terminology. In fact, you rarely see these words except in conversation, and let's face it, how many Latin dialogues do you expect to have riding on the elevator at work?

Practice Makes Perfect 5

Look back at the previous "Practice Makes Perfect" section and turn the sentences into questions. Then translate them into English.

The Least You Need to Know

◆ Adjectives make our writing more defined and interesting.

◆ Adjectives agree with the noun they modify in number, gender, and case.

◆ Adjectives are sometimes used as nouns.

◆ Adjectives have degrees of comparison.

◆ The direct object is in the accusative case, which usually ends in *-m* or *-s*.

◆ Neuter nominative and accusative forms are always the same. The neuter plural nominative and accusative ending is *-a*.

◆ Asking questions in Latin can get you into trouble. When in doubt, just use the universal shrug.

8

Taking the Place of Nouns— Pronouns

In This Chapter

◆ Pronouns you should know

◆ First and second person pronouns and adjectives

◆ Third person pronouns, demonstratives, and adjectives

◆ Reflexive and intensive pronouns and adjectives

◆ The irregular verb *ire* (go)

If there were no pronouns, Shakespeare would have written:

> Friends, Romans, countrymen, lend Mark Antony the ears of the friends, Romans, and countrymen; Mark Antony comes to bury Caesar, not to praise Caesar.

Pronouns are linguistic shortcuts, allowing us to use nice, short replacements for long, cumbersome names. English speakers automatically change cases—"I see him," "he sees me," "we see them." So doing the same in Latin will be easy.

Words You Yourself Should Know

Personal pronouns are small and short, and just as in English, they come in various cases.

Latin Pronoun	Case	Person	Number	English
ego (*EH-goh*)	nominative	first	singular	I
me (*MAY*)	accusative	first	singular	me
nos (*NOHSS*)	nominative	first	plural	we
nos (*NOHSS*)	accusative	first	plural	us
tu (*TOO*)	nominative	second	singular	you
te (*TAY*)	accusative	second	singular	you
vos (*WOHSS*)	nominative	second	plural	you
vos (*WOHSS*)	accusative	second	plural	you

The *ego*, made famous by Freud, is the "I" or "self" of any person. We all know that it can be very huge and/or fragile.

First and Second Person Pronouns and Adjectives

The personal pronouns in the first and second persons are very similar to the English: *ego* (I), *me* (me), *tu* (you). The plural varies a little, but you can remember it by *nos*, meaning "us," and *vos*, meaning "you guys." Here are some examples:

Ego te amo.	I love you.
Tu me amas.	You love me.
Nos familia laeta sumus.	We are a happy family.

The personal pronoun is often omitted, as in this example: *Te amo* (I love you). When the personal pronoun is used, it shows emphasis: *Ego te amo* translates as "*I* love you," as opposed to your worst enemy, who does not love you.

Latin shows personal possession in the first and second person by using the possessive adjectives. Remember, they have to agree with the noun they modify and, therefore, have varied endings.

Adjective	Base	Meaning
meus (*MEH-us*)	me	my, mine
tuus (*TOO-us*)	tu	your (singular)
vester (*WHESS-ter*)	vestr	your (plural)
noster (*NOHSS-ter*)	nostr	our

For example, *tua barba*, "your beard," means only one of you and your beard. *Vestras barbas*, "your beards," means more than one of you with all your beards.

Noster can be seen in the French *nôtre*, where the circumflex (ˆ) over the *o* denotes the missing *s*. Likewise, *votre* comes from the Latin *vester*.

The Lord's Prayer is often referred to as the *Pater Noster*, the first two words.

Latin Today!

Words to take to the science lab: Upon discovering an unidentifiable speck under your microscope:

sui generis (*SOO-ee GEHN-ehr-is; JEH-ner-is* in English) Unique!

Practice Makes Perfect 1

Translate the following phrases into English:

1. Noster pater   _____

2. Tua soror   _____

3. Ego sum dictator.   _____

4. Nos populus   _____

5. Vestra epistula   _____

This, That, and Whatever—Third Person Pronouns and Demonstratives

Now for the third person pronouns—*he, she, it, they, her, his, its, their, him,* and *them.* As you can see from the English, this is a bit more complicated, mainly because the pronouns designate gender and case. The English cases are …

♦ Subjective (for the subject): *he, she, it,* and *they.*

♦ Possessive (to show ownership): *his, her, its,* and *their.*

♦ Objective (for the object of a verb or preposition): *him, her,* and *them.*

Latin uses the demonstrative pronouns (*this, that, these, those*) as the third person pronouns. Literally, Romans were saying *this man, this woman, this thing* or *that man, that woman, that thing* instead of *he, she, it.* A further distinction designates whether the third person is near the speaker, away from the speaker, or just anywhere. So we have *hic* (*HIHK*), *haec* (*HEYEK*), and *hoc* (*HOHK*) to designate a person near, *ille* (*IH-leh*), *illa* (*IH-lah*), and *illud* (*IH-lud*) for someone farther away.

For example, check out *Is te amat* (he loves you), *ea te amat* (she loves you), *nos te amamus* (we love you), *is eam amat* (he loves her) and on and on.

But hey, forget all that! Just remember that a very short word beginning with *h* has something to do with this person, him or her or them. Another short word beginning with *ill* also has something to do with that person, and a really short word beginning with *e* or *i* designates all the above. Don't be put off by all the forms, which are included here for reference. (See Appendix B for all the forms.)

Case	Singular	Plural
Nominative	hic, haec, hoc (*HIHK*), (*HEYEK*), (*HOCK*)	hi, hae, haec (*HEE*), (*HEYE*), (*HEYEK*)
Genitive	huius, huius, huius (*HYOO-ee-us*)	horum, harum, horum (*HOH-rum*), (*HAH-rum*)
Accusative	hunc, hanc, hoc (*HUNK*), (*HAHNK*), (*HOCK*)	hos, has, haec (*HOHSS*), (*HAHSS*), (*HEYEK*)
Nominative	ille, illa, illud (*IH-leh*), (*IH-lah*), (*IH-lud*)	illi, illae, illa (*IH-lee*), (*IH-leye*)
Genitive	illius, illius, illius (*IH-lee-us*)	illorum, illarum, illorum (*ih-LOH-rum*), (*ih-LAH-rum*)

Case	Singular	Plural
Accusative	illum, illam, illud (*IH-lum*), (*IH-lahm*), (*IH-lud*)	illos, illas, illa (*IH-lohs*), (*IH-lahs*), (*IH-la*)
Nominative	is, ea, id (*IHSS*), (*EH-ah*), (*IHD*)	ei, eae, ea (*EH-ee*), (*EH-eye*), (*EH-ah*)
Genitive	eius, eius, eius (*AY-yoos*)	eorum, earum, eorum (*eh-OH-rum*), (*eh-AH-rum*)
Accusative	eum, eam, id (*EH-um*), (*EH-ahm*), (*IHD*)	eos, eas, ea (*EH-ohs*), (*EH-ahs*), (*EH-ah*)

Just as adjectives can become nouns—*bona* (good things)—so these pronouns can be translated as nouns—*ea* (these things), *illa* (those things), *haec* (these things). Don't confuse *haec* (nominative, singular, feminine) with *haec* (nominative and accusative, plural, neuter).

So we have *Eas edere nolo* (I do not wish to eat them), *habetis eas* (you have them), or *Illa bona sunt* (those are good).

> ### Tene Memoria
>
> Remember that the genitive is translated *his, hers,* or *its.* So *eius, huius,* and *illius* are all translated like this. Of course, you have noticed that *his* looks a lot like *eius.*

Practice Makes Perfect 2

Translate the following into English:

1. Illa inquit.   _____

2. Is erat.   _____

3. Haec procumbit.   _____

4. Illi ambulant.   _____

5. Eius villa   _____

There is a related adjective—*idem* (*IH-dem*), *eadem* (*eh-AH-dem*), *idem* (the same). All you need to remember is that the suffix *-dem* translates as "the same." All the forms are very similar to the demonstrative pronoun *is, ea, id.*

All followers of Freud will recognize the *id*, the part of the psyche that is the source of unconscious and instinctive impulses.

An expression that's simply fun to say is *huc illuc*. This phrase—which can sound like a hiccough—can describe a tennis match, the promises of a politician, or a lawyer's arguments. *Huc illuc* means "this way and that."

Demonstrative pronouns can also be used as adjectives. These are recognized because there will be two words, and the adjective almost always comes first.

Adjective	Noun	Translation
hunc	librum	this book
hic	homo	this man
illae	arbores	those trees
eundem	modum	the same way
has	urinatores	these divers
ea	villa	this/that house

For example, look at *Ei eandem puellam amant* (they like the same girl) and *Illae capellae sub ea sedent* (those goats are sitting under it).

Cave!

Remember that these are adjectives and, therefore, have endings that agree with the noun they modify. So you see *tuum, nostro, vestris*, but they still translate as "your," "our," and "your."

Reflecting Back: Reflexive Pronouns

The English reflexive pronoun is *myself, yourself, himself, herself, ourselves, yourselves,* and *themselves*. It is used when the direct object refers to the subject of the sentence. In Latin, the personal pronoun accusative case is used for the first and second persons—*me, te, nos, vos*. But as usual, the third person has to be different. The reflexive pronoun *se* (SAY) or *sese* (SAYSAY) is used for both the singular and plural and, therefore, is surprisingly easy!

Subject	Verb	Pronoun	Translation
Ego	specto	me	I see myself.
Tu	audis	te	You hear yourself.
Nos	ornamus	nos	We decorate ourselves.
Vos	obruitis	vos	You bury yourselves.
Pueri	recipiunt	se	The boys retreat.
Illi	appellant	se	They call themselves.
Frater	pugnat	se	The brother fights himself.
Ostrea	applicat	se	The oyster attaches herself.

The reflexive adjective *suus* (*SOO-us*; base *su*) is similarly used for all parties of the third person. It is translated "his own," "her own," or "their own," depending on the subject of the sentence.

For example, consider *Puella suum librum legit* (the girl reads her own book) or *hirci suas barbas spectant* (the billy goats look at their own beards).

The reflexive pronoun is not used for the subject. If you want to say "I myself," use the intensive pronoun, *ipse* (*IHP-seh*). This is also sometimes translated as "very," as in *the very idea!* This word can also be used as an adjective or a pronoun, as in this example:

> Ipsa ad villam venit.
> She herself comes to the house.

Don't confuse the intensive with the reflexive:

> Se vidit in speculo.
> She saw herself in the mirror.

Here are the singular and plural forms of *ipse*.

Grammar Guru

The reflexive adjective *suus* (his/her/their own) agrees with the noun it modifies, *not* the person it is representing. So *suos agros* could be "his fields" if the subject is singular—*Curat suos agros* (he watches over his fields).

Singular		
ipse *(IHP-seh)*	ipsa *(IHP-sah)*	ipsum *(IHP-sum)*
ipsius *(IHP-see-us)*	ipsius	ipsius
ipsi *(IHP-see)*	ipsi	ipsi
ipsum *(IHP-sum)*	ipsam *(IHP-sahm)*	ipsum
ipso *(IHP-soh)*	ipsa *(IHP-sah)*	ipso

Plural		
ipsi *(IHP-see)*	ipsae *(IHP-seye)*	ipsa *(IHP-sah)*
ipsorum *(ihp-SOH-rum)*	ipsarum *(ihp-SAH-rum)*	ipsorum
ipsis *(IHP-sees)*	ipsis	ipsis
ipsos *(IHP-sohs)*	ipsas *(IHP-sahs)*	ipsa *(IHP-sah)*
ipsis	ipsis	ipsis

There is one more demonstrative adjective, *iste (IHS-teh)*, which has similar forms and is translated "that ———— of yours," often used in a derogative way, like "that mother-in-law of yours!": *Ista hecyra!*

Practice Makes Perfect 3

Translate the following sentences and phrases into English:

1. Ea apprehendit suum fratrem. _____

2. Hic ornat suum domum. _____

3. Eam calamitatem. _____

4. Illa res _____

5. Id rete _____

If you need to refer to the pronunciation guide, the vocabulary listing in Appendix A gives the chapter where the word occurs first with the phonetic spelling.

Many indefinite pronouns in Latin translate as "some," "any," "any at all," "any one you please," "some," "someone," "some few," "a certain one," "whoever," and "I don't know who." These are discussed in Chapter 14, together with relative pronouns, because for the most part, these have forms similar to the relative pronoun.

Hysteria's Herstory

Fulvia, the Roman wife of Antony before he became besotted with Cleopatra, was famous for her boldness and verve. When Cicero was beheaded by Antony's soldiers in 43 B.C.E., his head and hands were brought to the Roman Forum where they were on display for all to see. Fulvia made a public spectacle of herself and subsequently a place in history by taking a large hairpin from her hair and vehemently piercing the inanimate and now powerless tongue of Cicero. Ouch!

You Can Go Now!

The verb *eo, ire,* is as short and irregular as its English counterpart. Do not confuse the third personal pronoun *is, ea, id* with the irregular verb *ire* (to go). *Is* can also mean "you go," so try to use your common sense and the context of the sentence. Here is the complete present tense.

Present Tense			
eo (*EH-oh*)	I go	imus (*IH-mus*)	we go
is (*IHSS*)	you go	itis (*IH-tis*)	you go
it (*IHT*)	he, she, it goes	eunt (*EH-unt*)	they go

This little verb is often combined with prefixes:

exeo (*EHKS-eh-oh*) I go out	redeo (*REH-deh-oh*) I return	ineo (*IHN-eh-oh*) I go in

abeo	adeo	obeo
(*AH-beh-oh*)	(*AHD-eh-oh*)	(*OHB-eh-oh*)
I go away	I go toward	I go to meet, I run over

praetereo
(*preye-TEHR-eh-oh*)
I go over or beyond

A preterite tense is one wholly in the past. This word is used in many Romance languages to describe a past tense. *Preterition*, also from *praetereo*, is the Calvinistic doctrine that having elected to eternal life certain chosen ones, God passed over the rest, leaving them to eternal death. Bummer.

Notice that the second person singular ending is -*s* and the plural is -*tis*. You can now use these endings on all the verbs you've learned.

Practice Makes Perfect 4

Try translating these:

1. Doletis   _____

2. Consistis   _____

3. Audis   _____

4. Deletis   _____

5. Adicis   _____

The Least You Need to Know

- Personal pronouns are small and powerful, and you know some already, such as *ego* and *me*.

- The third person pronouns come in many shapes and forms but look a lot like the English "his," "it," "him," and … "hiccoughs."

- The reflexive pronoun is the beginning two letters in *self*, which is how it is translated.

Where? When? How Many?

In This Chapter

- ◆ A look at adverbs
- ◆ Add it up with Roman numbers
- ◆ Flip through the Roman calendar
- ◆ At Carthage—the locative case
- ◆ The dative and ablative cases

Imagine trying to determine your place and time without compass or digital watch. Imagine adding and subtracting Roman numerals with a few beads and wire. Fortunately, the Latin language makes up for some of those deficiencies by having many adverbs to describe when, where, and how as well as a specific case for location. Specific time, unfortunately, never quite caught on.

Adverbs

Adverbs are used to modify verbs, adjectives, and other adverbs. Many adverbs in English end in *-ly*, such as *largely*, *insipidly*, or *indisputably*. Other adverbs are simple words, often short, like *not*, *very*, or *easily*.

In Latin, many adverbs are also short words that do not have other forms. Some are really easy to remember.

Easy Adverbs

The following adverbs should be easy to remember by their familiar derivatives. And the good news—adverbs have only one form.

Adverb	Meaning	Derivative
foras (*FOH-rahs*)	out	forum, door
primum (*PREE-mum*)	for the first time	prime time
privatim (*pree-WAH-tim*)	privately	private

Primogeniture is "being the first born," formerly a good thing for the inheritance, nowadays not so good; the oldest child always seems to be breaking ground for younger siblings.

When and Where Adverbs

Adverbs are often used to add a little information to a sentence. They can tell us the when, where, and how of the word or phrase they modify. The following adverbs are a little harder to remember.

Adverb	Meaning	Adverb	Meaning
hic (*HEEK*)	here	olim (*OH-lim*)	once upon a time
hodie (*HOH-dee-ay*)	today	postquam (*POHST-kwam*)	after
interea (*ihn-TEH-reh-ah*)	meanwhile	semper (*SEHM-pehr*)	always
mane (*MAH-neh*)	in the morning	simul (*SIH-mul*)	at the same time
numquam (*NOOM-kwam*)	never	tum (*TOOM*)	then

Adverb	Meaning	Adverb	Meaning
umquam (*OOM-kwam*)	ever	unde (*OON-day*)	from where
nunc (*NUNK*)	now		

Apart from the popular *Semper Fidelis* of the Marine Corps, we see *semper* in *semper-virent*, an "evergreen," which we hope will stay sempervirent for a *sempiternity*.

Tell-Me-How Adverbs

Finally, we have a few adverbs that tell you how, in what way, or to what degree.

Adverb	Meaning	Adverb	Meaning
adeo (*ahd-EH-oh*)	to such a degree	paulo (*POW-loh*)	a little
etiam (*EH-tee-ahm*)	even, also	quot (*KWOHT*)	how many
ita (*EE-tah*)	in such a way	tamen (*TAH-men*)	nevertheless
itaque (*ee-TAH-kweh*)	and so, therefore	tot (*TOHT*)	so many
item (*EE-tem*)	at the same time, likewise	vero (*WAY-roh*)	truly

Try to be *veracious* and truthful, and not *voracious* or, heaven forbid, *bodacious*. *Ver* (true) can be confused with *vert* (turn), *ver* (spring), or *verb* (word).

Adverbs from Adjectives

The other method of forming adverbs is fairly consistent and logical, unlike the previous list. To form an adverb from an adjective, much like we do in English (with words such as *pretty, prettily, handsome, handsomely*), you change the ending of the *-us* adjective to *-e*, and the ending of an *-is* adjective to *-iter*. This doesn't always work, just as it doesn't always work in English, but it's a start.

Adjective	Meaning	Adverb	Meaning
calidus	warm	calide (*KAH-lih-day*)	warmly
fortis	brave	fortiter (*FOHR-tih-ter*)	bravely
humilis	humble	humiliter (*hoo-MIHL-ih-ter*)	humbly
iniquus	unfair	inique (*ihn-IH-kway*)	unfairly
iratus	angry	irate (*ih-RAH-tay*)	angrily
laetus	happy	laete (*LEYE-tay*)	happily
miser	unhappy	misere (*MIH-sehr-ay*)	unhappily

Practice Makes Perfect 1

Match the face with the adverb:

humiliter	absurde
laete	calide
sane	misere
innocenter	irate
suaviter	frigide

A final note on adverbs—like adjectives, adverbs have a comparative and superlative degree. You can say *angrily, more angrily,* and *most angrily.* This is done by adding *-ius* for the comparative and *-issime* for the superla-tive. As with adjectives, the object of compari-son can be in the ablative. The word *quam* is also used. For example:

> He writes more clearly than I.

Translates as:

> Scribit clarius quam ego.

Or:

> Scribit clarius me.

Ten Little Carthaginians—Numbers

Roman numerals are used in the modern world to designate a classic. Super Bowl XXXIX is somehow a better thing, an event of stature, thanks to the addition of X's and I's. *Rocky II* is a movie to be seen because it has Roman numerals, not because it's a weak remake of the first *Rocky*.

Here are the basics of Roman numerals:

I	one	VIII	eight
II	two	IX	nine
III	three	X	ten
IV	four	L	fifty
V	five	C	one hundred
VI	six	D	five hundred
VII	seven	M	one thousand

Cave!

Watch out! The *-ius* ending can be a comparative neuter adjective—*melius* (better), a genitive singular of an irregular adjective, *ullius* (of another), or a comparative adverb, *miserius* (more miserably).

It is said that the shape of Roman numerals originated with the finger movements of early merchants and traders—one finger, two fingers, three fingers, four fingers, and then the V, shaped by the thumb and fingers. Crossed hands made a 10.

When writing Roman numerals, if two numbers are next to each other, the smaller is subtracted if on the left, the smaller is added if on the right. So XIX is 10 plus 1 from 10 (9) or 19. 2006 is MMVI.

The Romans used numerals for the same reason we use them—to count. But their method of counting, using an abacus, is light-years away from our methods today. The mind truly boggles at the difference. A Roman had to carefully put beads into the tens, hundreds, and thousands columns; whereas I, at the click of a mouse, can count every word, every character, every space, and every line in this book instantly.

Numbers are always tackled toward the end of the first year Latin textbook because they have several forms that are like irregular adjectives. Luckily, endings and the correct form are not top priority here, so we can enjoy this easy list of Latin words.

Number	Translation	Derivative
unus (*OO-nus*)	one	unify
duo (*DOO-oh*)	two	duplex
tres (*TRAYSS*)	three	triplets
quattuor (*KWAHT-tohr*)	four	quarter
quinque (*KWIN-kway*)	five	quintuplets
sex (*SEHKS*)	six	sextet
septem (*SEHP-tem*)	seven	September
octo (*AWK-toh*)	eight	October
novem (*NOH-wehm*)	nine	November
decem (*DEHK-ehm*)	ten	December

Number	Translation	Derivative
centum (*KEHN-toom*)	one hundred	century
mille (*MEE-leh*)	one thousand	millennium

Grammar Guru

Mille (1,000) is an indeclinable numeral. *Milia* (thousands of any number) is a noun and takes the partitive genitive. So you have to say 2,000 soldiers, *duo milia militum*, but 1,000 soldiers, *mille milites*.

A.U.C., B.C., A.D., C.E., and B.C.E.—the Roman Calendar

What year is it really? We passed through the millennium without any ruckus because everyone has a different idea of what the date really is! The Romans counted the years from the founding of Rome (*ab urbe condita*), 753 B.C.E. in our reckoning. So their date for the assassination of Caesar was A.U.C. 710. When the calendar was established for Christianity, the Latin *Anno Domini* (A.D.) was used and nowadays we have another choice, Before the Common Era (B.C.E.).

Just in case you want to convert our modern years to the Roman way of thinking or vice versa, here are the formulae:

- If the A.U.C. date is 753 or less, subtract it from 754 for a B.C.E. date.
- If the A.U.C. date is 754 or more, subtract 753 from it for a C.E. date.
- If the year is B.C.E., subtract it from 754 for an A.U.C.
- If the year is C.E., add it to 753 for an A.U.C.

Beware the Ides ...

The Romans had a calendar that would give you a headache. Every day was reckoned from three fixed dates—the *Kalends*, the *Nones*, and the *Ides*. Unfortunately, the Nones was sometimes on the fifth and sometimes on the seventh, whereas the Ides was sometimes on the thirteenth, other times on the fifteenth. Romans had to count backward from the Kalends to find out the dates after the Ides, and it really wasn't worth all that trouble.

Tene Memoria

To remember when the Ides occurs, either on the thirteenth or the fifteenth, here's a time-tested jingle:

In March, July, October and May,
The Ides falls on the fifteenth day.

The Kalends, from which we get the word *calendar* the first day of the month, was purely a Roman invention. It was also the day when payments for bills were due. If someone didn't want to pay up, he would promise to pay on the Greek Kalends (because there was no such thing). We've heard this before: "The check's in the mail!"

The Romans reckoned the hours of the day by the hours after sunrise. So 3 o'clock in the winter was at a different time than 3 o'clock in the summer.

The Roman Year

Romans had several versions of the calendar from early times, all beginning the year in March. Julius Caesar made several revisions. Following the Egyptian method, he used a 365-day year, adopted a leap day in every fourth February, and began his new year on the Kalends of January 45 B.C.E. He changed the month of Quinctilius, previously the fifth month, to July and later the sixth month was named by Augustus for himself. This explains why September, although derived from *septem*, is actually the ninth month in the year.

At Carthage—the Locative Case

Romans used special endings to show "at" someplace. *Romae* means "at Rome"; *Carthagini* means "at Carthage." These are locative case endings. For nouns of the first and second declension, the locative is like the genitive; for third declension, like the ablative, or sometimes dative; and for plural words and names of cities, small islands, and towns …

But hey, forget all that! Just remember that sometimes, by changing a word ending, you can say "at Rome," *Romae;* "at Carthage," *Carthagini;* "at Brundisium," *Brundisii;* "at Ostia," *Ostiae;* or "at home," *domi.*

The Last of the Cases

You've noticed by now that the endings on nouns give you a clue as to how the word can be translated and how it is used in the sentence. The nominative case shows that the word is the subject. The genitive case shows possession and is translated "of." The accusative case is the direct object or the object of certain prepositions. The locative case shows location. Have courage! Only two more to go.

The Dative Case

The dative case is used for the indirect object and sometimes for possession. The indirect object usually occurs with verbs of giving, showing, or telling.

For example:

> I give the cup to him.
>
> I give him the cup.

Translates as …

> Do poculum ei.

The cup is the direct object; it is what I give. *Him* is the indirect object; it is to whom I give the cup.

The dative of possession is seen most often in the expression *Mihi nomen est Marcus* (My name is Marcus, or literally, The name Marcus is for me).

The dative case is also used with the passive periphrastic (see Chapter 6) to show by whom the thing must be done. For example, *Mihi notandum est* (It must be noted by me) or *Illa capella omnibus laudanda est* (That nanny goat should be praised by everyone).

Here are the various singular and plural dative endings for all five declensions.

1st decl.		2nd decl.		3rd decl.		4th decl.		5th decl.	
s.	*pl.*	*s.*	*pl.*	*s.*	*pl*	*s.*	*pl.*	*s.*	*pl.*
ae	is	o	is	i	ibus	ui	ibus	ei	ebus

The Ablative Case

Notice that the ablative endings in the singular are simply one vowel. In the plural, they are identical to the dative in all declensions. The ablative is the last case and is a kind of catchall. You can do just about anything in the ablative case.

Here's a list of the various singular and plural ablative endings.

1st decl.		2nd decl.		3rd decl.		4th decl.		5th decl.	
s.	*pl.*	*s.*	*pl.*	*s.*	*pl*	*s.*	*pl.*	*s.*	*pl.*
a	is	o	is	e	ibus	◆	ibus	e	ebus

The ablative case is used in the following ways:

◆ **Means or instrument.** To show with what instrument, tool, object, or thing something is done. For example:

He improves the house with a shower.

Translates as:

Villam balneo mangonicat.

◆ **Agent.** The person by whom something is done, especially with passive verbs, is indicated by the preposition *a* or *ab* and the ablative. For example:

The house is improved by the landlord.

Translates as:

Villa a domino mangonicatur.

◆ **Time.** To show when something is done. For example:

He improves the house in the second year.

Translates as:

Villam secundo anno mangonicat.

◆ **With prepositions.** Many prepositions are followed by the noun in the ablative case, especially prepositions denoting place or from. For example:

Wine is in the cup.

Translates as:

Vinum in poculo est.

◆ **Manner.** To show how something is done. For example:

> I drink the wine with a great noise.

Translates as:

> Vinum magno clamore bibo.

◆ **Comparison.** Used with the comparative degree of an adjective or adverb to make a comparison between two things. For example:

> The pig is fatter than a horse.

Translates as:

> Porcus pinguior equo est.

◆ **Degree of difference.** Used with comparisons to show how much or little a difference there is. For example:

> The pig is a lot fatter than a horse.

Translates as:

> Porcus multo pinguior equo est.

The personal pronouns also have dative and ablative endings:

Dative:

mihi   nobis   tibi   vobis   ei, eis   huic, his

Ablative:

me   nobis   te   vobis   eo, ea, eis   hoc, hac, his

For example:

> I am wiser than he.

Translates as:

> Sum sapientior eo.

And:

> These girls are wiser than those girls.

Translates as:

> Hae puellae illis sapientiores sunt.

Practice Makes Perfect 2

Translate the following phrases and sentences:

1. Today, not in the morning   _____

2. Never at the second hour   _____

3. Angrily   _____

Now translate the Latin into English:

1. Duo et duo faciunt quattuor   _____

2. Nunc aut numquam   _____

3. Tum et nunc   _____

The Least You Need to Know

- Adverbs answer the questions of where, when, and how and do not have a lot of confusing endings.

- We are indebted to the Romans for the word *calendar*, the months of July and August, and that crazy leap year.

- When in Rome, use the locative case.

- The dative case is used for the indirect object, and the ablative case is used for everything else.

Expanding the Time Frame— Past and Future Tenses

In This Chapter

◆ Verbs' principal parts

◆ The imperfect tense

◆ A peek into the future

◆ Active and passive perfect tenses

◆ The perfect infinitive and the perfect passive participle

◆ Command with the imperative

It's time to look at verbs in their entirety. Dictionaries, vocabularies, and textbooks give four parts to every verb—unless the verb is missing a part or two, in which case it's called defective. This doesn't mean there's anything wrong with the verb. It just isn't all there, like your second cousin Ollie.

The Principal Parts of Verbs

Latin has six tenses—present, imperfect, future, present perfect, past perfect, and future perfect—and they all come in both active and passive voices. The four principal parts give all the bases for the tenses, so you really need to know what principal parts are and how to use them:

- **First principal part.** *Amo* (*AH-moh*; I love), first person singular, present tense. Every verb is listed under this form.

- **Second principal part.** *Amare* (*ah-MAH-reh*; to love), the present active infinitive. By dropping the *-re* ending, you've got the present stem; the basis for the present, imperfect, and future tenses, both active and passive.

- **Third principal part.** *Amavi* (*ah-MAH-wee*; I have loved), the first person singular, present perfect tense, active voice; by dropping the *-i*, the perfect stem is created, the basis for all the perfect active tense forms.

- **Fourth principal part.** *Amatus* (*ah-MAH-tus*; having been loved), the perfect passive participle and the basis for all the perfect passive tense forms.

Verbs with Easy Third Principal Parts

When the third principal part has the same base as the first, it really is not a good thing, because then, how can you tell *ascendimus* (we climb) from *ascendimus* (we have climbed)? Answer: you can't, and you'll just have to deal with it.

Except for a few changes in the fourth principal part, the following verbs are easily recognized in all tenses.

First	Second	Third	Fourth	Meaning	Derivative
ascendo (*ahs-KEHN-doh*)	ascendere (*ahs-KEHN-deh-reh*)	ascendi (*ahs-KEHN-dee*)	ascensus (*ahs-KEHN-sus*)	climb	ascend
invado (*in-WAH-doh*)	invadere (*in-WAH-deh-reh*)	invadi (*in-WAH-dee*)	invasus (*in-WAH-sus*)	invade	invasion
invenio (*in-WEHN-ee-oh*)	invenire (*in-wehn-EE-reh*)	inveni (*in-WEHN-ee*)	inventus (*in-WEHN-ee*)	come upon	invent

First	Second	Third	Fourth	Meaning	Derivative
moveo (*MOH-weh-oh*)	movere (*moh-WAY-reh*)	movi (*MOH-wee*)	motus (*MOH-tus*)	move	motion
prandeo (*PRAHN-deh-oh*)	prandere (*prahn-DAY-reh*)	prandi (*PRAHN-dee*)	pransus (*PRAHN-sus*)	eat	prandial
respondeo (*rehs-POHN-deh-oh*)	respondere (*rehs-pohn-DAY-reh*)	respondi (*rehs-POHN-dee*)	responsus (*rehs-POHN-sus*)	answer	response
venio (*WEHN-ee-oh*)	venire (*wehn-EE-reh*)	veni (*WAY-nee*)	ventus (*WEHN-tus*)	come	venture
video (*WIH-deh-oh*)	videre (*wih-DAY-reh*)	vidi (*WEE-dee*)	visus (*WEE-sus*)	see	vision
vinco (*WIHN-koh*)	vincere (*WIHN-keh-reh*)	vici (*WEE-kee*)	victus (*WIHK-tus*)	conquer	victory

Many English derivatives come from the fourth principal part: *motion, vision, response, convention.*

What Latin words are the basis for *application? appellation? concoction? diffuse? ornate? petition? relate?* See Chapter 5 for answers.

Verbs with Slightly Changed Third Principal Parts

These verbs often follow a pattern within the conjugation. The first-conjugation verbs end fairly regularly in *-are* (AH-reh), *-avi* (AH-wee), and *-atus* (AH-tus). Second-conjugation verbs (remember the ones whose first form ends in *-eo?*) often have a third principal part ending in *-ui* (OO-ee). Third-conjugation perfect stems often end in *-s* or *-x*. Fourth-conjugation verbs often end in *-ire* (EE-reh), *-ivi* (EE-wee), *-ii* (EE-ee), or *-itus* (EE-tus). Many of these verbs you have seen before.

It's good practice to just say aloud the principal parts, following the models of the verbs in the preceding table.

First	Second	Third	Fourth	Meaning	Derivative
amo	amare	amavi	amatus	love	amative
dico	dicere	dixi	dictus	speak	diction
dissimulo	dissimulare	dissimulavi	dissimulatus	pretend	dissimulate
habeo	habere	habui	habitus	have	habit
habito	habitare	habitavi	habitatus	live	inhabit
includo	includere	inclusi	inclusus	include	include
invito	invitare	invitavi	invitatus	invite	invite
laboro	laborare	laboravi	laboratus	work	labor
mitto	mittere	misi	missus	send	mission
moneo	monere	monui	monitus	warn	admonition
peto	petere	petivi	petitus	beg, ask	petition
porto	portare	portavi	portatus	carry	portfolio
quaero	quaerere	quaesivi	quaesitus	search	inquire
praetereo	praeterire	praeterivi	praeteritus	pass over	preterite

Your *portfolio*—the one with your artwork, not the one at your broker's—is used to carry around your work. A *portmanteau* is your traveling bag, and *porter's beer* is what your porter, the man who carries your stuff, drinks when off duty. Porter beer is made from a weak stout rich in sugar with 4 percent alcohol.

A word of caution: *praetereo* looks like a second-conjugation verb ending in *-eo*, but looks are misleading; the verb is, in fact, a compound of *praeter* and *eo*, which is a fourth-conjugation verb.

Verbs with Principal Parts You Really Need to Know

The following verbs are frequently used and have third and fourth principal parts that you might not recognize as remotely belonging to the first principal part. Most people won't find the word in the dictionary because it's listed under the first principal part. My advice is to always look around the dictionary page at the complete entries. Sometimes you'll find the mystery word listed as a third or fourth principal part. Most of these words were mentioned in Chapters 5 and 6.

First	Second	Third	Fourth	Meaning	Derivative
ago	agere	egi (*AY-gee*)	actus (*AHK-tus*)	do, drive, live	agent
capio	capere	cepi (*KAY-pee*)	captus (*KAHP-tus*)	capture	capture
do	dare	dedi (*DEH-dee*)	datus (*DAH-tus*)	give	data
facio	facere	feci (*FAY-kee*)	factus (*FAHK-tus*)	do, make	fact
fero	ferre	tuli (*TOO-lee*)	latus (*LAH-tus*)	carry	elate
iacio	iacere	ieci (*YAY-kee*)	iactus (*YAHK-tus*)	throw	reject
possum	posse	potui (*POH-too-ee*)	—	be able	potent
sto	stare	steti (*STEH-tee*)	status (*STAH-tus*)	stand	status
sum	esse	fui (*FOO-ee*)	futurus (*foo-TOO-rus*)	be	future
volo	velle	volui (*WOH-loo-ee*)	—	want	volunteer

So many English words come from the fourth principal part: *status, data, future, fact, act. Jactation* is the tossing to and fro, jerking and twisting of the body or its parts. Something like dancing?

It's an Imperfect World

The imperfect tense is so named because it denotes action that's not finished, not perfected. It is translated "was/were ———ing," "kept ———ing," or "used to ———."

The imperfect is formed in Latin by adding *bam, bas, bat, bamus, batis,* or *bant* to the present stem. Following are the imperfect tense of the verb *sto, stare* (to stand). Remember, the accent goes on the first syllable unless there are more than two. Then it goes on the second to last. So it's *STAH-bahm* but *stah-BAH-tis*.

stabam	I was standing	stabamus	we were standing
stabas	you were standing	stabatis	you were standing
stabat	he was standing	stabant	they were standing

The imperfect is the same for all conjugations and is easy to recognize.

Unfortunately, irregular as always, the imperfect tense of the verb *esse* (to be) is as follows (use the same pronunciation rules as given earlier):

eram	I was	eramus	we were
eras	you were	eratis	you were
erat	he was	erant	they were

As you can see, this is consistent and will be used as a helping verb in the past perfect tenses, active and passive.

Practice Makes Perfect 1

Translate the following verb forms into English:

1. Faciebamus   _____

2. Ferebant   _____

3. Eramus   _____

4. Dabat   _____

5. Agebatis   _____

What's in Your Future?

The future tense tells what will be. In the first and second conjugations, look for *-bo*, *-bi*, or *-bu* added to the present stem.

Here is the future tense of the verb *amare* (to love) (remember that the accent is on the second-to-last syllable):

amabo	I will love	amabimus	we will love
amabis	you will love	amabitis	you will love
amabit	he will love	amabunt	they will love

Unfortunately, the third and fourth conjugations couldn't follow that simple rule. Instead, they have *a* in the first person and *e* in all the rest. Now if you say that a few times, stressing the *a* first and then *e*, you'll have a little thing going that you can sing in the shower or hum in the subway.

> **Cave!** _____
>
> Watch out! Second-conjugation present tense looks exactly like the third- and fourth-conjugation future tense: *habet* (he has), *mittet* (he will send). Remember that the second-conjugation verb has an *-eo* ending on the first principal part.

Here is the future tense of *mittere* (to send):

mittam (*MIH-tahm*)	I will send	mittemus (*mih-TAY-mus*)	we will send
mittes (*MIH-tayss*)	you will send	mittetis (*mih-TAY-tis*)	you will send
mittet (*MIH-teht*)	he will send	mittent (*MIH-tent*)	they will send

The future tense of *esse* (to be) is characterized by *eri*. These forms apply to all compounds of *esse*, such as *possum* (to be able), *absum* (to be away), and *adsum* (to be present). The same pronunciation rules apply: *EH-roh eh-RIH-mus*.

ero	I will be	erimus	we will be
eris	you will be	eritis	you will be
erit	he will be	erunt	they will be

Practice Makes Perfect 2

Now translate these verb forms into English:

1. Dices   _____

2. Erimus   _____

3. Amabo   _____

4. Poteritis   _____

5. Habebunt   _____

At this point, then, you are able to talk about something happening in the past, the present, and the future, using the imperfect, present, and future tense forms. What else could there be?

The Perfect Tenses, Active and Passive

The perfect tenses (all happening in the past) in English use the verb *has/have* as a helping verb. The present tense of *have* is used for the present perfect (*he has gone*), the past tense of *have* for the past perfect (*he had gone*), and the future tense of *have* for the future perfect (*he will have gone*).

In Latin, the verb ending changes to indicate the tense. All the perfect active tenses use the third principal part, and all the perfect passives use the fourth principal part.

So let's put together the present perfect active (a.k.a. perfect active tense) of the verb *videre* (to see). Note the slightly different endings for the second person:

vidi (*WEE-dee*)	I have seen, I saw, I did see
vidisti (*wee-DIHS-tee*)	you have seen, saw, did see
vidit (*WEE-dit*)	he has seen, saw, did see
vidimus (*wee-DIH-mus*)	we have seen, saw, did see

vidistis (*wee-DIHS-tis*)	you have seen, saw, did see
viderunt (*wee-DAY-runt*)	they have seen, saw, did see

You can see immediately that the *-t*, *-mus*, *-tis*, and *-nt* endings are still there to remind you of *he*, *we*, and *they*. The *-i*, *-isti*, *-istis*, and *-erunt* endings and the third principal part are the only indications that this is a perfect and, therefore, a past tense.

The past and future perfect tenses are not used as frequently as the present perfect, and they are easy to spot. They use a helping verb, the imperfect of *esse* and the future of *esse*, but it is added to the perfect stem like an ending.

Here is the past perfect active (a.k.a. pluperfect tense) of the same verb (same pronunciation rules apply):

videram	I had seen	videramus	we had seen
videras	you had seen	videratis	you had seen
viderat	he had seen	viderant	they had seen

And here is the future perfect active tense:

videro	I will have seen	viderimus	we will have seen
videris	you will have seen	videritis	you will have seen
viderit	he will have seen	viderint	they will have seen

The perfect passive tenses use the fourth principal part, the perfect passive participle, and the verb *to be* as a helping verb, although, because this is Latin, the helping verb is out of order. It follows the participle as opposed to English, where the helping verb comes first.

> **Tene Memoria**
>
> Just remember: third principal part, past tense. Third principal part with *era*, "had ———ed."

Here is the present perfect passive tense of *videre*. The three endings on the participle are for a masculine, feminine, or neuter subject:

visus/a/um sum	I have been seen
visus/a/um es	you have been seen
visus/a/um est	he/she/it has been seen
visi/ae/a sumus	we have been seen

visi/ae/a estis	you have been seen
visi/ae/a sunt	they have been seen

So if the subject is feminine, for example, the verb would be *visa sum* and if plural, *visae sunt*. If the subject is neuter, then *visum est* or *visa sunt*. So *homo visus est* (The man has been seen); *Mensa visa est* (The table has been seen).

Here is the past perfect passive tense:

visus/a/um eram	I had been seen
visus/a/um eras	you had been seen
visus/a/um erat	he/she/it had been seen
visi/ae/a eramus	we had been seen
visi/ae/a eratis	you had been seen
visi/ae/a erant	they had been seen

The future perfect passive, should you ever use it, follows the same pattern:

visus/a/um ero	I will have been seen
visus/a/um eris	you will have been seen
visus/a/um erit	he/she/it will have been seen
visi/ae/a erimus	we will have been seen
visi/ae/a eritis	you will have been seen
visi/ae/a erunt	they will have been seen

Grammar Guru

The perfect passive participle, like all participles, can be used as a noun or adjective. Sometimes it is translated in a clause: *visus* is "which has been seen" or "the seen" (thing, person). But you are always correct to translate the fourth principal part as "having been ———ed."

But hey, forget all that! Just watch for those third principal parts that will transport you to the past, and remember that *i* actually means "I," and you will have—or have had or had had—the perfect tense!

One last note: there's a perfect active infinitive that is easy to identify; *-isse* on the perfect stem translates "to have ———ed."

The perfect passive infinitive uses the fourth principal part and the infinitive form of "to be," *esse*. For example:

amavisse	to have loved
amatus esse	to have been loved

Practice Makes Perfect 3

Now translate the following:

1. Quaesivi   _____

2. Deportavit   _____

3. Noluit   _____

4. Antecesserat   _____

5. Commoverat   _____

The Imperative—a Commanding Lead

Although the Romans often used the subjunctive (see Chapter 14) for a gentle command in the third person—*Fiat lux!* (Let there be light!)—or an encouragement in the first person plural—*Eamus!* (Let's go!)—they used the imperative form to give commands. And because commands are usually urgent, they made up a short imperative form, the present stem for the singular, and added *-te* for the plural. So if your employees were wasting time around the water cooler, you could yell, *Laborate!* (*lah-boh-RAH-tay*). Or if your mother-in-law was not moving fast enough, you could give her a little shove and say, *Festina!* (*fehs-TEEN-ah*).

There are some irregular imperatives: *duc!* (*DOOK*; lead!) and *fac!* (*FAHK*; Do!) are regular in the plural.

Negative commands took a little more time. *Noli* (*NOH-lee*; singular) and *nolite* (*NOH-lee-tay*; plural) plus the infinitive get people to stop doing something—*Noli circumstare!* (Stop standing around!), *Nolite cantare!* (Stop singing!).

Vocative Case and Direct Address

While we're speaking directly to people, you might as well know that you use the vocative case, which is just like the nominative case ending. "Woman!" *femina!*

"Caesar!" *Caesar!* Second declension men end in *-e*. "Marcus!" *Marce!* If your name ends in *-ius*, then your vocative ending is *-i*. "Lucius!" becomes *Luci!* which looks and sounds like Charlie Brown's friend Lucy except, remember, the *c* is always hard—*LOO-key*.

If you're important enough to address more than one person, just use the nominative plural.

Practice Makes Perfect 4

Now try yelling these commands and then translate them:

1. Prandite!
   (*PRAHN-dee-tay*)   _____

2. Move!
   (*MOH-way*)   _____

3. Noli movere!
   (*NOH-lee moh-WAY-reh*)   _____

4. Ite!
   (*EE-tay*)   _____

5. Porta!
   (*POHR-tah*)   _____

Hysteria's Herstory

The Empress Poppaea, wife of Nero, will be remembered for her permanent wave. She sat for 2 weeks with her hair bound in curlers and packed in clay and mud. When the mud dried and was cracked off, her hair was rippling like the sea. Nero was so entranced he had his hair waved likewise, setting off a trend. Of course, a bust of Poppaea survives to this day, making her hairdo really permanent.

Practice Makes Perfect 5

Identify the person, number, tense, and voice and then translate the verb; the first one is done for you. (If this is too onerous, just translate.)

1. Fuimus   1st person, plural, present perfect active, we have been

2. Misit   _____

3. Veni   _____

4. Veniebant   _____

5. Potueram   _____

6. Amavit   _____

7. Factum est   _____

8. Data erant   _____

9. Steti   _____

10. Ceperint   _____

Study Tips

The way to learn a language is to use it. Review the list at the beginning of this chapter, and cover the English and try to repeat the meaning. Or have a friend read the Latin or English and you give the translation.

When you have identified words you can't remember, write them on cards or paper. Put the list over the kitchen sink, over your desk at the office, or on the bathroom mirror. Read and repeat. Read and repeat.

Some people remember words better if they associate the words with pictures. Organize a picture party: have everyone bring old magazines and find pictures that illustrate those words you can't remember. Cut out the picture, paste it onto construction paper, and write the Latin word prominently on the back of the picture. Keep these picture vocabulary cards near you.

Try to use the Latin derivatives as often as you can. When you read, note the words and expressions that are Latin or derived from Latin. Keep an eye out for articles about the Roman Empire or about Latin in education.

And above all, read Chapter 11. There we finally get to read phrases, clauses, and entire sentences in Latin.

The Least You Need to Know

♦ The third principal part is very important.

♦ The imperfect is translated as "was/were ———ing."

♦ The future tense of the third and fourth conjugations has *a* in the first person and *e* in all the rest.

♦ Perfect tenses are past history.

♦ Commands are short.

Part 3

Expressing Yourself in Latin

Part 3 is all about Latin phrases, clauses, and sentences. Phrases, although incomplete grammatically, are often used for whole thoughts—*like, whatever!* Although hindered by a lack of verb, some phrases can still pack a punch—*under 21?*—or keep you going—*nice work!*—or make you very happy—*no school!*

Then there are those combinations of words that express a complete thought grammatically. A sentence is the coming together of all the parts of speech, a joining of those words, clauses, and phrases to make a statement about life, about nothing, about anything. The good news is that every sentence has a subject and predicate, so there's something going on in a logical and complete way. The bad news is that sentences can be complicated.

Locutiones–Phrases

In This Chapter

- ◆ Prepositions and prepositional phrases
- ◆ Prepositions as prefixes
- ◆ Interjections!

Here are some definitions for the hard-core grammarian: a *phrase* is a group of words that does not have a subject and verb. A *clause*, on the other hand, has a subject and verb, although it may not always be a complete sentence. A *prepositional phrase* is a group of words that begins with a *preposition*, a word that shows a relationship of a noun or pronoun to some other word in the sentence.

But hey, forget all that! A prepositional phrase begins with a little word, a preposition, and is followed by other words.

There used to be a grammatical rule: don't end a sentence with a preposition. That's because a preposition is wedded to its object, the word that follows it. So you're not supposed to say, *Which car is the president in?* Instead, you should say, *In which car is the president?* As far as English goes, this rule probably went out with the undershirt; in Latin, however, you can count on the preposition and its object being very close together.

Words Without Which You Cannot Do

Some prepositions denote *coming toward*, or if you are not looking, *running into*. These generally are followed by the accusative case. *Ad murum* means "toward the wall," and *in murum* translates as "into the wall."

Other prepositions describe a *going away from—a muro* (away from the wall), *de muro* (down from the wall), and in case you are a mouse or termite, *e muro* (out of the wall). These generally take the ablative case. The following table lists many common prepositions.

Preposition	Case	Meaning	Derivative
a/ab (*AH*)/(*AHB*)	ablative	away from	abience
ad (*AHD*)	accusative	to, toward	adience
ante (*AHN-teh*)	accusative	before	anteroom
contra (*KOHN-trah*)	accusative	against	contradict
cum (*KOOM*)	ablative	with	compress
de (*DAY*)	ablative	down from	deride
e/ex (*AY*)/(*EHKS*)	ablative	out of	extract
in (*IHN*)	ablative	in, on, into	insider
in	accusative	into, onto, against	invective
inter (*IHN-ter*)	accusative	between	intermission
per (*PEHR*)	accusative	through	perfume
post (*POHST*)	accusative	behind, after	postlude
praeter (*PREYE-ter*)	accusative	past, beyond	preterite

Preposition	Case	Meaning	Derivative
pro (*PROH*)	ablative	before, for	prosecute
prope (*PROH-peh*)	accusative	near	propinquity
propter (*PROHP-ter*)	accusative	on account of	—
sine (*SIH-neh*)	ablative	without	sinecure
sub (*SUHB*)	ablative/ accusative	to the foot of, under	suburb
supra/super (*SOO-prah*)/ (*SOO-per*)	accusative	over, above	superego
trans (*TRAHNS*)	accusative	across	transatlantic

Remember the *ego* and the *id?* The *superego* is the third part of Freud's psyche, which is partly unconscious and develops from the ego. It is *above the ego* partly to protect it from those nasty id impulses.

While we're psychoanalyzing, *abience* is that avoidance behavior we're all so fond of, whereas *adience* is the tendency to approach willingly a stimulus or situation. To avoid writing, I engage in abient behavior: walking the dog, cleaning the floor, ironing T-shirts, or reading junk mail.

A *sinecure* is a job without work, if such a thing is possible.

The following table lists some common nouns and adjectives you need to read the selections in Part 4. Notice that *agricola* is masculine, even though it belongs to the first declension.

Noun	Genitive	Gender	Meaning	Derivative
agricola (*ah-GRIH-koh-lah*)	agricolae	m.	farmer	agriculture
alces (*AHL-kayss*)	alcis	m./f.	elk	elk

continues

continued

Noun	Genitive	Gender	Meaning	Derivative
articulus (*ahr-TIH-coo-lus*)	articuli	m.	joint	articulate
auxilium (*awks-IH-lee-um*)	auxilii	n.	aid	auxiliary
equus (*EH-kwuhs*)	equi	m.	horse	equine
iter (*EE-tehr*)	itineris	n.	journey, way	itinerary
magister (*mah-GIS-ter*)	magistri	m.	teacher	magistrate
regina (*reh-GEE-nah*)	reginae	f.	queen	regal
rex (*REKS*)	regis	m.	king	regal
sacerdos (*sah-KER-dohs*)	sacerdotis	m.	priest	sacerdotal
taberna (*tah-BER-nah*)	tabernae	f.	shop, bar	tavern
ursus/a (*OOR-sus*)/(*OOR-sah*)	ursi/ursae	m./f.	bear	ursine
parvus/a/um (*PAHR-wus*)	parvi/parvae/i	m./f./n.	small	parvitude
malus/a/um (*MAH-lus*)	mali malae/i	m./f./n.	bad	malediction

Tene Memoria

Remember that verbs whose first principal part ends in *-eo* are in the second conjugation. Other conjugations are determined by the infinitive: *-are*, first; *-ere*, third; and *-ire*, fourth.

To *articulate* is to unite with joints, and to be *articulate* is to be able to join your syllables, words, and phrases into meaningful sentences.

A *malediction* is the opposite of a *benediction* and is something to avoid.

Parvitude is the state of being little. My troubles, for example, can differ in multitude and parvitude.

Here are more verbs without which you cannot read Latin.

Verb and Principal Parts	Meaning	Derivative
animadverto, ere, verti, sus (*ahn-nee-mahd-WEHR-toh*)	notice	animadversion
cedo, ere, cessi, cessus (*KAY-doh*)	move, yield	secede
deporto, are, avi, atus (*day-POR-toh*)	deport	deport
intellego, ere, exi, ectus (*ihn-tel-LEH-goh*)	know	intelligent
narro, are, avi, atus (*NAH-roh*)	tell	narrate
opprimo, ere, pressi, pressus (*oh-PRIH-moh*)	oppress	oppress
pono, ere, posui, positus (*POH-noh*)	put, place	deposit
reicio, ere, eci, ectus (*reh-IH-kee-oh*)	reject	reject
remaneo, ere, mansi, mansus (*reh-MAHN-eh-oh*)	remain	remain
salio, ire, salii/salui, salitus (*sah-lee-oh*)	jump	salient
sedo, are, avi, atus (*SAY-doh*)	sedate, sooth	sedate
statuo, ere, ui, tutus (*sta-TOO-oh*)	decide	statute

Salient means "prominent," "conspicuous," "jumping," or "leaping." So if your salient talent is jumping and leaping, you could be famous for your salient salience.

In the Blink of an Eye—Coming or Going?

Two prepositions—*a, ab* and *e, ex*—have different forms for when the next word begins with a vowel or consonant, similar to the English *a* or *an* (for example, *a muro, ab arbore, e muro, ex arbore*).

Both *de* and *ex* are used with *numero* to mean "from the number of." *De* can also mean "about, concerning." For example, *aliqui ex numeo militum relinquebantui* (some from the number of soldiers were left behind), or *tres de pueris clamabant* (three of the boys shouted).

Ad followed by a participle can be translated "for the purpose of"—*Ad cavendum praesidium ponitur* (The guard is posted for the purpose of looking out).

A or *ab*, when used with a person, can mean "by"—*Ab puero canis amatur* (The dog is loved by the boy).

Cum is usually combined with the reflexive and personal pronouns—*mecum* (with me), *secum* (with himself), *tecum* (with you).

Finally, don't worry about getting the case correct. The object always follows the preposition closely, and what do you care what case it's in? The only word you might want to remember is *in*, and you should be able to tell by the context of the sentence whether the elephant is *in* the wall, or *running into* the wall.

Practice Makes Perfect 1

Try translating the following prepositional phrases:

1. Ad villam _____

2. A sorore _____

3. E numero concharum _____

4. Post cenam _____

5. Ab sacerdote _____

Prepositions as Prefixes—Preposterous!

The English language has thousands of words that begin with a Latin prefix, including *absent, adjunct, antedate, composite, excavate, invade,* and *submarine.*

Many words are compounded with a prefix in Latin, too. The compound words often change one letter or two, but generally they are easy to spot and translate. Here are a few formed from the prepositions you have learned already:

From *a/ab* …

abstineo, ere, inui, tentus	abstain
appendo, ere, di, sus	pay out, weigh out
abripio, ere, ripui, reptus	snatch away

From *ante* …

antecedo, ere, cessi, cessus	outdo, surpass
anteambulo, are, avi, atus	run before
antevenio, ire, veni, ventus	come before

From *con* (derived from *cum*, meaning "together, completely") …

commoveo, ere, movi, motus	move thoroughly
comprehendo, ere, si, sus	unite, hold together, know
comporto, are, avi, atus	bring together
compello, ere, pulsi, pulsus	drive together

From *de* …

decido, ere, cidi, cisus	cut down, fall down
decipio, ere, cepi, ceptus	take down
deduco, ere, duxi, ductus	lead down
deporto, are, avi, atus	carry away
desilio, ire, ui, itus	jump down

From *e/ex* …

excipio, ere, cepi, ceptus	make exceptions
excogito, are, avi, atus	think out

Grammar Guru

Watch out for the prefix *in-*, which sometimes carries a negative meaning, as in *incomprehensible*, *intolerant*, and *indefensible*. The same warning for *ante-*, not to be confused with the Greek *anti-*, "against." So be *anti- war* (against war), not *antebellum* (before the war).

Latin Today!

Words to take to the stadium: Try these at homecoming on your way to the game:
stadium (*STAH-dee-um; STAY-dee-um* in English)
colosseum (*koh-loh-SEE-um*)
pompa triumphalis (*POHM-pah tree-um-FAH-lis*)

From *in* …

induco, ere, duxi, ductus	lead in
infundo, ere, fusi, fusus	pour on
inicio, ere, ieci, iectus	inject, throw on
insto, are, steti, status	stand on
invenio, ire, veni, ventus	come upon, find, invent

From *per* (meaning thoroughly) …

perficio, ere, feci, fectus	complete, finish
permisceo, ere, mixi, mictus	mix completely
pernocto, are, avi, atus	spend the night
permuto, are, avi, atus	change completely

Practice Makes Perfect 2

Can you guess the meaning of these words made with prepositional prefixes?

1. Exit _____

2. Init _____

3. Inambulo _____

4. Pervenit _____

5. Abduxit _____

Hey! Interjections!

The word *interjection* comes from *iacio* (to throw) and *inter* (between). When thrown in between a conversation, sentence, thought, or even total silence, an exclamation becomes a part of speech, the interjection, and is always followed by an exclamation point.

Hysteria's Herstory

Pliny the Younger tells about a remarkable woman, Ummidia Quadratilla, who lived to be almost 80. She owned a company of pantomime dancers and enjoyed their performances more than the typical Roman noblewoman should. She brought up her grandson in her own home, supervising his education. Whenever she was about to either play checkers or watch the pantomimes, she sent him away to study. Way to go, Grandma!

Like all human beings, the Romans had strong emotions, and we have evidence of what they said in times of surprise, anger, shock, or sadness. Letters about deaths or expressing indignation often used interjections. But our best and most valid sources are plays, particularly of Plautus, as he wrote about the daily life of the common people.

Cave!

Don't confuse *Interjection* with *expletive*, an exclamation or oath that is frequently deleted. An expletive can also be that extra word in a sentence, like *there*, that really serves little purpose. For example: "There is a dog in the car."

In *The Pot of Gold*, Eunonia says: *Heia! hoc face quod te iubet soror* (Come on now, do what your sister orders).

And later, Megadora replies: *Neque edepol ego te derisum venio.* (Good heavens! I didn't come here to make fun of you).

Calling to someone, Megadora shouts: *Heus! Pythodicus!*

Here are some common interjections:

a, ah	alas! ah!
(*AH*)	
ecce	look!
(*EH-kay*)	

eugapae (*YOO-gah-peye*)	hooray!
hei, ei (*HAY*), (*AY*)	hey! (alarm)
eheu (*AY-hoe*)	alas!
io (*EE-oh*)	hurray! (joy) oh! (pain) ho there! (calling out)
ha, ha (*HAH*)	ha ha! (laughter, hysterical laughter)
ohe (*OH-hay*)	stop! enough!
oh (*OH*)	oh! (surprise, joy, grief)
oi (*oy*)	oh! oh, dear! (complaining, weeping)

At last, some answers:

ita (*EE-tah*)	yes!
ita vero (*EE-tah WAY-roh*)	yes, indeed!
non (*NOHN*)	no!
minime (*MIH-nih-may*)	not at all!

The Romans could and did swear, invoking the gods just as we do today. We, however, tend to curse the one God, whereas the Romans had a grand panoply of deities to call on. Plautus has his characters frequently say *Pol! Edepol! Ecastor!* These rather mild imprecations call upon the minor god Pollux and his brother Castor. The *ede* is probably the preposition *e*, meaning "from," and a shortened form of *deus*, "god."

Practice Makes Perfect 3

Choose an appropriate interjection from the previous list for …

1. Calpurnia calling out to Caesar on his way to the Senate: _____! Don't go! It's the Ides of March!

2. Caesar to Brutus: _____! Et tu, Brute?

3. Cleopatra to Antony: _____! Our ship is sinking!

4. A friend of Caesar, on hearing of his assassination: _____!

5. An enemy of Caesar, on hearing of his assassination: _____!

6. One Roman barfly to another: Did you hear the one about … _____!

7. Roman thief calling to victim: _____!

8. Victim, being beaten by thief: _____!

Using your Latin answers, respond in Latin:

1. Esne architectus? _____

2. Amasne asparagum? _____

3. Elephantusne arborem ascendit? _____

4. Habitasne in piscina? _____

5. Amasne legere? _____

6. Estne agricola bonus vir? _____

7. Habitatne Regina Shebae in tua villa? _____

The Least You Need to Know

◆ Prepositional phrases begin with a preposition and end shortly.

◆ Prepositions can be prefixes.

◆ Unlike injections, interjections can be fun.

◆ Now you can say "yes," "no," and "definitely!"

Articuli–Clauses

In This Chapter

- ◆ More nouns and adjectives
- ◆ Temporal clauses
- ◆ The ablative absolute
- ◆ Deponent verbs

A clause is a group of words that contains a subject and a verb. There are two basic kinds of clauses: independent clauses and subordinate clauses. The *independent clause* is like your oldest son and can stand alone. The *subordinate clause* is like your dog and depends on just about everybody to make his life meaningful.

A sentence is an independent clause. Two independent clauses can be joined to make one sentence. Another sentence can include both a subordinate and an independent clause.

But hey, forget all that! I go into more detail in Part 4. Just try to learn the following words.

Absolutely Necessary Words

The following nouns and adjectives are from four different declensions. Remember that the fourth declension nouns have the genitive ending in *-us*.

Nominative	Genitive	Gender	Meaning	Derivative
astrum (*AHS-trum*)	astri	n.	star	astrology
auris (*OW-ris*)	auris	f.	ear	auricular
consuetudo (*kohn-sway-TOO-doh*)	consuetudinis	f.	custom	consuetude
cornu (*KOHR-noo*)	cornus	n.	horn	corniform
hortus (*HOHR-tus*)	horti	m.	garden	horticulture
lana (*LAH-nah*)	lanae	f.	wool	lanolin
manus (*MAH-nus*)	manus	f.	hand, band	manuscript
mas (*MAHS*)	maris	m.	male	masculine
metus (*MEH-tus*)	metus	m.	fear	—
miles (*MEE-lehs*)	militis	m.	soldier	military
plebs (*PLEHBS*)	plebis	f.	commoners	plebeian
puer (*POO-ehr*)	pueri	m.	boy	puerile
sapiens (*SAH-pee-ayns*)	sapientis	m./f./n.	wise	sapient
stola (*STOH-lah*)	stolae	f.	dress	stole
urbs (*UHRBS*)	urbis	f.	city	urban
via (*WEE-ah*)	viae	f.	road	viaduct

Nominative	Genitive	Gender	Meaning	Derivative
longus/a/um (*LOHN-gus*)	longi/ae/i	m./f./n.	long	long
mortuus/a/um (*mohr-TOO-us*)	mortui/ae/i	m./f./n.	dead	mortuary
novissimus/a/um (*noh-WISS-ee-mus*)	novissimi/ae/a	m./f./n.	latest	novice
transversus/a/um (*trahns-WEHR-sus*)	transversi/ae/a	m./f./n.	lying	transverse across

Consuetude means custom or use, a useful term for not tipping—"It's not my consuetude." If your bicycle got run over by a truck and is now *corniform* (in the shape of a horn), that is probably not a good thing. A *cornada* is not a good thing, either; it's a wound inflicted by a bull in bullfighting.

Lanolin, used for ointments and cosmetics, is actually refined wool fat.

Here are some more useful verbs; remember that verbs with an *-eo* ending on the first principal part are second conjugation.

First	Second	Third	Fourth	Meaning	Derivative
affero (*ah-FEH-roh*)	afferre	attuli	allatus	carry to	afferent
alo (*AH-loh*)	alere	alui	alitus	eat	aliment
canto (*KAHN-toh*)	cantare	cantavi	cantatus	sing	cantabile
constituo (*kohn-stih-TOO-oh*)	constituere	constitui	constitutus	decide	constitute
exanimo (*eks-AH-nee-moh*)	exanimare	exanimavi	exanimatus	weaken	exanimate
excogito (*eks-COH-gee-toh*)	excogitare	excogitavi	excogitatus	think up	cogitate
gero (*GEH-roh*)	gerere	gessi	gestus	wear	gesticulant

continues

continued

First	Second	Third	Fourth	Meaning	Derivative
lego (*LEH-goh*)	legere	legi	lectus	choose, read	lectern
placo (*PLAH-koh*)	placare	placavi	placatus	please	placate
recipio (*reh-CIH-pee-oh*)	recipere	recepi	receptus	receive, with *se*, to retreat	receipt
rideo (*RIH-day-oh*)	ridere	risi	risus	laugh	risible
rodo (*ROH-doh*)	rodere	rodi	rosus	wear down	erode
se recipio	recipere	recepi	receptus	retreat	receipt
scio (*SKEE-oh*)	scire	scivi	scitus	know	science
specto	spectare	spectavi	spectatus	look at	spectator
spero	sperare	speravi	speratus	hope	aspiration
tardo	tardare	tardavi	tardatus	slow down	retard

An *afferent* nerve conveys an impulse to the central nervous system.

Exanimo means "to knock the breath out of, tire, weaken, kill, or scare the wits out of." So if your spouse comes home and appears *exanimate*, he's probably had a very bad day.

Some people can't seem to talk without punctuating their thoughts with their fingers, waving their arms, and generally causing a lot of distraction with gestures. A nice way of describing this person is *gesticulant*.

And *risible* is a favorite on SAT tests. It means "laughable," so don't confuse it with *erasable*.

Time for Temporal and Causal Clauses

Temporal clauses are introduced by words denoting time: *ubi* (when), *antequam* (before), *postquam* (after), *quamquam* (although), *quod* (because), *simul* (at the same time as).

Tene Memoria

Remember that if there is no noun subject, the personal ending of the verb is the subject; *-o* translates "I," *-s* translates "you," *-t* translates "he," *-it* translates "she," *-mus* translates "we," *-tis* translates "you," and *-nt* translates "they."

Practice Makes Perfect 1

Translate the following. Note they are all sentence fragments.

1. Ubi astrum spectas   _____

2. Antequam librum lego   _____

3. Postquam miles trans viam ambulat   _____

4. Simul cantant   _____

5. Quamquam via longa est   _____

The Clause of Much Confusion—Ablative Absolute

The word *absolute* comes from *ab* and *solvo*, "to loosen" or "let go." Caesar uses *absolvo* to describe the letting go of the ships from their moorings. In English, your church *absolves* or *frees* you from your sins (should you have any).

In English grammar, an absolute is a phrase, usually a noun and a participle, that is not connected grammatically to the rest of the sentence. Absolutes are often used to add specifics to a generalization. For example: "Feet propped up on desk, light turned off, music turned on, George was ready for work."

In Latin, the ablative absolute is a similar construction but is often translated as a clause. The ablative absolute consists usually of a noun and perfect passive participle, but sometimes has a present participle, sometimes two nouns, and is always in the ablative case. It can express time, circumstance, cause, condition, concession, means, or manner.

Grammar Guru

Remember that a phrase is a group of words that do not have a verb and a subject. A clause, on the other hand, does.

But hey, forget all that! Just remember that you can translate the ablative absolute with "after," "when," "since," "although," "because," "if," or "in the time of." Common sense is another key to translating the ablative absolute. Take a look at the following examples:

Inauribus gestis, omnes risimus.

> The earrings having been worn, we all laughed.

> Because the earrings were worn, we all laughed.

> When the earrings were worn, we all laughed.

> Although the earrings were worn, we all laughed.

> Since the earrings were worn, we all laughed.

M. Antonio et Cicerone consulibus, Roma urbs magna erat.

> In the consulship of Antonius and Cicero, Rome was a large city.

Rosa carne omni, margaritae ad imum cadunt.

> All the meat having been worn away, the pearls fall to the bottom.

> When all the meat has been worn away, the pearls fall to the bottom.

> Because all the meat has been worn away, the pearls fall to the bottom.

Latin Today!

Words to take to the concert:
Going to a Bon Jovi concert?
Sing along in Latin:

musica (*MOO-sih-kah*)

cantare (*kahn-TAH-reh*)

auscultare (*ows-kul-TAH-reh*)

turba (*TUHR-bah*)

All these translations, although different in meaning, are grammatically correct. Which one do you use? The one that fits best the context of the sentence or paragraph. This is the curse of Latin: 2 words, 200 possible translations. The following phrase is from the selection in Part 4 on "How to Catch an Elephant":

Novissimo totius agminis elephantorum spectato ...

> The last of the whole line of elephants having been seen ...

> When the last of the line of elephants is seen ...

Cave!

The ablative singular feminine often looks like the nominative singular feminine. Look to other words in the phrase for hints that it's an ablative.

Remember that the ablative absolute can be translated many different ways. But it will always be in the ablative (duh) and most often is separated from the sentence with commas.

Practice Makes Perfect 2

Translate these sentences:

1. Cane alito, iter fecimus.   _____

2. Agricola placata, equi ex urbe ducti sunt.   _____

3. Toga induta, senator ex villa ambulavit.   _____

4. Domino nato, in ecclesia cantamus.   _____

5. Servata republica, Cicero laudatus est.   _____

Or ... Deponent Verbs

It's time to review the passive forms of verbs. The passive voice is formed by adding special passive endings to the base. You learned the first person (*or*) and third person (*tur*) singular as well as the third person plural (*ntur*) in Chapter 5. Here is the complete passive conjugation.

Present Tense Ending	Imperfect Ending	Future Ending (1st and 2nd/3rd, io, 4th)
-or	-bar	-bor/-ar
–ris	-baris	-beris/-eris
–tur	-batur	-bitur/-etur
–mur	-bamur	-bimur/-emur
–mini	-bamini	-bimini/-emini
-ntur	-bantur	-buntur/-entur

For example: *amaris* (you are loved), *relinquemini* (you will be left behind), *laudamur* (we are praised), *capientur* (they will be seized).

Present Perfect	Past Perfect	Future Perfect
4th prin. part plus	*4th pr. part plus*	*4th pr. part plus*
sum	eram	ero
es	eras	eris
est	erat	erit
sumus	eramus	erimus
estis	eratis	eritis
sunt	erant	erunt

For example: *allata sunt* (they have been carried away), *ductus eram* (I had been led), *recepti erimus* (we will have been received).

Hysteria's Herstory

The Emperor Augustus was devoted to his wife, Livia Drusilla, and died in her arms on August 29, 14 C.E. When asked how she kept the love and affection of such an important and influential man, she replied, "My secret is simple: I have made it the work of my life to please him."

Deponent comes from the Latin *depono*, "to put aside," because these verbs have put aside all their active voice forms. Deponent verbs have passive endings but are translated in the active voice. So *loquor* means "I speak," not "I am spoken," even though it has a passive ending.

Or … you can just remember that if the first principal part ends in *-or*, it's deponent and always active, even though it has those passive endings. Here's a partial list of deponents. Notice that the infinitive is the present passive: the *e* of the present active infinitive changes to *i* except for the third conjugation, which has to do something different.

1st Principal Part	2nd Principal Part	3rd Principal Part	Meaning	Derivative
arbitror	arbitrari	arbitratus sum	think	arbitration
loquor (*LOH-kwohr*)	loqui	locutus sum	speak	loquacious
morior (*MOH-ree-ohr*)	mori	mortuus sum	die	mortuary
nascor (*NAHS-kohr*)	nasci	natus sum	be born	natal

1st Principal Part	2nd Principal Part	3rd Principal Part	Meaning	Derivative
palor (*PAH-lohr*)	palari	palatus sum	wander	—
patior (*PAH-tee-ohr*)	pati	passus sum	suffer	patient
polliceor (*poh-LIK-eh-ohr*)	polliceri	pollicitus sum	promise	pollicitation
proficiscor (*proh-fih-KISS-kohr*)	proficisci forward	profectus sum	leave, go	proficient
sequor (*SEH-kwohr*)	sequi	secutus sum	follow	sequel

Morior means "to die, pass away, die out." It is slightly more definitive than *exanimo*.

Pollicitation is a promise that is not accepted. If, for example, your neighbor dies and wills you her extremely scrawny and mean cat and you reject the offer, that is a *pollicitation*. Don't confuse this with *solicitation*, which has only one *l* but could also contain a promise.

Practice Makes Perfect 3

Translate the following clauses:

1. Natus est.   _____

2. Ego loquor.   _____

3. Proficiscebantur.   _____

4. Passus sum.   _____

5. Palarisne?   _____

More Deponent Verbs

The Romans loved prefixes and sprinkled them liberally around their language. Three deponent verbs offer excellent examples of this make-another-word-with-a-prefix syndrome.

Prefix	Verb and Parts	Meaning	Derivative
	loquor, loqui, locutus	to speak	locution
ad	alloquor	speak to	allocution
con	colloquor	speak with	colloquy
ex	eloquor	speak out	eloquence
	gradior, gredi, gressus	to step, walk, go	
ad	aggredior	approach	aggressive
con	congredior	come together	congress
ex	egredior	go out	egress
in	ingredior	go in	ingredient
	sequor, sequi, secutus	to follow	sequence
ad	assequor	go after	—
con	consequor	pursue	consequent
ex	exsequor	follow out	executive

The Least You Need to Know

◆ Temporal clauses indicate time and are fragments.

◆ Absolutes are separated from the sentence with commas.

◆ Deponent verbs are passive in form and active in meaning.

◆ If you want your deeds to be eternal, write them in stone.

The Theory of Relative Clauses

In This Chapter

- ◆ Useful words to learn
- ◆ The relative clause
- ◆ The relative pronoun
- ◆ Indefinites, intensives and interrogatives

Your relatives are people you're pretty much stuck with. They're connected to you for birthday parties, family reunions, and obligatory correspondence like congratulations or condolences. Although you're closely related, your life would go on without them. So it is with relative clauses. The sentence is complete without them, but the relative clause brings information and adds a little excitement to the sentence, just as Uncle Edwin does to Thanksgiving dinner.

Words That Must Be Learned

The following table lists just a few new words you need to learn so you can read the relative clauses in the Latin selections in Part 4.

Latin	Parts	Meaning	Derivative
apud (*AH-puhd*)	(preposition with acc.)	among, at the home of	—
bos (*BOHSS*)	bovis, m./f.	ox, cow	bovine
casus (*CAH-sus*)	casus, m.	chance	casual
celer (*KEHL-ehr*)	celeris, celere	swift	celerity
cervus (*KEHR-wus*)	cervi, m.	deer	cervicorn
creo (*KREH-oh*)	creare, avi, atus	create	create
crux (*KRUHKS*)	crucis, f.	cross	crucify
fleo (*FLEH-oh*)	flere, flevi, fletus	cry	flow
magnopere (adv.) (*mahg-NOH-peh-reh*)		greatly	magnificent
nam (conj.) (*NAHM*)		for	—
nomen (*NOH-men*)	nominis, n.	name	nomenclature
novus (*NOH-wus*)	nova, novum	new	novice
obtineo (*ob-TIHN-eh-oh*)	ere, tinui, tentus	occupy	obtain
scribo (*SKRIH-boh*)	ere, scripsi, scriptus	write	scripture
sella (*SEH-lah*)	sellae, f.	chair	—
teneo (*TEH-neh-oh*)	ere, tenui, tentus	hold	tenet

A *tenet* is a belief you hold dearly.

And let's hope that poor Uncle Edwin, who is nasicorn, hirsute, and nasute, is not also *cervicorn*, because then to add to his troubles, he'd have antlers on his head.

Review time! In the following table, cover the column on the right and provide the correct translation. You've seen these words before.

> **Tene Memoria**
>
> Remember, you can study words by sticking them on your fridge, TV, bathroom mirror, or the back of your cell phone.

Latin	Meaning
ago, agere, egi, actus	do, drive, live
illa	she, that woman
ille	he, that man
inaures, ium, f. pl.	earrings
licuit	it was permitted
margarita, ae, f.	pearl
mensa, ae, f.	table, meal
murena, ae, f.	eel
natus, a, um	born, taken from
terra, ae, f.	earth

Recognizing Your Relatives

Remember that clauses are more complicated than phrases because they have a subject and a verb. An independent clause can stand alone, but a subordinate clause depends on the rest of the sentence for meaning.

There are several kinds of subordinate clauses, one of which is the relative clause. Relative clauses are found within complete sentences. The relative pronoun takes the place of a noun, its antecedent, and acts within its own clause.

But hey, forget all that! Just remember:

♦ A relative clause begins with a relative pronoun: who, whose, whom, which, that.

♦ You can put mental (or real) parentheses around the relative clause and still have a meaningful sentence.

And to get your exercise regimen started, pick out the relative clause from these four sentences:

1. I saw the boy who was eating peanuts.

2. The eel which was in the bathtub frightened the man.

3. My country, which I love, is America.

4. The car in which the president was riding turned the corner.

The other problem: you have to identify the antecedent. The antecedent (coming from the Latin *antecedo*, "go before") is the word directly before the pronoun. This is not difficult. In sentence 1, the antecedent is *boy*; in sentence 2, *eel*. The other antecedents are *country* and *car*.

In English, how do you know when to use *who, whom, whose, which,* or *that?* Some people don't know, or use the relative pronouns incorrectly. Here are some rules:

♦ **First rule.** Use *who, whom,* or *whose* for people and *which* or *that* for things.

♦ **Second rule.** *Who*, the nominative/subjective form, is used for the subject of the clause. *Whose*, the genitive/possessive form, is used to show possession. *Whom*, the accusative/objective form, is used as the object of the verb or object of a preposition.

♦ **Most important rule.** Decide the case by its use in its own clause.

For example:

The boy whose father is a teacher eats peanuts.

If you replace *whose* with its antecedent, the clause reads "The boy's father is a teacher." Obviously, the *'s* shows possession and, hence, the genitive form.

Another example:

The girl whom I see is strong.

If you replace *whom* with its antecedent, the clause reads "I see the girl." *Girl* is the direct object of the verb and, therefore, in the accusative/objective form.

This is the reason you say *to whom*. You need to use the objective form because the pronoun is the object of a preposition.

Practice Makes Perfect 1

Fill in the blanks with the correct relative pronoun:

1. The bike _____ is locked isn't stolen.

2. The person of _____ you speak is Caesar.

3. I saw your girlfriend _____ was walking down the street with your best friend.

4. Your girlfriend _____ I saw was walking down the street.

5. Dali, _____ paintings are very modern, had a prodigious mustache.

Whoosier Relative Pronoun?

In Latin, the relative clause is a little more complicated because of the cases. The relative pronoun must agree with its antecedent in number and gender, but, just as in English, it takes its case from its use in its own clause.

Here are the forms of the relative pronoun. Note how similar they are to the demonstrative pronoun *hic*. (See Appendix B for the complete table of forms.)

	Singular			Plural		
Case	**m.**	**f.**	**n.**	**m.**	**f.**	**n.**
Nominative	qui	quae	quod	qui	quae	quae
Genitive	cuius	cuius	cuius	quorum	quarum	quorum
Dative	cui	cui	cui	quibus	quibus	quibus
Accusative	quem	quam	quod	quos	quas	quae
Ablative	quo	qua	quo	quibus	quibus	quibus

Note the pattern in the relative pronoun forms: *-ius* for genitive singular, and *–i* for dative singular like the demonstrative pronouns. The dative and ablative plurals are always the same. The ablative singulars end in single letters, and the accusatives are reminiscent of the declensions.

Look at these examples:

Vidi Caesarem qui ab Gallia venit.
I saw Caesar who came from Gaul.

Vidi Caesarem cuius filia Julia appellata est.
I saw Caesar whose daughter was called Julia.

Vidi Caesarem cui honor datur.
I saw Caesar to whom honor is given.

Vidi Caesarem quem omnes laudant.
I saw Caesar whom all praise.

Vidi Caesarem ab quo laudor.
I saw Caesar by whom I am praised.

Grammar Guru

Remember, nominative case, subject; genitive case, possession; dative case, indirect object; accusative case, direct object; ablative case, everything else.

Cave!

The nominative singular masculine relative pronoun and nominative plural masculine are spelled the same: *qui*. Ditto for the nominative feminine forms: *quae*.

The relative pronoun agrees with its antecedent in number and gender. Imagine that the pronoun is taking the antecedent's place; if the antecedent is a woman, then the pronoun should be feminine, and if the antecedent is two men, then the pronoun should be masculine plural. But because the pronoun is doing something in its clause, either being the subject or the direct object or object of a preposition, then its case is determined by its behavior in its own clause.

Practice Makes Perfect 2

Fill in the blanks, using the words from the following pool of words: *Caesar, cervus, bos, epistula, vir, femina.*

Several answers are correct, but common sense probably excludes the cow from jumping or the letter being given food.

1. _____ qui salire amat.
   (Hint: the noun is singular and masculine because *qui* is singular. How do you know? The verb has a singular ending.)

2. _____ quae domum remanet.
   (Hint: the noun is singular and feminine because *quae* is singular, feminine.)

3. _____ quam scripsi.
   (Hint: *quam* is singular, feminine.)

4. _____ qui in piscina cecidit.

5. _____ cui cibum datum est.

6. _____ ab quo canes vocati sunt.

Practice Makes Perfect 3

Translate the following clauses; remember, they are subordinate clauses and, therefore, are not complete thoughts. You will see these clauses and the rest of their sentences in the Latin selections in Part 4.

1. Versiculum in quo me admones   _____

2. Illam, cui Quintus mensam misit   _____

3. Ego qui ab ostreis abstinebam   _____

4. Nuclei qui margaritae sunt   _____

5. Is qui primus pensiles balineas invenit   _____

Indefinites, Intensives, Interrogatives ... Whatever

The words in the next table follow the pattern set by the relative pronoun: genitive in *-ius*, dative ending in *-i*, accusatives following the first and second declension, dative and ablative plurals with third declension *-ibus*.

Nominative (m., f., n.)	Meaning
aliquis, aliquis, aliquid (*AH-lih-kwis*)	someone, anyone
ipse, ipsa, ipsum (intensive) (*IHP-seh*)	-self
quidam, quaedam, quiddam (*KWIH-dam*)	a certain person

continues

Nominative (m., f., n.)	Meaning
quis, quis, quid (interrogative) (*KWISS*)	who? what?
quinam, quinam, quidnam (*KWIH-nam*)	who, pray? what?
quisque, quisque, quidque (*KWISS-kweh*)	each, every
quisquis, quisquis, quidquis (*KWISS-kwiss*)	whoever
quisvis, quisvis, quidvis (*KWISS-wees*)	whomever you want

It's lists like this that make you curse the Roman precision. They were maddeningly detailed, even about being indefinite!

You don't have to learn every form for every pronoun, because the endings are similar to the relative pronoun and often the prefix or suffix hints as to the meaning. For example:

- Aliquis is made up of *alius* (other) and *quis* (who).

- Quinam has the suffix *-nam* (for), adding a little urgency to the question.

- Quisvis has the suffix *-vis* (you want).

The interrogative pronoun is used to ask a question. The forms are just a little different from the relative pronoun. Here's the singular.

Case	m. and f.	n.
Nominative	quis	quid
Genitive	cuius	cuius
Dative	cui	cui
Accusative	quem	quid
Ablative	quo	quo

The plural is exactly like the relative pronoun. For example, *Quis es?* (Who are you?), *Quid est?* (What is it?), *Qui sunt?* (Who are these people?).

The interrogative adjective—"what god," "what road," "what gift"—is declined completely like the relative pronoun *qui deus, quae via, quod donum.*

Latin Today!

Words to take to the library: Put these in your spiral notebook:

liber (*LEE-behr*)   silentium (*see-LEHN-tee-um*)

legere (*LEH-geh-reh*)   scribere (*SKREE-beh-reh*)

addenda (*ahd-DEHN-dah*)   corrigendum (*koh-rih-GEN-dum; koh-rih-JEN-dum* in English)

Practice Makes Perfect 4

Translate the following into English:

1. Quidam cervus nasum rubicundum habet.   _____

2. Quae bos super lunam salit?   _____

3. Invitate quemvis.   _____

4. Caesar ipse catapultum habuit.   _____

Hysteria's Herstory

During the siege of Saguntum by Hannibal, after all the food was gone, the people piled up a heap of all their treasures in the center of town. Then the men made a last-ditch foray against the Carthaginians, who promptly slaughtered them all. Upon hearing of the disaster, the women set fire to the pile and cast themselves and their children on it to avoid capture and dishonor. This was not a good thing and began the Second Punic War.

The Least You Need to Know

♦ The relative clause begins with a relative pronoun.

♦ The relative pronoun begins with *qu-* or *cu-* just as the English relative pronoun begins with *wh-*.

♦ Many Latin words have *quis* with a suffix or prefix.

♦ Now you can say "Whatever." "Quicquid."

Chapter 14

Closing In on Clauses

In This Chapter

- ◆ Words to learn
- ◆ Subjunctive mood
- ◆ Subordinate conjunctions
- ◆ Purpose clauses
- ◆ Result clauses
- ◆ Clauses of fearing
- ◆ Temporal clauses

Let's face it. Some days you're in a good mood; others, not so hot. Verbs, too, have their moods. The imperative mood is bossy, the indicative mood is just your everyday normal state, and the subjunctive mood is wistful and dreamy. You've already learned the indicative and imperative. It's time for the subjunctive.

Words to Learn in Order to Be Educated

The following words have been grouped according to parts of speech—nouns, adjectives, adverbs, and verbs. Some should be included in the easy category, such as *fabula* (story) or *figura* (figure).

Nominative	Genitive	Gender	Meaning	Derivative
canis (*CAH-nis*)	canis	m./f.	dog	canine
cibus (*KIH-bus*)	cibi	m.	food	ciborium
civis (*KEE-wis*)	civis	m./f.	citizen	civil
concilium (*kohn-KIHL-ee-um*)	concili	n.	council	council
exspectatio (*eks-pehk-TAH-tee-oh*)	exspectationis	f.	anticipation	expect
fabula (*FAH-boo-lah*)	fabulae	f.	story	fabulous
figura (*fih-GOO-rah*)	figurae	f.	shape	figure
frons (*FROHNS*)	frontis	f.	forehead	front
ludus (*LOO-dus*)	ludi	m.	game, school	ludicrous
nihil (*NIH-hil*)	—	—	nothing	nil
os (*OHSS*)	oris	n.	mouth	oral
officium (*oh-FIH-kee-um*)	offici	n.	duty	office
patria (*PAH-tree-ah*)	patriae	f.	fatherland	patriotic
pellis (*PEH-liss*)	pellis	f.	skin, hide	pelt
pondus (*POHN-dus*)	ponderis	n.	weight	ponderous

Nominative	Genitive	Gender	Meaning	Derivative
quies (*KWEE-ays*)	quietis	f.	quiet, rest	quiet
radix (*RAH-diks*)	radicis	f.	root	radical
ramus (*RAH-mus*)	rami	m.	branch	ramification
senatus (*sen-AH-tus*)	senatus	m.	senate	senate
species (*SPEH-kee-ays*)	speciei	f.	sight	species
venter (*WEHN-tehr*)	ventris	m.	stomach	ventral

The *ciborium* is a permanent canopy over an altar. More aptly, it is also the vessel for holding the consecrated bread or sacred wafers for the Eucharist (see Chapter 22).

You *ponder* while thinking weighty thoughts, and you will become *ponderous* if you eat doughnuts at the same time. Other *ramifications?* An enlarged *ventral* area.

> ### Tene Memoria
> The genitive case, the second word in vocabulary lists, is translated *of* or *'s*.

Practice Makes Perfect 1

To be sure it all sticks, translate the following genitives:

1. The anticipation of school _____

2. The hide of the deer _____

3. The food of the dog _____

4. The shape of the forehead _____

5. The quiet of leisure _____

Adjective/Adverb	Genitive	Meaning	Derivative
alius (*AH-lee-us*)	alii	other	alias
cotidie (*koh-TIH-dee ay*)	—	daily	—
deinde (*day-IHN-day*)	—	then, next	—
dulcis (*DOOL-kiss*)	dulcis	sweet	dulcimer
excelsus (*eks-KEL-sus*)	excelsi	high, lofty	excel
fictilis (*fik-TIH-lis*)	fictilis	clay, earthenware	fictile
imus (*EE-mus*)	imi	deepest	—
iniquus (*IH-nih-kwus*)	iniqui	unfair	iniquity
istuc (*IHSS-took*)	—	there, to that place	—
lenis (*LEH-nis*)	lenis	gentle, kind	lenient
magis (*MAH-gis*)	—	more	magnify
mirus (*MIH-rus*)	miri	wonderful	miracle
mitis (*MIH-tis*)	mitis	sweet, gentle	mitigate
mutuus (*MOO-too-us*)	mutui	borrowed	mutual
praeceler (*preye-KEH-ler*)	praeceleris	very swift	celerity
praecipuus (*preye-KIP-oo-us*)	praecipui	special	—
sic (*SEEK*)	—	thus	—
sollertius (*soh-LEHR-tee-us*)	sollertii	skilled	—

Adjective/Adverb	Genitive	Meaning	Derivative
subinde (*sub-IHN-day*)	—	immediately afterward	—
subito (*SUH-bih-toh*)	—	suddenly	—
vetustus (*weh-TUHS-tus*)	vetusti	old	veteran

Several other words come from *dulcis; dulcet* is an adjective meaning "pleasant to listen to," *dulcify* means "to make more agreeable," and a *dulcinea* is a sweetheart or girl-friend, named for Dulcinea, the ladylove of Don Quixote.

Principal Parts	Meaning	Derivative
committo, committere, commisi, commissus (*KOH-mih-toh*)	begin	commit
conspicio, conspicere, conspexi, conspectus (*kohn-SPIH-kee-oh*)	catch sight of	conspicuous
curo, curare, curavi, curatus (*KOO-roh*)	care for	curative
libero, liberare, liberavi, liberatus (*LEE-beh-roh*)	free	liberate
salveo, salvere (*SAHL-weh-oh*)	be in good health	salve
sedeo, sedere, sedi, sessus (*SEH-deh-oh*)	sit	session
terreo, terrere, terrui, territus (*TEH-reh-oh*)	frighten	terror
trado, tradere, tradidi, traditus (*TRAH-doh*)	hand over	trade
vereor, vereri, veritus sum (*WEH-reh-or*)	fear	—
vivo, vivere, vixi, victus (*WEE-woh*)	live	vivacity

Romans greeted each other with *Salve!* (Be well!). Other derivatives are *salutation*, *salubrious*, and *salutary*.

Cave! _____

Don't confuse *saltation* (jumping) with *salutation* (welcoming), although the two often happen simultaneously, especially with your dog.

Let's Get This! The Subjunctive Mood

So far all the tenses of the finite verbs (those with personal endings) have been in the indicative mood. The indicative mood indicates something is definitely happening—*it is*, *it was*, *it will be*, and *it has been*. No discussion.

The subjunctive is used to show that the action is not straightforward. The subjunctive mood shows action that might happen, would happen, should happen if all goes well, or just wishful thinking. It is also used for first and third person commands *Fiat lux!* (Let there be light!) and *Eamus!* (Let's go!). When used to command, it's called the hortatory subjunctive. In English, the hortatory subjunctive is formed with the helping verb "let" or "may," as in "Let's think about this," or "May you always be remembered."

Latin Today!

Words to take to the dining hall: Institutional food may need some spicing up:

    cibus (*KIH-bus*)   alere (*AH-leh-reh*)
    condere (*KOHN-deh-reh*)   sal (*SAHL*)

And remember: de gustibus non est disputandum (*DAY GOOS-tih-bus non est dihs-poo-TAHN-dum*; there's no disputing about tastes).

The subjunctive mood, a whole new set of endings for verbs, is used frequently in subordinate clauses.

Here's a list of what you need to form the subjunctive:

- **Present active subjunctive.** Use *e* in the first conjugation, *a* in all the rest. For example, *portet* (he might carry), *mittat* (he might send), or *audiam* (I may hear).

- **Present passive subjunctive.** Add passive endings. For example, *portetur* (he might be carried), *mittatur* (he might be sent), or *audiar* (I may be heard).

- **Imperfect active.** The present infinitive plus an ending. For example, *portaret* (he was carrying) or *mitterem* (I was sending).

- **Imperfect passive.** Add passive endings. For example, *portaretur* (he was being carried).

- **Perfect active.** Add *eri* and endings to the perfect stem. This will look a lot like the future perfect. For example, *portaverim* (I carried) or *dederint* (they gave).

Grammar Guru

The subjunctive is often translated exactly like the indicative. Other times it can be translated "may," "might," "in order to," or "should," depending on the construction.

- **Perfect passive.** Fourth principal part plus the subjunctive of the verb *esse* (to be). For example, *portatus sim* (I have been carried) or *portati sint* (they have been carried).

- **Pluperfect active.** The perfect infinitive plus endings. For example, *portavissem* (I had carried) or *monuisset* (he had warned).

- **Pluperfect passive.** Fourth principal part plus the imperfect subjunctive of the verb *esse* (to be). For example, *portatus essem* (I had been carried) or *moniti essemus* (we had been warned).

The subjunctive of *esse* is easily recognized.

Present		Imperfect	
sim	simus	essem	essemus
sis	sitis	esses	essetis
sit	sint	esset	essent

The following table presents the first and second conjugation. All the other conjugations form the subjunctive exactly like the second.

amo, amare, amavi, amatus (to love)

Active		Passive	
		Present	
amem	amemus	amer	amemur
ames	ametis	ameris	amemini
amet	ament	ametur	amentur

continues

amo, amare, amavi, amatus (to love)   (continued)

Active		Passive	
Imperfect			
amarem	amaremus	amarer	amaremur
amares	amaretis	amareris	amaremini
amaret	amarent	amaretur	amarentur
Perfect			
amaverim	amaverimus	amatus sim	amati simus
amaveris	amaveritis	amatus sis	amati sitis
amaverit	amaverint	amatus sit	amati sint
Pluperfect			
amavissem	amavissemus	amatus essem	amati essemus
amavisses	amavissetis	amatus esses	amati essetis
amavisset	amavissent	amatus esset	amati essent

moneo, monere, monui, monitus (to warn)

Active		Passive	
Present			
moneam	moneamus	monear	moneamur
moneas	moneatis	monearis	moneamini
moneat	moneant	moneatur	moneantur

All other tenses are formed exactly like the first conjugation.

Subordinate Conjunctions

Here is a list of conjunctions that will introduce a subordinate clause, usually in the subjunctive mood.

Conjunction	Meaning	Derivative
antequam (*AHN-teh-kwam*)	before	—
cum (*KOOM*)	when, since, although	—
donec (*DOH-nek*)	until	—
dum (*DOOM*)	while	—
quanto (*KWAHN-toh*)	how much	quantify
quo (*KWOH*)	where	—
si (*SEE*)	if	—
sic (*SEEK*)	thus	—
tam (*TAHM*)	so	—
tantum (*TAHN-tum*)	so great	tantamount
ut (*OOT*)	in order that, that	—
veluti (*weh-LOO-tee*)	just as	—

Hysteria's Herstory

Twenty-four letters from Cicero to his wife, Terentia, survive and reveal that as a dutiful Roman wife, she kept a home for him until he became obsessed with the idea that she was stealing his money and divorced her in 46 B.C.E. He was probably turned off by her strong will and independence. Cicero had arranged two marriages for his daughter Tullia, but Tullia and her mother chose the third husband while Cicero was away.

Unlike the hapless Cicero, whose head and pierced tongue ended up impaled on the Forum, Terentia was said to have lived to the ripe old age of 103.

Clauses with a Purpose

Purpose clauses begin with "in order that," "with the purpose of," or just plain "to." For example:

> I went into the bar to drink wine.

> I went into the bar in order to drink wine.

In Latin, the verb in the purpose clause is in the subjunctive. For example:

> In tabernam ivi ut vinum biberem.

Sometimes the purpose clause begins with a relative pronoun, translated "who were to ..." For example:

> Servos in tabernam misi qui vinum ad me exportarent.
> I sent the slaves into the bar to bring out the wine.

The negative purpose clause is introduced by *ne*. For example:

> Epistulam mittit ne fleas.
> He sends a letter in order that you not cry.

Practice Makes Perfect 2

Now it's your turn. Translate these sentences:

1. Multi alios laudant, ut ab aliis laudentur.

   _____

2. Multi alios laudabant, ut ab aliis laudarentur.

   _____

3. Servos in tabernam misit ut amicum occuparent.

   _____

Clauses with a Result

Subordinate clauses of result sometimes follow a word or phrase such as "in such a way," "so that," "so much," "to the point that," or "so great," and begin with "with the result that" or sometimes simply "that." Result clauses are always in the subjunctive. For example:

> Pisces tantum condiunt ut nemo edere possit.
> They season the fish so much that no one is able to eat.

Now translate the following sentences:

1. Ita clamorem fecit ut exire necesse esset.

   _____

2. Amabat murenam adeo ut in piscina sederet.

   _____

The negative result clause uses *ut … non*. For example:

> Tanta fabula fuit ut ego ei credere non possem.
> The story was of such a kind that I was not able to believe it.

Clauses of Fear

These aren't clauses to be afraid of; these are clauses that show fear and are always in the subjunctive. Even more perverse, they use *ut* for the negative and *ne* for the positive. For example:

> Vereor ut taberna vinum habeat.
> I fear that the bar may not have wine.

> Verebatur ne hostes urbem occuparent.
> He was afraid that the enemy would seize the city.

When? Why? What If? Clauses

Subordinate clauses that indicate time are usually in the indicative. For example:

> Ubi magister haec audivit, ridens decidit.
> When the teacher heard these things, he fell down laughing.

Quod can introduce main clauses that indicate cause. These are also in the indicative. For example:

Quod has soleas emi, meas sunt.
Because I bought these flip-flops, they are mine.

Clauses that indicate conditions are sometimes indicative and sometimes subjunctive. If it is an open condition, where there is no doubt as to its fulfillment or probability, the indicative is used. For example:

Si spirat, vivit.
If he is breathing, he is living.

If, on the other hand, there is some doubt as to the actuality, if it is contrary to fact, then the subjunctive is used. For example:

Si ex rupe urinavisses, territus essem.
If you had dived off a cliff, I would have been frightened.

Practice Makes Perfect 3

Choose a clause that would complete the sentence:

1. He was a general	a. Si meus canis abesset
2. We go shopping	b. Cum fabulam audimus
3. The men took the rope	c. Ut cervum caperent
4. We have fun	d. Quod praecipuus erat
5. I would cry	e. Cum nihil facere sit

Now translate the following sentences, all of which you will find in Part 4:

1. Cum Caesar haec audiret, se recipere
   milites iussit.   _____

2. Quae cum ita sint, Romam ibo.   _____

3. Haec feci, dum licuit.   _____

4. Dum haec agebantur, servi discesserunt. _____

5. Mane domum donec redibo.   _____

6. Si stat, vivit.   _____

The Least You Need to Know

- ◆ Subjunctive forms are not like the indicative.

- ◆ If it's not real, it's subjunctive.

- ◆ Latin has many conjunctions.

- ◆ Clauses complete thoughts and complicate sentences.

15

Simple and Not-So-Simple Sentences

In This Chapter

- Words to learn
- Start basic: simple sentences
- Ask questions with interrogative sentences
- Get complex with more advanced sentences

Sentences can be as short as one word—*Go!*—or as long as William Faulkner's sentences that stretch from Mississippi to Tennessee. But every sentence has at least one subject and one predicate, because that's what makes the complete thought.

Sentences work in different ways. Some declare their thoughts and are called *declarative* sentences. Others ask questions and are *interrogatives*. Still others give commands and are called *imperative* sentences. Imperative sentences often have the subject, *you*, understood (that is, not written), like the imperative sentence in the first paragraph: *Go!*

I Will Learn These Words

Here are more verbs to learn and enjoy! Watch out for the fourth principal part that sometimes looks like an alien. There are deponent verbs as well; these end in *-or* and have passive forms but active meanings.

Principal Parts	Meaning	Derivative
absum, abesse, afui, afuturus (*AHB-sum*)	be away	absent
ambulo, ambulare, avi, -atus (*AHM-boo-loh*)	walk	ambulatory
condo, condere, condidi, conditus (*KOHN-doh*)	to found	condition
credo, credere, credidi, creditus (*CRAY-doh*)	believe	credible
delinquo, delinquere, -liqui, -lictus (*deh-LIN-kwoh*)	fall short of standards	delinquent
exeo, exire, exii, exitus (*eks-EH-oh*)	go out	exit
excipio, excipere, excepi, exceptus (*eks-KIH-pee-oh*)	take out	exception
gaudeo, gaudere, gavisus sum (*GOW-deh-oh*)	rejoice	gaudy
incido, incidere, incidi, incissus (*in-KEE-doh*)	cut into	incisor
iubeo, iubere, iussi, iussus (*YOO-beh-oh*)	order	jussive
lacrimo, lacrimare, avi, atus (*LAH-krih-moh*)	cry	lachrymose
miror, mirari, miratus sum (*MIH-rohr*)	wonder	miracle
soleo, solere, solui, solitus (*SOH-leh-oh*)	be accustomed	—
taceo, tacere, tacui, tacitus (*TAH-keh-oh*)	be quiet	taciturn
traho, trahere, traxi, tractus (*TRAH-hoh*)	draw, drag	traction

Principal Parts	Meaning	Derivative
tutor, tutari, tutatus sum (*TOO-tohr*)	watch over	tutor
valeo, valere, valui, valiturus (*WAH-leh-oh*)	be well	value

If you're an *ambulatory* patient, you're walking around, unlike the British babies, who are pushed around in a *perambulator*.

Don't confuse *condio, ire, ivi, itus* (to season), with *condo, ere, didi, ditus* (to found). Garlic may be the foundation of your soup, but you can't found a city with it.

 Cave! ___

Exeo, although it ends in *-eo,* is not a second declension verb. Another of those pesky exceptions.

Lachrymose means "teary," having those wet things coming from your *lacrimal* glands and causing much *lacrimation*.

Here are some nouns and adjectives you will need.

Word and Base	Meaning	Derivative
ager, agri (m.) (*AH-gehr*)	field	agriculture
bellum, belli (n.) (*BEH-lum*)	war	bellicose
brevis, breve (*BREH-wiss*)	short	brief
caper, capri (m.) (*KAH-pehr*)	goat	capricious
caput, capitis (n.) (*KAH-put*)	head	capital
corpus, corporis (n.) (*KOHR-pus*)	body	corporal
cubile, cubilis (n.) (*koo-BEE-leh*)	bed	concubine
culpa, culpae (f.) (*KOOL-pah*)	fault	culpable

continues

continued

Word and Base	Meaning	Derivative
deceptus, decepta, deceptum (*day-KEP-tus*)	deceived	deception
derectus, derecta, derectum (*day-REK-tus*)	straight	direct
domus, domus (f.) (*DOH-mus*)	house	domestic
frigidus, frigida, frigidum (*FRIH-gih-dus*)	cold	frigid
iucundus, iucunda, iucundum (*yoo-KUN-dus*)	happy	jocund
luna, lunae (f.) (*LOO-na*)	moon	lunar
lupus, lupi (m.) (*LOO-pus*)	wolf	lupine
nemo, neminis (m./f.) (*NAY-moh*)	no one	—
nox, noctis (f.) (*NOHKS*)	night	nocturnal
onus, oneris (n.) (*OH-nus*)	burden	onerous
palla, pallae (f.) (*PAH-lah*)	dress	—
servus, servi (m.) (*SEHR-wus*)	slave	servile

Grammar Guru

Remember, every noun has a gender. Adjectives, on the other hand, have forms for all three genders. Numbers, like adverbs, blessedly have only one form.

Corporal punishment relates to blows to the body, whereas *capital* punishment afflicts the head and is, therefore, more deadly.

Domus is slightly irregular, sometimes seen with a fourth declension genitive, *us*, and sometimes with a second declension, *i*. It usually appears as *domi* (at home), *domum* (to home), or *domo* (from home).

Adverb	Meaning
diu (*DEE-oo*)	for a long time
iam (*YAHM*)	now, already
igitur (*IH-gih-tur*)	therefore
mox (*MOHKS*)	soon
quoque (*KWOH-kweh*)	also
saepe (*SEYE-peh*)	often
statim (*STAH-tim*)	immediately
ubi (*OO-bee*)	where, when
utinam (*OO-tih-nam*)	would that

Simple Sentences: *I Can Learn Latin.*

Simply put, every sentence has a subject and a verb. The subject is always in the nominative case.

Remember, nominative case endings are often one of the following: *-a, -ae, -r, -us, -um, -i, -a, -es.* Unfortunately, the maverick third declension (nominative singular) can end in any letter. In Latin, sometimes the subject is attached to the verb. The personal pronoun is indicated by the following: *-i* or *-o* (I), *-s* or *-isti* (you), *-t* (he, she, it), *-mus* (we), *-tis* (you pl.), and *-nt* or *-erunt* (they).

The passive personal endings are *-or* (I), *-eris* or *-re* (you), *-tur* (he, she, it), *-mur* (we), *-mini* (you pl.), and *-ntur* (they).

Here's a translation tip: look for a noun in the nominative case. If there is none, look for the verb, usually at the end of the sentence. Use the personal pronoun ending for your subject. Take, for example, *Viros invitabo.* Because *viros* is not nominative, look at *invitabo* and begin the sentence "I will invite …"

Practice Makes Perfect 1

Translate these simple sentences:

1. Nihil vidi.   _____

2. Ad transversum versiculum venio.   _____

3. Caudam apprehendunt.   _____

4. Ex Arpinati profecti sumus.   _____

5. Nervos caedit.   _____

Some sentences have a subject and a direct object. The verbs in these sentences have a transitive verb, a verb that *transits* or *goes across* to an object. Because of the lackadaisical attitude toward word order, the reader must distinguish the nominative from the accusative endings. For your review, here are the accusative endings: *-am, -as, -um, -os, -a, -em, -es,* and *-us.* For example:

> Bellum agros delebat.

The obvious accusative is *agros. Bellum* could be in the accusative because it's a neuter noun. But there is no conjunction to show that something destroys fields and war and, furthermore, that just doesn't make sense. It is more sensible to use *bellum* as the subject.

Another helpful hint is to check out the verb. It is singular, third person, agreeing very nicely with *war.*

Finally, some sentences don't have a direct object because their verb is intransitive, *not going across* to an object. Often these verbs are followed by a predicate noun, a word that renames the subject and, therefore, is in the nominative case.

Typical intransitive verbs that take a predicate noun are *is, am, are, was, were, feel, be called,* and *seem.*

Other intransitive verbs are action words or states of being, like *run, jump, stand,* and *happen.* For example:

> Vicinus discipulus esse videtur.

You can see that the two nouns are in the nominative. So either of the following is correct:

The neighbor seems to be a student.

The student seems to be a neighbor.

Practice Makes Perfect 2

Translate the following sentences, all of which you will find in the Latin selections, Part 4:

1. Lauti fungos, helvellas, herbasque condiunt. _____

2. Homo nobilis hoc simulacrum deportat. _____

3. Sergius Orata vivaria invenit. _____

4. Uxor inaures addidit. _____

5. Troglodytae arbores conscendunt. _____

6. Diligenter quaesivi. _____

7. Alii singuli sunt. _____

8. Silentium est. _____

9. Unum cornu exsistit. _____

10. Nuclei decidunt. _____

Interrogative Sentences: *Can I Learn Latin?*

Interrogative sentences are questioning sentences. Latin has many interrogative words that can begin a question. For example:

Quo vadis?
Where are you going?

Quot fratres habes?
How many brothers do you have?

Tene Memoria

I covered interrogative sentences in Chapter 7. If you need a refresher on questions, please look there.

Other useful interrogative words are as follows:

quotiens	how many
quanto	how much
quanam	by what route
quam diu	how long
quam ob rem	for what reason

Complex Sentences: *Although I Am a Complete Idiot, I Can Learn Latin.*

A complex sentence is a simple sentence that contains a subordinate clause. There are four ways you can recognize a subordinate clause in Latin:

♦ A relative pronoun begins the clause. The forms of the relative pronoun begin with *qu-* or *cu-*. The clause usually ends with its own verb. For example:

Video poculum quod in mensa est.

The simple sentence is *video poculum*, "I see the mug." The subordinate clause, which you can lift out and still have a complete thought, is "which is on the table."

♦ The clause begins with *ut* or *ne*, followed by the subjunctive and is translated "for the purpose of" or "with the result that." For example:

Tantum vinum bibit ut ebrius fiat.

Words like *tantum*, *ita*, *adeo*, and *tam* often signal a result clause. "He drank so much wine that he became drunk."

♦ A subordinate conjunction begins a clause. *When, since, although,* and *while* are frequently used. For example:

Dum magister abest, discipuli non laborant.

♦ The clause contains the ablative absolute—two or three words, usually set off by commas, in the ablative case, without any recognizable connection to the sentence. For example:

Viris captis, feminae clamabant.

Remember, the ablative absolute can be translated with a subordinate conjunction, even though there is none there in the Latin. For example, "Because the men were captured, the women were shouting."

<table><tr><td>**Latin Today!**</td></tr></table>

Words to take to the theatre: Both literally and figuratively, you may see a …

　deus ex machina (*DAY-us EKS MAH-keen-ah*)

With any complex sentence, you can remove the clause and still have a complete thought.

Hysteria's Herstory

Upper-class Roman women used cosmetics extensively. They painted the under lid of their eye green and blackened the upper lid, eyelashes, and eyebrows. They painted their fingernails and toenails red and often used an orange-red dye to color the palms of their hands and the soles of their feet. White lead was used to beautify their faces, but because women often became sick from lead poisoning, they substituted chalk.

Practice Makes Perfect 3

Your turn again. Translate the following sentences into English, all of which come from the mouth of Cicero via his letters:

1. Venio ad transversum versiculum in quo me admones.

2. Dies fecit (made it happen) ut Quintus in Arcano maneret.

3. Illa inquit, "Ego ipsa sum hospita," quod antecesserat Statius ut prandium nobis videret.

4. Discubuimus omnes praeter illam, cui Quintus mensam misit.

5. Lauti volunt in honorem adducere terra nata quae lege excepta sunt.

The Least You Need to Know

◆ Simple sentences have a subject and verb.

◆ Complex sentences contain a subordinate clause.

◆ Yes/no questions are indicated by the suffix *-ne* on the first word.

Compound Sentences and Beyond

In This Chapter

◆ More words to learn and memorize

◆ Simple and complex compound sentences

◆ Compound-complex sentences

◆ Indirect statements, questions, and commands

Most first-time readers of Cicero's orations curse his use of clauses within clauses. His famous periodic sentences are also infamous for their length. Students struggling through Caesar's *Gallic Wars* will agree that all his sentences are too complex and wonder why he doesn't have shorter thoughts.

A reader of original Latin has to get used to stopping at the conjunctions and breaking up some of those long sentences into more readable, understandable ideas.

More Words to Learn and Memorize

Many of these conjunctions you have seen before. Remember that coordinating conjunctions join two independent clauses. Subordinating conjunctions have one clause that depends on the other to complete its meaning.

The good news is, conjunctions have only one form.

Coordinating	Meaning	Subordinating	Meaning
at	but		
aut	or	antequam	before
aut ... aut	either/or	cum	when, since, although
autem	moreover, nevertheless, on the other hand	donec	until
et	and	dum	while
et ... et	both/and	ita	in such a way
		quamquam	although
etiam	also	si	if
-que	and	sic	thus
sed	but	tam	so
sicut	just as	tantum	so great
		unde	whence
		ut	in order to, that
		veluti	just as

You've seen a few forms of two irregular verbs. The following tables list the complete conjugation of *volo, velle, volui* (be willing, wish) and *nolo, nolle, nolui* (be unwilling).

volo, velle, volui

Present			
volo	I wish	volumus	we wish
vis	you wish	vultis	you wish
vult	he wishes	volunt	they wish

Future

volam	I will wish	volemus	we will wish
voles	you will wish	voletis	you will wish
volet	he will wish	volent	they will wish

All other forms of *volo* are regular.

nolo, nolle, nolui

Present

nolo	I do not want	nolumus	we do not want
non vis	you do not want	non vultis	you do not want
non vult	he does not want	nolunt	they do not want

Future

nolam	I will not want	nolemus	we will not want
noles	you will not want	noletis	you will not want
nolet	he will not want	nolent	they will not want

All other forms are regular.

Remember that the imperative form of *nolo*, *noli* (singular), and *nolite* (plural) is used with an infinitive for the negative command. For example:

> Noli in via stare.
> Don't stand in the road.

> Nolite clamare.
> Don't shout (you all).

The other irregular verb is *fio, fieri, factus sum*.

This verb is actually the passive of *facio, facere* (do or make). As such, it is translated as "become," "be done," "be made."

Cave!

The second person singular and plural of *nolo* is different. Remember, it has two words, *non vis* and *non vultis*.

Latin Today!

Words to take to the final exam:
tempus fugit (*TEM-pus FOO-giht; FU-jit* in English)

Present			
fio	I become	fimus	we become
fis	you become	fitis	you become
fit	he becomes	fiunt	they become

The future is like a third conjugation, and all other tenses are regular.

Compound Sentences

Compound sentences have two or more simple sentences joined by a coordinating conjunction. In English, we can use the semicolon, an idea not yet in vogue for the Roman scribes. For example:

> Musica tibia canet et omnes cantant.
> The musician plays the flute; everybody sings.

Practice Makes Perfect 1

Translate the following compound sentences. (These have been culled from the original Latin selections in Chapters 18 and 19.)

1. In nobile civitate Ephesi, Graeci habitaverunt et lex iniqua constituta esse dicitur.

   _____

2. Architectus publicum opus recipit et pretium dat.

   _____

3. Figura alcis similis capro est sed magnitudine paulo antecedit.

   _____

4. Ad arbores se applicant et ita quietem capiunt.

   _____

---

5. Aut arbores ab radicibus subruunt aut eas accidunt.

   _____

6. Infirmas arbores pondere affigunt atque ipsae concidunt.

   _____

7. Troglodytae Aethiopiae solo venatu se alunt et cotidie arbores ascendunt.

   _____

8. Pedes stipat in sinistro femine itaque poplitem dextra caedit.

   _____

9. Elephantus crure tardatur et breve tempore mortuus est.

   _____

10. Itaque id me commoverat sic illa aspere responderat.

   _____

Compound-Complex Sentences

Compound-complex sentences are those compound sentences that also include clauses. Latin writers were fond of putting clauses into clauses into clauses *ad infinitum*, all of which were in the subjunctive. For example:

> Musica tibia canet et omnes qui in atrio sunt cantant.
> The musician plays the flute and all who are in the hall sing.

 Grammar Guru

The English subjunctive uses "were," "be," and "would," among others, to show contrary-to-fact conditions and other nonrealistic states. For example, "If I were a complete idiot, would I be reading this book?"

> **Practice Makes Perfect 2**
>
> Your turn again. Translate the following gems:
>
> 1. Si non amplius quam quarta sumptui in opere consumitur, ad aestimationem eam addit neque ulla poena tenetur.
>
>   _____
>
> 2. Neque quietis causa procumbunt neque, si quo afflictae casu conciderunt, erigere sese ac sublevare possunt (si quo = "if any").
>
>   _____

Indirect Statements

An indirect statement comes after verbs of stating—"say," "know," "think," "tell," "believe,"—and reports a direct statement in a subordinate clause introduced by *that*. For example:

> *Direct statement:* The catapult is illegal.
>
> *Direct statement:* He said, "The catapult is illegal."
>
> *Indirect statement:* He said that the catapult is illegal.

In English, we sometimes omit the introductory word *that:*

> He said the catapult is illegal.

In Latin, there is no introductory word. Instead, we have the subject of the indirect statement in the accusative case and the verb in the infinitive. For example:

> Dixit catapultam illicitam esse.
> He said that the catapult was illegal.

Notice that the present infinitive *esse* is used here, although it's translated in the past. The infinitive in an indirect statement shows a relationship between the main verb and the subordinate verb. The present infinitive shows that both verbs are going on at the same time. For example:

> Dicit catapultam illicitam esse.
> He says that the catapult is illegal.

Dixit catapultam illicitam esse.
He said that the catapult was illegal.

The perfect infinitive is used to show time before that of the main verb:

Dicit catapultam illicitam fuisse.
He says that the catapult was illegal (but has since been legitimatized by catapult lobbyists).

Dixit catapultam illicitam fuisse.
He said that the catapult had been illegal.

The future infinitive is used to show time after that of the main verb:

Dicit catapultam illicitam futuram esse.
He says the catapult will be illegal (if catapult control advocates have anything to do with it).

Dixit catapultam illicitam futuram esse.
He said that the catapult would be illegal (but what did he know back in 1825?).

Practice Makes Perfect 3

Translate these indirect statements from ancient authors:

1. Quintus mihi narravit illam secum dormire non voluisse. (Cicero)

   _____

2. Sapientissimum esse dicunt eum cui quod opus sit ipsi veniat. (Cicero)

   _____

3. Credula spes vitam fovet et futurum esse melius cras semper dicit. (Tibullus)

   _____

4. Nemo enim est tam senex qui annum vivere se posse putet. (Cicero)

   _____

Indirect Questions

Like the indirect statement, the indirect question comes after a verb of stating, knowing, thinking, or asking, but instead of the accusative and infinitive, it takes the subjunctive. For example:

> Quaesit qui ad cenam veniat.
> He asks who is coming to dinner.

Some words that introduce an indirect question are *qui* (who), *quid* (what), *quomodo* (how), *unde* (wherefrom), and *quantum* (how much).

Practice Makes Perfect 4

Try translating these sentences from Latin authors:

1. Ne mireris unde hoc accideret et quomodo commiserim. (Cicero)

   _____

2. Pollicetur dicere quantus sumptus futurus sit. (Vitruvius)

   _____

3. Nescire quid antequam natus sis acciderit, id est semper esse puerum. (Cicero)

   _____

4. Nunc scio quid sit amor. (Vergil)

   _____

5. Multi dubitabant quid optimum esset. (Cicero)

   _____

Indirect Commands

Although indirect commands can come in the guise of the accusative and an infinitive, they also come with *ut* or *ne* plus the subjunctive. The most common verbs implying an act of will or command are *mando* (command), *rogo* (ask), *peto* (ask), *persuadeo* (persuade), *moneo* (warn), *hortor* (urge), and *permitto* (permit). Note that each verb deals with the person involved differently. For example:

Caesarem hortor ut …	I urge Caesar (accusative) to …
Caesari mando ut …	I command Caesar (dative) to …
Ab Caesare peto ut …	I ask Caesar (ablative) to …
Caesarem moneo ut …	I warn Caesar (accusative) that …
Caesari persuadeo ut …	I persuade Caesar (dative) to …
Caesari permitto ut …	I allow Caesar (dative) to …

Practice Makes Perfect 5

Time to hand the pen to you again. Translate the following sentences:

1. Quintus in Arcano remansit.

    _____

2. Aquinum ad me postridie mane venit.

    _____

3. Mihi narravit nec secum illam dormire voluisse.

    _____

4. Cum discessura esset, ea fuit eius modi qualem ego eam vidissem.

    _____

Hysteria's Herstory

When Pliny the Younger was 40, he married a young girl, Calpurnia. He was inordinately proud of this model wife who was sensible and thrifty and took an interest in literature, especially Pliny's writings. He boasted that when he gave public readings of his works, she would station herself behind a curtain and listen carefully to the praise heaped upon him. She even took his poetry, set it to music, and then serenaded her husband with his own poems. No wonder he thought she was terrific!

The Least You Need to Know

◆ In spite of all the grammatical terminology, thoughts can be broken down into bits.

◆ Indirect statements take the subject in the accusative case and the verb in the infinitive.

◆ Indirect questions and commands take the subjunctive.

◆ If the Romans wanted to string their thoughts into one unbroken, tediously long sentence, we are up to the challenge of reading them.

Part 4

Reading Latin—Selections from Ancient Authors

In Part 4, you get some practice reading Latin. The selections in this part are arranged in chronological order and represent various aspects of life: art, politics, sports, natural history, family life. The readings show that contractors underestimated their bids, wives were insulted by their husbands' behavior, some people had to watch what they ate, and there was more than one way to catch an elephant. It's hard to imagine that some of these events happened 2,000 years ago and not yesterday.

Selections from Republican Rome

In This Chapter

- ◆ Terence and his writings
- ◆ Caesar and his writings
- ◆ Cicero and his writings

After the expulsion of the kings in 509 B.C.E. and the formation of the republic, the inhabitants of Rome gradually expanded their power and influence, first throughout Italy and then to the whole Mediterranean world. By 166 B.C.E., the time of Terence, many Romans had become well-educated citizens, knowing Greek as well as their own developing language, Latin.

The literature that remains from early Rome through the fall of the republic is wonderfully varied. Letters, although often edited for publication, reveal personal life. The *Commentaries* from Caesar are the first written record of Western Europe. Through Cicero's letters, orations, and essays, we see a rich picture of the contemporary mind. Terence's plays give us a taste of the language and behavior of the people in the street.

Vita Terentii (The Life of Terence)

At the end of the second century B.C.E., Rome had expanded her power from Spain to Africa and from Asia Minor to Macedonia. Roman life was imitated in art and architecture, politics and government. Some Roman citizens became wealthy. They had slaves to do the housework and take care of business. Money was rolling in from the provinces. What was left to do? Luckily, some talented people could write plays, and the wealthy citizens were quick to sponsor such endeavors.

Publius Terentius Afer was born in Carthage in 185 B.C.E. and came to Rome as a slave of a senator who educated him and then gave him his freedom. Sponsored by Scipio Africanus Minor, Terence wrote many plays, which were adapted into the Latin language from Greek.

My Play! Listen Up!

The following selection is from the prologue, 21–36, to *Hecyra* (*The Mother-in-Law*) and shows how plays attracted all kinds of people in the streets. At this time, there were no theaters, so plays were produced on hastily built stages that were often dismantled at the end of the day.

With the help of the following notes, you should be able to read this adaptation from *Hecyra*. Remember to find the subject and verb, and if it seems like Greek to you, sneak a peek at the translation that follows.

The speaker is also the producer.

Latin	Form	Meaning
hecyram (*heh-KIH-rahm*)	acc. singular, f.	mother-in-law
refero	first per. s. pres.	I bring back
eam (*EH-ahm*)	acc. s. fem.	it (referring to *Hecyra*)
erit	third per. s. future	it will be
pugilum	gen. pl.	of the boxers
fecerunt (*fay-KAY-runt*)	third per. pl. perf.	made it so
tutari	pres. inf.	(deponent verb) to save

Hecyram ad vos refero, quam mihi in silentio numquam agere licuit. Ita eam oppressit calamitas.

Eam calamitatem vestra intellegentia sedabit, si erit adiutrix nostrae industriae. Cum primum eam agere coepi, pugilum gloria, funambuli exspectatio, comitum conventus, strepitus, clamor mulierum fecerunt ut ante tempus exirem foras.

Refero denuo. Primo actu placeo. Cum interea rumor venit de gladiatoribus, populus convolat, clamant, pugnant de loco; ego interea meum non potui tutari locum.

Nunc turba non est; otium et silentium est. Agendi tempus mihi est.

I bring to you "The Mother-in-Law," which I have never been able to do in silence. Disaster has overwhelmed it [the production] thusly. Your understanding will appease this calamity if there will be a sympathizer of our work. When first I began to produce it, the glory of boxers, the expectation of a tightrope walker, the gathering of friends, noise, and the shouting of women made it so I had to leave before it was time.

I bring it again. I am pleased to get through the first act. Meanwhile, rumor comes about gladiators, people fly around, they shout, they fight for a place; I am not able to keep a safe place.

Now there is no crowd; there is peace and quiet. The time has come for me to present my play.

The Worried Father

The following lines are adapted from Act 1 of Terence's play, *Adelphoe* (*The Brothers*) and are spoken by Micio, who is worried about his adopted son who has been out all night. (Do things *ever* change?)

Hic ex me natus non est, sed ex meo fratre. Meus frater dissimilis mihi ab adulescentia fuit; ego hanc vitam urbanam atque otium secutus sum et, quod fortunatum illi putant, uxorem numquam habui. Ille contra haec omnia; ruri agit vitam; uxorem duxit; nati filii duo; inde ego hunc maiorem adoptavi mihi; eduxi a parvolo, habui, amavi, pro meo; solum id est carum mihi.

He is not my son, but my brother's. My brother has been unlike me from adolescence; I follow a city life and pursuit of leisure and; what some people say is a good thing, I have never had a wife. He is the opposite in all these things; he spends his life in the country, he married and had two sons. And so I adopted the older one for myself. I brought him up since boyhood. I considered him, and I loved him as my own. He is the only thing dear to me.

Caesar: More Than Just a Salad

Gaius Iulius Caesar, renown for his military conquests, his mastery over a certain Egyptian queen, and his role in a Shakespearean play, was born in 100 B.C.E. He rose through the ranks of Roman politics and maneuvered himself into a consulship and later membership in the first triumvirate. The Roman authorities, fearful of Caesar's growing power, gave him the province of Gaul, hoping he would cross the Alps, hit a snowdrift, and find it difficult to return. But Caesar spent seven years building camps, taking over the barbarian cities, strengthening his army, and annexing much of western Europe to the Roman state. While he was gone, Pompey had also built up an army and was threatening to take over Rome. More than a little miffed, Caesar crossed the Rubicon with his army, thus breaking the law against entering Rome accompanied by thousands of troops.

With those immortal words, *Alea iacta est* (The die is cast), he proceeded to take over the known world; fix up the calendar by adding a month with his name, July; and give a dinner for 22,000 people. Now that's a lot of salad.

Cave!

In Latin, the illustrious leader's name is pronounced *KEYE-sahr*, from which come *kaiser* and *tsar*.

The *Commentarii de Bello Gallico* was written while Caesar was in Gaul. It was intended as a report to the Roman people that Caesar, though far away across the Alps, was alive and well and conquering up a storm. (You can see more in Appendix C.)

The Smart Elks

Julius Caesar's prose has been read by Latin students for centuries, because it is clear and fairly simple. You have already translated the first line of his *De Bello Gallico*. With the help of a few notes, you should read this selection with ease. This selection, VI, 26–27, describes the remarkable animals found in the Hercynian forest in Germany.

Latin	Form	Meaning
cornu	nom. s. neuter	horn
his	abl. pl. n.	modifies cornibus
quo	abl. s.	(after si) if any
quarum	gen. pl. fem.	of these
consuerint (*kohn-soo-EH-rint*)	third pl. perf. subj.	were accustomed

Est bos cervi figura cuius a media fronte inter aures unum cornu exsistit excelsius magisque derectum his quae nobis nota sunt cornibus; ab eius summo sic ut palmae ramique late diffunduntur. Eadem est feminae marisque natura, eadem forma magnitudoque cornuum.

Sunt item quae appellantur alces. Harum est consimilis capris figura et varietas pellium; sed magnitudine paulo antecedunt mutilaeque sunt cornibus et crura sine nodis articulisque habent, neque quietis causa procumbunt neque, si quo afflictae casu conciderunt, erigere sese ac sublevare possunt. His sunt arbores pro cubilibus; ad eas se applicant atque ita paulum modo reclinatae quietem capiunt. Quarum ex vestigiis cum est animadversum a venatoribus quo se recipere consuerint, omnes eo loco aut ab radicibus subruunt aut accidunt arbores, tantum ut summa species earum stantium relinquatur. Huc cum se consuetudine reclinaverunt, infirmas arbores pondere affligunt atque una ipsae concidunt.

There is an ox in the shape of a deer, from whose forehead between the ears one horn stands out, higher and straighter than these horns that are known to us. From the top of this horn it spreads out widely like palm branches. The same nature is for both male and female, the same shape and size of the horns.

There are also those called elks. The figure of these is similar to goats, and they have a variety of pelts. But they are a little bigger and have broken horns and legs without joints and nodes; neither do they lie down for the sake of rest, nor, if by some chance they are afflicted and fall down, are they able to stand themselves up. These use trees for beds; to which they lean and, thus, leaning, get a little rest. When it is known from the tracks of these by hunters where they are accustomed to rest, they root up all the trees in the place or cut the trees so that the exact appearance of standing trees remain. Here, when they lean according to their custom, they knock the trees over with their weight and fall down with them.

Hysteria's Herstory

Less well known to us but certainly known to the Romans of Cicero's day was Clodia, a woman of noble lineage. In 61 B.C.E., she was 33 years old and a widow. Catullus, age 27, fell madly in love with her and wrote many blistering love poems to his *Lesbia*. After 3 years, Clodia dropped him like a hot potato for an even younger man, Caelius. Unfortunately, after 2 years, Caelius dropped her, and the vengeful Clodia brought trumped-up murder charges against him. Cicero successfully defended him in court, and Clodia disappeared from history forever.

Vita Ciceronis (The Life of Cicero)

Marcus Tullius Cicero was a consul, senator, provincial governor, and lawyer. Through his voluminous writings, he gives us an intimate glimpse of life with Caesar, Pompey, Antony, and many of the movers and shakers during the fall of the republic. We can almost hear him wonder, *Whom shall I support? What's Brutus up to? How should I treat Caesar when I see him for dinner?*

Cicero is especially interesting because he was born into a middle-class family and became a self-made man. Although born at Arpinum, 60 miles southeast of Rome, and considered a country bumpkin, his father brought him to Rome for his later education. At age 25, he began his career in the law courts. After a trip to Greece to rest his voice and gain weight (baklava, anyone?), he returned to politics in Rome. In 76 B.C.E., he was selected to be *quaestor* in Sicily, which gave him automatic membership in the senate. His honest and attentive administrative skills were appreciated by the Sicilians, and in 70 B.C.E., the Sicilians asked Cicero to prosecute a corrupt governor, Verres. His successful prosecution led to more pleadings in the courts. In 66 B.C.E., Cicero supported the Manilian law, which gave Pompey military authority in Asia Minor.

In 63 B.C.E., Cicero was elected consul, the highest office in Rome. He defeated Catiline, who did not take defeat lightly and plotted to assassinate Cicero and take over the city.

Cicero called an emergency meeting of the senate in the temple of Jupiter Stator on the Capitoline hill. There he delivered an address that includes the line, *O tempora, o mores* (Oh the times, oh the ways), bewailing the lawlessness of the times and pointing to the brooding Catiline, who sat apart from the crowd (at least according to the picture in my high school Latin classroom).

Catiline eventually left the city. His co-conspirators were apprehended, and Cicero asked for the death penalty. They were hastily executed without trial.

The senate declared a thanksgiving in Cicero's name and called him *pater patriae*, "father of his country." It was a high point of his life—and it was all downhill from there.

All his life, Cicero tried to promote a *concordia ordinum* (a harmony of the orders), a first-century rainbow coalition between the nobles and the equestrians, but with no success. Nice thought, though.

When the first triumvirate of Pompey, Crassus, and Caesar was formed, Cicero was left out. Worse, his sworn enemy, Clodius, got himself elected tribune and promptly passed a law that condemned to exile anyone who put a citizen to death without a trial. Oops! Guess who that would be?

So Cicero hightailed it to Greece, where he fretted and fumed for a year until Pompey revoked the law.

In 56 B.C.E., Cicero retreated to the country to write and read philosophy. Five years later, he was sent to Cilicia in Asia Minor as the provincial administrator and commander of the army. He didn't really command the army, however; like the president of the United States, he had professional military to do that.

When he returned to Rome, Crassus had died, Caesar had crossed the Rubicon, and all Hades had broken out. Cicero was courted by both Caesar and Pompey, but in the end, he sided with Pompey. It turned out to be a bad idea, because Pompey was defeated. Cicero retired again.

At this time, Cicero decided to dump his wife of 20 years because she was spending a lot of money and married his young ward, Publilia, who had a lot of money. This unfortunate union lasted only a few months—a mother-in-law is sometimes credited with the breakup—and Cicero was left poorer than ever. His daughter Tullia died in 45 B.C.E., and he tried to work through his grief by more study and philosophical reading.

But Cicero was quickly back on his feet when Caesar was assassinated in 44 B.C.E. He returned to Rome to deliver a series of stinging speeches berating tyrants, dictators, and Marc Antony.

Unfortunately, Octavian and Antony had joined forces, and along with Lepidus, formed the second triumvirate. To stabilize their positions, they made lists of proscriptions—men to be eliminated, not medicines to be taken. Of the 200 names,

Cicero's topped the list. Cicero attempted to escape to the sea in a curtained litter but was overrun by Antony's men. As he stuck his head out to see what was happening, he lost it.

Dining Room Scene

The following selection is from the *Epistulae ad Familiares VII*, 26, written in 46 B.C.E. from Cicero's villa in Tusculum. He had been corresponding with Gallus, a friend, but had to desist all work while recovering from a severe case of diarrhea. He probably didn't actually write anything himself, but rather dictated all his letters to his faithful slave, Tiro.

Grammar Guru

The second person (you) passive ending is *-ris* or *-re*, making it look a lot like the present active infinitive—but it's *not!*

Don't let Cicero's word order confuse you. Sometimes the subject is in the verb.

Word	Form	Meaning
cautiores (*kow-tee-OH-rays*)	nom. pl.	more cautious
deceptus sum	first s. pres. perf. pass.	I was taken down
diarroia (*dee-ah-ROY-ah*)	nom. s.	diarrhea
helvellas (*hel-WEH-lahs*)	accusative plural	greens
litoteta (*lih-toh-TAY-tah*)	nom. s. fem.	simplicity
mirere (*mih-RAY-reh*)	second per. pres. pass.	you wonder
nata	neuter pl. part.	things born from

At tamen, ne mirere, unde hoc acciderit, et quomodo commiserim. Lex sumptuaria, quae videtur litoteta attulisse, ea mihi fraudi fuit. Nam volunt isti lauti terra nata, quae lege excepta sunt, in honorem adducere. Fungos, heluellas, herbas omnes ita condiunt, ut nihil possit esse suavius. Cum incidissem in cena apud Lentulum, tanta me diarroia arripuit, ut hodie primum videatur consistere. Ita ego, qui me ostreis et muraenes facile abstinebam, a beta et a malva deceptus sum. Post hac igitur erimus cautiores.

Anyhow, lest you wonder when this happened and how I began—the sumptuary law, which is seen to have brought simplicity, was a problem for me. For those gourmets want to honor food born from the earth [foods] which is exempted from the law. So they season mushrooms, boiled greens, all greens in such a way that nothing is able to be more tasty. When I fell into them at a dinner at the house of Lentulus, such awful diarrhea attacked me that today is my first day well. And so I, who abstain easily from oysters and eels, was taken down by a beet and a marrow. Therefore, after this, I will be more cautious.

My Sister-in-Law!

Cicero wrote many letters to his friend Atticus, spanning from 68 to 43 B.C.E. T. Pomponius Atticus was well known for his writings on Greek literature and culture. He wrote commentaries on Greek poets and translated many Greek plays into Latin. His surname was given to him because of his love and devotion to Greece.

The following letter (*Ad.Att.*V.1) was written in 51 B.C.E. Cicero was going from friend's villa to friend's villa, wending his way to Brundisium, from where he would sail to Cilicia for his year of governing. Cicero spent several weeks tying up loose ends, so to speak—paying debts, establishing political friendships, and basically dallying around before his big trip.

In this letter he speaks of having dinner with his brother, Quintus, who is married to Atticus's sister.

Letters can reveal how the Romans actually spoke. It is probable that the *nosti* (you know) of his conversation was as used and overused as it is today.

Word	Form	Meaning
quae	relative fem. s. nom.	this
se habet (*say HAH-beht*)	third, s., pres.	is how it is
mite (*MIH-TAY*)	acc. n. s.	gentle, modifies nihil
dies (*DEE-ays*)	nom. s. m.	festival day
nosti (*NOHS-tee*)	second s. pres.	you know

continues

continued

Word	Form	Meaning
quo	rel. abl. s.	there
lenius (*LEH-nee-us*)	comparative m. s.	more kind
ducenda	gerund abl. s.	leading to marriage

Nunc venio ad transversum illum extremae epistulae tuae versiculum in quo me admones de sorore. Quae res se sic habet. … Nihil tam vidi mite, nihil tam placatum quam tum meus frater erat in sororem tuam … Postridie ex Arpinati profecti sumus. Ut in Arcano Quintus maneret, dies fecit, ego Aquini, sed prandimus in Arcano. Nosti hunc fundum. Quo ut venimus, humanissime Quintus, "Pomponia" inquit, "tu invita mulieres, ego arcivero viros." Nihil potuit, mihi quidem ut visum est, dulcius idque cum verbis tum etiam animo ac vultu. At illa audientibus nobis "Ego ipsa sum" inquit "hic hospita," quod antecesserat Statius, ut prandium nobis videret. Tum Quintus, "En" inquit mihi "haec ego patior cotidie." Dices: "Quid, quaeso, istuc erat?" Magnum: itaque me ipsum commoverat; sic absurde et aspere verbis vultuque responderat. Dissimulavi dolens. Discubuimus omnes praeter illam, cui tamen Quintus mensam misit. Illa reiecit. Quid multa? Nihil meo fratre lenius, nihil asperius tua sorore mihi visum est; et multa praetereo … Quintus in Arcano remansit et Aquinum ad me postridie mane venit mihique narravit nec secum illam dormire voluisse.

Now I come to the little note written across the end of your letter, in which you warn me about your sister. This is how it is. I have seen nothing so gentle, nothing so pleasing as my brother was at that time to your sister. … On the next day, we set out from Arpinum. A festival made Quintus remain in Arcanum, I in Aquinum, but we dined in Arcanum. You know this place. As we arrived there, Quintus said most politely, "Pomponia, you invite the women, I will invite the men." Nothing was able, as indeed it seemed to me, to be sweeter with words as well as in intention and countenance. But she, while we were listening, said, "I am myself a guest here" … because Statius had gone ahead to prepare dinner for us. Then Quintus said to me "Oh, I suffer these things daily." You'll say, "What, if you please, was the problem?" Much; and so she upset me, too; so absurdly and harshly she had responded with words and countenance. Sadly, I pretended otherwise. We all reclined except her, to whom nevertheless Quintus sent a tray. She refused it. What more? Nothing seemed to me more kind than my brother,

nothing more harsh than your sister; and I omit a lot … Quintus remained in
Arcanum and on the next morning came to me at Aquinum and told me that she
had refused to sleep with him.

In a later letter (*Ad Att.* XIV.13.5), after Pomponia and Quintus had divorced, Cicero
states:

Abhorret a ducenda autem uxore: "Nihil iucundius libero lecto est."

He shies away from marrying again: "Nothing is more pleasant than an empty
bed."

My House!

While Cicero was in exile, Clodius seized his house on the Palatine hill, burned it to
the ground, and offered his belongings for sale. He then had the property dedicated
to a goddess, Liberty, so the spot was sanctified and no private person could ever buy
it. Clodius's brother-in-law, recently returned from a lucrative visit to Greece, performed the ceremony and evidently added a statue to the loot.

In the end, of course, after Clodius was murdered, Cicero did recover his property.
This selection is from *De Domo Sua xliii.*

Latin	Form	Meaning
meretrix (*MEH-reh-triks*)	nom. s.	prostitute, woman of the street
simulacrum (*sih-moo-LAH-krum*)	nom. s	statue
sepulcro (*seh-PULL-krow*)	abl. s.	tomb
sacerdote (*sah-kehr-DOH-tay*)	abl. s.	priest
aedilitatis (*eye-dih-lih-TAH-tihs*)	gen. s.	of his aedilship
cogitarat (*koh-gi-TAH-raht*)	third. s. perf.	he thought
muneris	gen. s.	of his gift
fanis (*FAH-nees*)	abl. pl	shrines

At unde est inventa ista (statua) Libertas? Quaesivi enim diligenter. Tanagraea quaedam meretrix fuisse dicitur. Eius non longe a Tanagra simulacrum e marmore in sepulcro positum fuit. Hoc quidam homo nobilis (Appius Clodius, frater Publii Clodii) non alienus ab hoc religioso Libertatis sacerdote, ad ornatum aedilitatis suae deportavit. Etenim cogitarat omnes superiores muneris splendore superare. Itaque omnia signa, tabulas, ornamentorum quod superfuit in fanis et communibus locis, tota e Graecia atque insulis omnibus honoris populi Romani causa sane frugaliter domum suam deportavit.

But where did that statue of Liberty come from? I asked around carefully. There is said to have been a certain woman of the streets at Tanagra. Not far from the city her statue from marble had been placed on a tomb. A certain noble man, not unconnected to this religious priest of Liberty, carried it to decorate his aedilship. And so he thought to surpass all his predecessors by the splendor of his gift. And so all statues, pictures, and furniture which were left over in the shrines and public places in all of Greece and every island, for the sake of the honor of the Roman people, wisely and frugally he brought to his own home.

Latin	Form	Meaning
iterum (*IH-teh-room*)		again
obtigisset (*ohb-tih-GIHS-set*)	third sing perfect subj.	it fell to his lot
vesperum (*WEHS-peh-room*)	acc. sing.	evening
filiolam (*fih-lee-OH-lahm*)	acc. sing. object of osculans	little daughter
periit (*PEH-rih-it*)	third sing. perfect	has died
complexus	past participle	having embraced
catellus	nom. sing.	puppy

The Least You Need to Know

- ◆ Terence wrote plays that were performed on the street.

- ◆ Caesar wrote a description of the Gallic Wars in which he comes out looking pretty good.

- ◆ Cicero wrote 900 letters with the help of a word processor named Tiro.

Chapter 18

Selections from Vitruvius *et al.*

In This Chapter

- ◆ Vitruvius and his writings
- ◆ Livy and his writings
- ◆ Pliny and his writings
- ◆ The Fables of Phaedrus

Blissfully unaware that he was making the transition from 1 B.C.E. to 1 C.E., Augustus attempted to establish a "pax Augusta," peaceful times that enabled poets, writers, and essayists to produce at a prodigious rate. Generous patronage continued, and writers became more independent of their Greek predecessors. National consciousness was high, as seen in Vergil's and Livy's works, but then slowly ebbed away to a more personalized, private outlook. Histories, literary criticism, technical writing, and compilations were only part of the empire's contributions to Latin literature.

Vitruvius and His Works

Marcus Pollio Vitruvius was a celebrated architect and engineer. About his personal life we know only that he lived in the first century B.C.E. His treatise on his profession, dedicated to Augustus, is the only book on architecture surviving from ancient times. Topics include how to build a city, covering everything from walls to bricks to entire buildings; how to create colors; the physics of water; and a series of descriptions of ancient machines such as the water organ, water wheels, catapults, siege machines, and a water pump.

A Good Law

In the following passage from the preface, Vitruvius describes a law regarding bids and contractors.

Latin	Form	Meaning
civitate (*kih-wih-TAH-tay*)	abl. s.	in the city
constitua esse	perf. inf. (with dicitur)	to have been instituted
dura condicione (*DOO-rah kohn-dih-kee-OWN-ay*)	abl. s.	with a hard condition
cum	when	
tradita aestimatione (*TRAH-dih-tah eyes-tihm-ah-tee-OWN-ay*)	abl. abs.	estimate having been handed over
bona	nom. pl. n.	goods

Nobili Graecorum et ampla civitate Ephesi lex vetusta dicitur a maioribus dura condicione sed iure non iniquo constituta esse. Nam architectus cum publicum opus curandum recipit, pollicetur, quanto sumptui futurum sit. Tradita aestimatione magistratui bona eius obligantur, donec opus perfectum sit. Absoluto autem, cum ad dictum inpensa respondit, decretis et honoribus ornatur. Item si non amplius quam quarta in opere consumitur, ad aestimationem est adicienda et de publico praestatur, neque ulla poena tenetur. Cum vero amplius quam quarta in opere consumitur, ex eius bonis ad perficiendum pecunia exigitur.

Utinam dei immortales fecissent, ea lex etiam Populo Romano non modo publi-
cis sed etiam privatis aedificiis constitutua esset.

In the noble and large city of Ephesus of the Greeks, an old law is said to have
been instituted by the forefathers, with a hard condition, but not unfair. For the
architect, when he receives a public work to be done, promises how much the
cost will be. The estimate is handed over and his goods are earmarked to the
magistrate until the work is finished. At completion, moreover, when the cost
responds to the contract, he is decorated with decrees and honors. Likewise,
if it is no more than a quarter more than the estimate, it must be added to the
estimate and paid for by the public. Nor is any penalty paid. But when it is more
than a quarter over, the money is exacted from his own goods for finishing.

Would that the immortal gods would make it that this law be instituted for the
Roman people, not only for public buildings, but for private ones as well!

The Life of Livy and Selections

Titus Livius lived from 59 B.C.E. to 17 C.E., spending his whole life either in Padua,
his birthplace, or Rome. He wrote a monumental opus, *Ab Urbe Condita* (*From the
Founding of the City*), a readable history of Rome in 142 books, only 35 of which exist
today.

His work and reputation brought him to the attention of Octavian, later known as
Augustus, who hired him to help his young nephew Claudius with his writing.

This selection from Book 2 relates an incident from 494 B.C.E. The plebeians of
Rome, determined to escape the tyranny of the patricians, withdrew from the city.
Tired of paying taxes and dying for a city that
did not even grant them basic civil rights, they
marched to a field about 3 miles from Rome.
The patricians, wondering who would defend
Rome if an enemy were to attack, sent
Menenius Agrippa to convince the plebeians to
return. Livy repeats the words of Menenius and
the result.

Tene Memoria
The genitive plural ending for the third declension is *-um*, much like the accusative singular of other declensions.

Latin	Form	Meaning
egit	third s. perfect	did
Meneni Agrippae (*meh-NEH-nee ah-GRI-peye*)	gen. s.	of Menenius Agrippa
consulum	genitive pl.	of the consuls; they were the highest political officers
membra	accusative pl.	members

Corpus humanum multa membra habet inter quae manus, os, dentes, venter sunt. Olim reliquae partes corporis iratae erant, quod venter omnia accepit sed nihil sibi egit. Tum inter se hoc consilium ceperunt. Dentes nullum cibum mandere statuerunt; os, nullum cibum accipere, manus nullum cibum ad os ferre. Itaque venter ali non poterat, et totum corpus e vita excessit. Nolite, O cives, propter discordiam vestram patriam eodem modo delere.

Necesse erat corpus humanum omnes partes habere; necesse erat patriam et patres et plebem habere. Plebs fabulam Meneni Agrippae intellexit et condiciones pacis accepit. Novi magistratus creati sunt quorum erat officium contra violentiam consulum plebi auxilium semper dare.

The human body has many members, among which are the hands, mouth, teeth, and stomach. Once upon a time, the rest of the parts of the body were angry because the stomach received everything but did nothing for himself. Then they made this plan together. The teeth decided not to chew the food, the mouth not to receive food, and the hands not to bring food to the mouth. And so the stomach was not able to be fed and the whole body died. Do not, O citizens, on account of your discord, destroy your country in the same way.

It was necessary that the human body have all parts. It was necessary that the country have both patricians and plebeians. The plebeians understood the story of Menenius Agrippa and accepted the conditions of peace. New magistrates were created whose duty was to always give aid to the plebeians against the violence of the consuls.

Grammar Guru

The word *candidate* comes from the Latin *candidatus*, which means "dressed in white." Men seeking public office in republican days wore the *toga candida*, a plain white toga that was sometimes made more white by the use of chalk. Let's hope they were more candid than our candidates today, who can't hold a candle to the ancient politicians' candor.

The Life of Pliny and Selections

Gaius Plinius Secundus was born in 23 C.E. in Verona to a noble family. He held the office of augur and was governor of Spain, although he probably delegated the office work to an educated slave so he could spend his whole life making lists. He was known to have servants read to him while he ate so he could continue to take notes. He always appeared in Rome with his secretary and was courted and admired by two emperors, Titus and Vespasian.

Pliny was the commander of the fleet at Misenum when Vesuvius erupted in 79 C.E. He set sail in a small vessel to investigate the phenomenon and landed on the coast. He stayed overnight with a friend, intending to return the next day. But an earthquake and contrary winds kept him on shore, where he was finally overcome by smoke and ashes and died.

Of all his voluminous note taking and list making, only 37 books remain. Treatises on stars, heavens, wind, rain, hail, minerals, trees, flowers, plants, all living beasts, a geographical description of every place known to man, a history of every art and science, commerce, and navigation are just a small part of his work. His lists of sources and titles make up one book. He consulted 160 sources, 362 Greek authors, and 146 Roman authors.

Book 8, for example, covers mammals, both wild and domesticated; snakes, crocodiles, and lizards; and the appearance, behavior, history, and habitations of these animals. Book 9 describes aquatic species, including Nereids (they exist?), Tritons, sea serpents, the use of fish as food, pearls, dyes obtained from fish, and the physiology of aquatic animals.

> **Latin Today!**
>
> *Words to take on your jungle safari:*
>   elephantus (*el-eh-FAHN-tus*)
>   captare (*kahp-TAH-ray*)
>   magnum opus (*MAHG-num OH-pus*)

How to Catch an Elephant

The first selection is adapted from *Natural History*, VIII.viii.26.

Latin	Form	Meaning
novissimo (*noh-WIH-see-moh*)	abl. s.	last
spectato (*spehk-TAH-tow*)	abl s. abl. absolute	having been seen

continues

continued

Latin	Form	Meaning
totius (*TOH-tee-us*)	gen. s.	of the whole
praeacuta bipenni (*preye-ah-KOO-tah*)	abl. s.	with a sharp knife
cuncta (*KUNK-tah*)	acc. pl. n.	all things

Trogodytae Aethiopiae, qui se hoc solo venatu alunt, propinquas conscendunt arbores, inde totius agminis novissimo spectato, extremas in clunes desiliunt; laeva adprehendunt caudam, pedes stipant in sinistro femine; ita pendens alterum poplitem dextra caedit praeacuta bipenni. Crure tardato, alterius poplitis nervos caedit, cuncta praeceleri pernicitate peragens.

The cavemen of Ethiopia, who feed themselves by hunting alone, climb the nearest trees and from there, having seen the last of the whole line of elephants, jump down on the last hindquarters; they grasp the tail with their left hand, plant their feet on the left thigh; hanging in such a way, he cuts one of the hamstrings with his right hand with a very sharp two-edged knife. When the elephant is slowed down by his leg, he cuts the nerves of the other knee, doing it all with amazing speed.

The Sad Fate of Oysters

This adaptation is from Pliny's *Natural History*, IX, lv.

Latin	Form	Meaning
veluti		just as
duces mirae	nom. pl.	admirable leaders
sunt		they are
obruunt (*awb-ROO-unt*)		they bury
rosa carne omni	abl. absolute	all meat having been gnawed away

Ita, sicut apibus, alii e numero concharum, singuli magnitudine et praecipui vetustate sunt. Veluti duces mirae ad cavendum sollertiae sunt. Urinantes has cura magna petunt. Illis captis, facile ceteras palantes retibus includunt. Deinde, eas obruunt sale in vasis fictilibus; rosa carne omni, nuclei corporum qui margaritae sunt in ima decidunt.

Thus, as with bees, some of the shells are singular in size and unusual in old age. Just as admirable leaders they are skillful in evading capture. Divers look for these with great care. These having been captured, the divers, with nets, easily catch the rest who are wandering. Then they bury them in salt in clay vases. All the meat is gnawed away and the kernels of the bodies, which are pearls, fall to the bottom.

Hysteria's Herstory

Pliny tells the story of Cleopatra and Antony and the mother of all banquets. Cleopatra boasted that she could create a banquet that would cost 10 million sesterces. Bets were taken, and on the very next day, Cleopatra presented her lover with a rather ordinary dinner. But for dessert she ordered a cup of vinegar, took one of her huge pearl earrings off, dropped it into the cup, and when it was dissolved, drank it. Lucius Plancus, who was overseeing the event, placed his hand on the other pearl when the queen was preparing to destroy it in a similar way and declared that Antony had lost the battle—an ominous remark that came true.

After Cleopatra's death, the other pearl was cut in half and brought to Rome to beautify the ears of a statue of Venus in the Pantheon.

Fishponds and Showers

This selection is from Pliny's *Natural History Book*, IX.lxxix and lxxxi.

Latin	Form	Meaning
balineas (*bah-LIHN-eh-ahs*)	acc. pl.	baths
Servius Orata (*SEHR-wee-ahs oh-RAH-tah*)		(proper name)
mutua appendit	third s. perf.	loaned out

continues

continued

Latin	Form	Meaning
quidem		any
amor	nom. s. f.	love
orator	nom. s. m.	(subject of habuit)
qua	abl. s.	(piscinam is antecedent)
dilexit	third s. perf.	loved
vivarium	n.	fishpond

Tene Memoria

Showers, or hanging baths, were around long before modern plumbing. A fourth-century B.C.E. piece of artwork depicts a bevy of women enjoying water piped into overhead devices and spraying out through showerheads shaped like boars and lions.

The word for shower comes in two versions: *balineum, i,* n., and *balinea, ae,* f.

Primus omnium Sergius Orata ostrearum invenit. Et is qui primus pensiles balineas invenit, ita mangonicatas villas subinde vendendo.

C. Hurrius ante alios murenarum vivarium privatim excogitavit. Is cenis triumphalibus Caesaris dictatoris sex milia in numero murenarum mutua appendit; nam permutare quidem pretio noluit aut alia merce. Invasit deinde singulorum piscium amor. Apud Baulos in parte Baiana piscinam habuit Hortensius orator in qua murenam adeo dilexit ut exanimatam flevisse credatur. In eadem villa Antonia, uxor Drusi, murenae quam diligebat, inaures addidit.

First of all, Sergius Orata invented the fish hatcheries. And it is he who first invented hanging baths [showers] and in such a way improved the appearance of houses for immediate sale.

C. [Caius] Hurrius, before others thought up the private fishpond for eels, loaned out for the triumphal dinners of Caesar the Dictator 6,000 eels. For he did not want to exchange them for a price or any other merchandise. Next, love of single fish came into vogue. At Baulos, in a part of Baiana, Hortensius the orator had a fishpond in which he loved an eel to such an extent that he is believed to have wept when it died. In the same house, Antonia, wife of Drusus, put earrings on an eel she was fond of.

The Fables of Phaedrus

Phaedrus, born in Macedonia and brought to Italy as a slave, obtained his freedom from Augustus. He is most well known for his Latin translations of Aesop's fables. There are 93 extant fables, including some originals written by Phaedrus himself. I've revised the following fable once again for even more readability.

De Capellis Barbatis (The Nanny Goats and the Beards)

The original eight-line poem has been revised into dialogue form for your enjoyment. Get your bearded friends to take part!

Latin	Form	Meaning
plorare	present infinitive after noli	whine
gratias (*GRAH-tee-ahs*)	acc.pl.	thanks
impares	nom. pl.	unequal
fortitudini (*fohr-tih-TOO-dih-nee*)	dative s.	in strength
aspectu	ablative s.	in appearance
virtute	ablative s.	in merit

Capellae: Nos barbas volumus! Nos barbas volumus! Nos barbas similes barbis hircorum volumus!

Iuppiter: Nolite plorare! Ecce! Habetis vestras barbas.

Capellae: Eugepae! Tibi gratias maximas agimus.

Hirci: Eheu! Nunc infirmae capellae similes nobis sunt!

Iuppiter: Pares sunt vobis vultibus, sed impares vobis fortitudini.

Sententia: Qui par aspectu est, non semper par virtute.

Nanny Goats: We want beards! We want beards like the guy goats!

Jupiter: Don't whine. Look! You have your beards.

Nanny Goats: Hooray! We thank you so much.

Billy Goats: Alas! Now those weak girl goats look like us!

Jupiter: They may be equal to you in appearance, but they are not equal in strength.

Moral: Those who are similar in appearance are not always similar in merit.

The Least You Need to Know

◆ Augustus was the first of a long line of emperors, all calling themselves Caesar.

◆ Vitruvius was an engineer and architect.

◆ Livy wrote a long history of Rome.

◆ Pliny wrote about everything.

◆ Goats can talk—in Phaedrus's writings, anyway.

Chapter 19

Look, Ma! I'm Reading Latin!

In This Chapter

- More reading practice: sentences, stories, and Psalms
- Case and verb syntax review
- Translation hints

The old Latin textbooks, the ones without pictures, were divided into phonology, morphology, and syntax. Phonology discussed the letters and pronunciation of Latin. Morphology described the forms of Latin words, and syntax prescribed the rules for using those words. Nowadays, we have forms and usage.

In this chapter, you practice your vocabulary and forms while translating some more Latin sentences. In the process, you can review the syntax and usage rules as well.

Review: Sentences and Cases

The ending on a noun, pronoun, or adjective tells the reader how the word is used in the sentence.

The subject of the sentence is in the nominative case. The subject sometimes has modifiers, appositives, adjectives, or a noun in the genitive. Here are some examples:

1. Romulus rex moritur.

2. Bonus rex lacrimavit.

3. Libri Sanctarum Scripturarum saepe leguntur.

4. Is est in tua provincia.

> **Hysteria's Herstory** _____
>
> Roman mothers did not enjoy the status and reverence bestowed on mothers today, and mothers are not mentioned much in literature. Many women died in childbirth. Divorce was simple, and men often just walked out of a marriage and took the kids with them. Fathers had complete control over the people in the household. No Mother's Day! No Mommy dearest! No Mom and apple pie!

The accusative case is used for the direct object, the object of a preposition, the subject of an infinitive for indirect statement, time, and extent of space and exclamations. For example:

5. Marius Italiam liberavit.

6. Trans flumen transivit.

7. Dicunt Platonem in Italiam venisse.

8. Romulus septem et triginta annos regnavit.

9. Me miserum!

The dative case is used for the indirect object; with verbs of *favor, help, please, trust, persuade,* and the like; and to show possession:

Grammar Guru _____

Remember that the demonstrative pronouns can also be the third personal pronoun: *he, she, it,* or *they.*

10. Signum militibus dedit.

11. Ego numquam mihi placui.

12. Facile Helvetiis persuasit.

13. Mihi nomen est Caesar.

The genitive case is used to show possession and to show a part:

14. Officium consulis est mandata dare.

15. Clunis elephanti magnus est.

16. Mille militum misit.

17. Horum omnium fortissimi Belgae sunt.

The ablative case is used for everything left over. It primarily, however, shows *from* or *by*, *in* or *at*, means, time, or use in an absolute. It is also used with comparisons without *quam*. Here are some examples:

18. Ex concha margarita venit.

19. Ab eis amatur.

20. Nihil est iucundius vita.

21. Cornibus alces se tutantur.

22. Venatu solo vivunt.

23. Anno ipso Ennius natus est.

24. Agro capto, partem militibus Caesar dedit.

Nouns and adjectives agree in number, gender, and case. If an infinitive is used as a noun, it is neuter singular, as in these examples:

25. Dolere malum est.

26. Errare humanum est.

27. Haec vasa aurea in mensa sunt.

Verb Usage Review

Every sentence has a verb. The complications begin when the verb has attachments—adverbs, clauses, direct and indirect objects, or prepositional phrases.

Just remember that the verb agrees with the subject in person and number. Also, the verb is frequently at the end of its clause or sentence. Here are some examples:

1. Romulus urbem condidit.

2. Gloria saepe laborem sequitur.

3. Sapientes laete vivunt.

4. In urbe Epheso, rex Graecus cum regina remansit.

5. Ego ad te scribam.

Verbs appear in six tenses. The present, imperfect, and future are formed from the second principal part; the perfect active tenses are formed from the third principal part; and the perfect passive tenses are formed from the fourth principal part. So when you see the fourth principal part followed by some form of the verb *esse* (to be), you know you have a verb that translates "has/have/had been ———ed." Also, the participle has an ending that agrees with the subject. To refresh your memory, take a look at these examples:

6. Castor et Pollux ex equis pugnare visi sunt.

7. Vir a puero ab aqua tractus erat.

8. Strepitus a turba auditus est.

The verb *esse* is often omitted, as in these examples:

9. Rara avis.

10. Quot homines, tot sententiae.

11. Ars longa, vita brevis.

12. Quid hoc ad me?

The imperative mood is used to give commands. Negative commands use *noli, nolite* with the infinitive. The subjunctive mood shows unreal conditions and commands of the first and third persons. The subjunctive is often used on clauses within clauses. Here are some examples:

13. Libera rem publicam metu.

14. Nolite velle quod fieri non potest.

15. Vincat.

16. In mundo deus est qui regat, qui gubernet, qui cursus astrorum conservet.

Passive verb forms have *r, mini*, and perfect tense forms with two words. Deponent verbs are always passive but have active meanings, as shown in these examples:

17. A deo mundus aedificatus est.

18. Rex magnopere amatur.

19. Hoc mirabar.

20. Homines id quod volunt credunt.

21. Amicitiae nostrae memoriam spero sempiternam fore.

More Hints for Translating

Here are some more hints that will help with your Latin skills:

♦ **Read the whole sentence.** Put mental (or real) parentheses around relative clauses, result or purpose clauses, prepositional phrases, or any other groups.

♦ **Find the verb.** The verb will also lead you to the subject. If the verb is in the first or second person, you already have a subject: *I, you,* or *we.* If the verb is in the third person, look for a noun in the nominative that is in the same number. If the verb is third-person plural, look for a plural nominative. If the verb is in the third-person singular, look for the nominative singular. Remember that sometimes a phrase or clause or infinitive can also be the subject.

♦ **Determine word order.** The usual word order is: subject (and attachments), indirect object, object, adverb and prepositions, and verb. For example:

Si vincimus, omnia tuta erunt.

Fortuna fortes adiuvat. (The verb tells you which is the subject.)

Nihilne te nocturnum praesidium Palati, nihil urbis vigiliae, nihil timor populi, nihil concursus bonorum omnium, nihil hic munitissimus habendi senatus locus, nihil horum ora vultusque moverunt?

The *nihil* has the force of *non.* The subjects are all nicely in the nominative case, the verb is at the end, and the direct object is the second word.

Tene Memoria

Remember that every letter counts in pronouncing Latin. Except for diphthongs (*ae, au, oe* being the most common), all vowels and consonants are separate sounds. When all else fails, just read with confidence. It will be a *rara avis* who corrects you!

◆ **Think like a Roman.** The way *not* to translate is to write all the English meanings on pieces of paper and try to arrange them to make sense. This will not work and will lead to hours of frustration, not to mention an incorrect translation.

Stories to Read in Latin

Here are some words you have not seen.

Latin	English
altus, a, um	high, deep
caelum, i, n. (*KEYE-lum*)	sky
defessus, a, um	tired
dis, ditis (*DEES*)	rich
flumen, fluminis, n.	river
fluo, ere, fluxi, fluxus (*FLOO-oh*)	flow
fortasse	perhaps
glaber, ra, rum (*GLAH-behr*)	bald
harena, ae, f. (*hah-RAY-nah*)	sands
lapis, lapidis, m.	stone
lavo, lavare, lavi, lautus (or lotus)	wash
mare, maris, n.	sea
navis, navis, f.	ship
nimbus, i, m.	cloud, rain cloud
oculus, i, m.	eye
ossum, i, n.	bone
paro, parare, avi, atus	prepare
pluit, pluere, pluit	it rains

Latin	English
scelus, sceleris, n.	crime
somnus, i, m.	sleep
stupeo, ere, stupui (*STOO-peh-oh*)	be silent
tergum, i, n.	back
tristis, is, e	sad
turpis, is, e	ugly, nasty, disgraceful
ubique (*oo-BEE-kweh*)	everywhere
unda, ae, f.	wave
velo, are, avi, atus	veil, wrap, put on
verto, ere, verti, versus	turn
vix	scarcely (*wicks*)

Midas

This famous tale begins when Silenus, the drunken old man who accompanies Bacchus, god of wine, wanders into Midas's rose garden. Midas leads him back to where he belongs and is duly rewarded.

Olim Bacchus Midae, regi Phrygiae, donum dedit. "Quid vis, tibi dabo," dixit. Midas sic respondit: "Quicquid meo corpore contigero, id aurum sit." Cui deus dixit, "Ita sit." Midas laetus domum redivit. Vix bonae fortunae credens, portas tangit, quae in aurum vertuntur. Deinde domum percurrit, lectos, mensas, sellas, manu tangens. Brevi tempore omnia sunt aurea. Tum vero quicquid cibi rex ore contingit, id statim in aurum vertitur. Etiam vinum in aureum flumen vertitur. Midas attonitus dites effugere temptat sed frustra. Sic tandem secum dicit: Tam stultus fui! Et ditissimus et pauperrimus mortalium sum!

Inde Midas Bacchum diem noctemque quaerebat. Tandem defessus Midas deum invenit.

Tum dixit, "Quaeso, ab hoc crudeli fato me eripe." Cui deus respondet: "Vade ad flumen Pactolum et te lava in aqua." Rex Midas ad flumen succedit atque in aquam se mergit. Statim, mirabile dictu, aurum de eius corpore in flumen cedit. Usque ad hoc tempus Pactolus aureis harenis fluere dicitur.

Once upon a time, Bacchus gave a gift to Midas, king of Phrygia. "What you want, I will give you," he said. Midas answered, "Whatever I touch with my body, let it become gold." The god said, "So be it." Midas happily returned home. Scarcely believing his good fortune, he touched the doors, which turned into gold. Then he ran through the house, touching with his hand beds, tables, chairs. In a short time everything was gold. Then whatever food the king brought to his mouth, it, too, turned to gold. Even wine turned into a river of gold. The astonished Midas tried to escape the riches, but in vain. Then finally he said to himself, "I was so foolish. I am both the richest and poorest of mortals."

From there Midas sought Bacchus day and night. Finally, exhausted, Midas found the god.

Then he said, "Please, take me from the cruel fate." The god responded, "Go to the river Pactolus and wash yourself in the water." King Midas went to the river and immersed himself in the water. Immediately, miraculous to say, the gold fell from his body into the river. And up to this time, the Pactolus is said to flow with golden sands.

Biblical Translations

The Bible has been translated into many languages, but the Latin version has a certain quality that recalls the age when Christianity began. Be sure to read these two familiar Psalms (Psalm 23 and Psalm 100) aloud and imagine yourself in a monastery high in the mountains of Italy, reading the daily devotionals and dedicating your life to God.

Psalmus Davidis XXIII

1. Jehova pastor meus est, non possum egere.

2. In caulis herbidis facit ut recubem, secundum aquas lenes deducit me.

3. Animam meam quietam efficit: ducit me per orbitas iustitiae, propter nomen suum.

4. Etiam cum ambularem per vallem lethalis umbrae, non timerem malum quia tu mecum es: virga tua et pedum tuum, ipsa consolantur me.

5. Instruis coram me mensam e regione hostium meorum: delibutum reddis unguento caput meum, poculum meum exuberans.

6. Nihil nisi bonum et benignitas prosequentur me omnibus diebus vitae meae: et quietus ero in domo Jehovae, quamdiu longa erunt tempora.

1. The Lord is my shepherd, I shall not want.

2. He makes me lie down in green pastures; He leads me beside still waters.

3. He restores my soul; He guides me in the paths of righteousness for his name's sake.

4. Even though I walk through the valley of the shadow of death, I fear no evil: for Thou art with me; Thy rod and Thy staff, they comfort me.

5. Thou dost prepare a table before me in the presence of my enemies: Thou hast anointed my head with oil; My cup overflows.

6. Surely goodness and mercy will follow me all the days of my life, and I will dwell in the house of the Lord forever.

Psalmus Pro Gratiarum Actione C

1. Clangite Jehovae, omnes incolae terrae.

2. Colite Jehovam cum laetitia, venit in conspectum eius cum cantu.

3. Agnoscite Jehovam esse Deum, ipsum effecisse nos (non autem nos ipsos) populum suum et gregem pastus sui.

4. Ingredimini portas eius cum gratiarum actione, atria eius cum laude: gratias agite ei, benedicite nomini eius.

5. Nam bonus est Jehova, in seculum est benignitas eius: et usque ad generationem quamque fides eius.

1. Shout joyfully to the Lord, all the earth.

2. Serve the Lord with gladness; come before Him with joyful singing.

3. Know that the Lord Himself is God; it is He who has made us, and not we ourselves; we are His people and the sheep of His pasture.

4. Enter His gates with thanksgiving and His courts with praise. Give thanks to Him, bless His name.

5. For the Lord is good; His loving kindness is everlasting and His faithfulness to all generations.

The Least You Need to Know

♦ Every sentence has a subject and a predicate.

♦ Case endings indicate how the word is used in the sentence.

♦ Verb endings indicate who, when, and what mood the verb is in.

♦ Sorting all the Latin words in a sentence alphabetically will not get you a translation. You must look at the endings.

Part 5

Coping with Latin in the Modern World

Latin is all around you, whether you realize it or not. If you drive through upstate New York, you'll pass through Rome, Greece, Syracuse, Utica, Ithaca, Troy, and Ilion. Latin lives on in quotations, mottoes, and classical references. Latin is in legal documents, botanical species, prescriptive medicine, and almost every part of your life except maybe McDonald's. In Part 5, I show you how to cope with Latin in your everyday life.

Chapter 20

Legal Latin

In This Chapter

- ◆ More words to learn
- ◆ Legal terms and meanings
- ◆ Law-school-paper Latin
- ◆ Law sayings and quotations
- ◆ Ancient Roman law

When a lawyer stands before a jury to present his case, he's not going to spout Latin. But when conversing with other lawyers or the judge, or when reading law books, he needs to know some Latin. Many terms in documents and legal writings are in Latin. You will hear Latin when you watch *Court TV*—or, heaven forbid, you are in court yourself.

In this chapter, I include the more frequently used terms in courts or in legal papers. Remember that these terms have for the most part become English, and, therefore, the English pronunciation can be found in any dictionary.

Words to Learn or Learn Again

Lawyers themselves say that pronunciation of the following Latin terms differs from place to place. The Latin pronunciation is never wrong, but because many of the terms have become part of the English language, the Anglicized version is correct also. Meanwhile, here are the original Latin words with their etymological information.

Latin	Forms	Meaning	Derivative
caveo	cavere, cavi	cautus	take care, beware
curia	curiae, f.	senate house	court
delictum	delicti, n.	fault, misdeed	delict
facies	faciei, f.	face, appearance	face
factum	facti, n.	deed	fact
flagrans	flagrantis	flaming	flagrant
fructus	fructus, m.	fruit	fructify
hic	haec, hoc	this	this
ius	iuris, n.	right, justice	jury
matrimonium	matrimoni, i, n.	marriage	matrimony
par	paris	equal	parity
operor	ari, atus sum	work hard	operator
pando	pandere, passus	spread out	expand
primus	prima, primum	first	prime
tempus	temporis, n.	time	temporal
usus	usus, m.	use	usage
vinculum	vinculi, n.	chain	invincible

Legal Latin Terms and What They Mean

Here's a list of legal Latin terms you may have come across at some point in your life. The pronunciation guide is the English version if it differs from the Latin. The English is probably the way you will hear it pronounced in court.

***Ad hoc* (to this)**   The preposition *ad* takes the accusative case, and in this instance, the neuter accusative singular. This expression designates a specific purpose: the ad hoc committee, for example, for abolishing homework.

***Amicus curiae* (ah-mee-KUS KYU-ree-eye; friend of the court)**   *Curiae* is in the genitive singular, first declension. An *amicus curiae* is a person who is neutral to specific action and gives advice on matters not before the court. Often this is done when the case may be setting legal precedent.

***A vinculo matrimonii* (ah VIN-kyu-loh mah-trih-MOH-nee-ee; from the chain of marriage)**   The preposition *a/ab* takes the ablative case. *Matrimonii* is in the genitive, *of*. Harsh term! This is the legal term for a permanent decree of divorce.

Hysteria's Herstory

In republican times, there were no divorce courts, and a wife could not take her husband to court for adultery. However, if she was caught with the milkman, *in flagrante delicto*, she could be killed, beaten, or mutilated by her husband—legally! The milkman, too, could be legally killed by the husband. After Augustus' law concerning divorce in the late first century, it was not just *Res tuas tibi habeto* (Take your things and go). There had to be witnesses, contracts, restoration of dowry, and other considerations that only lawyers think of.

***Caveat* (KAH-vee-at; let him beware!)**   This is in the subjunctive mood, a third person command. A *caveat* is a formal warning to an officer or a court not to do a specified act—not to probate a will, for example—until the person can be heard in opposition.

***Corpus delicti* (KOHR-pus deh-LIK-teye; the body of the crime)**   *Corpus* is in the nominative case; *delicti* is in the genitive. The *corpus delicti* is the object upon which a crime has been committed, but of course it doesn't have to be a body, in spite of the Latin. It could be your car.

Grammar Guru

Legal-minded Romans used *ius, iuris* heavily. It was used for law, legality, the legal system or code; a rule; the binding decision of a magistrate; an oath; anything that is right; obligations from a relationship; one's due; or jurisdiction. Many of our legal terms come from this little, powerful word.

***De facto* (concerning the deed)**   A *de facto* situation is one that actually exists, whether it is legal or not.

Habeas corpus (**HAY-bee-uhs KOHR-pus; may you have a body**)   Note that this is the subjunctive in a command sense. It's not that you have a body. That would be indicative, *habes*. Instead, the subjunctive indicates that it is not actual but is definitely desired. A writ of *habeas corpus* is an order by a judge to have a prisoner brought to trial to determine the legality of his imprisonment.

In flagrante delicto (**while the crime is still burning**)   Caught in the act! *Flagrante* is an adjective of the third declension and in the ablative case after *in*.

J.D. (juris doctor)   This is a law degree.

Modus operandi (**MOH-dus oh-pur-AHN-deye; the way of working**)   This is the gerund form of the verb, translated as *-ing*. We are all creatures of habit, and a criminal's modus operandi often gives the police a lead.

Nolo contendere (**I do not wish to contest**)   Used primarily in criminal cases, the defendant declines to refute the evidence. In most situations, this response has the same effect as pleading guilty.

Prima facie (**PREYE-mah FAY-shee; on first appearance**)   At first glance or on the face of it. *Facie* is one of those rare fifth-declension nouns and appears here in the ablative case.

Pro bono publico (**for the public good**)   A lawyer takes a pro bono case and does not receive payment. The preposition *pro* can have several meanings: before, in front of, in the presence of, on behalf of, in favor of, in the service of, instead of, the same as, and for.

Pro forma (**for the form**)   Something is done as a matter of form, not because it is essential.

Pro tempore (**for the time being**)   This legalese term simply translates as "temporarily."

Subpoena (**sub-PEE-nah; under penalty**)   In Latin, this is really two words, *poena* being in the ablative case after *sub*. A subpoena is an order of the court that requires a person to be present at a certain time and place or suffer a penalty.

Latin in Your Law-School Papers

Any kind of research paper—whether high school, college, or beyond—requires some use of Latin. Whether you're writing or just reading a scholarly paper, knowledge of the following abbreviations will surely be helpful:

ca., circa **(about, approximately)**   Often used with dates when the exact date is unknown.

e.g., exempli gratia **(for the sake of example)**   Try to use this abbreviation correctly. It is easy to misuse e.g. and i.e. For example:

> Romance languages, e.g., French, Spanish, Italian

> Romance languages, i.e., languages derived from the Latin of the Roman Empire

et al., et alii **(and others)**   *Alii* is in the nominative plural masculine. Sorry, girls. When there is a mixed-gender group, the noun or adjective goes in the masculine gender. *Et al.* is often used to denote multiple authors.

et alia **(and other things)**   This is used when referring to anything other than people.

etc., et cetera **(and so forth)**   *Cetera* is neuter plural, meaning "the other things, the remaining things, the rest."

ibid., ibidem **(in the same place)**   This is used in legal papers, research papers, and bibliographies.

i.e., id est **(that is)**   This is usually followed by an explanation or a synonym, not examples. *See e.g.*

id., idem **(the same)**   This is used in footnotes and bibliographies to refer to persons except in law citations. According to Kate Turabian, in *A Manual for Writers*, references following legal style employ *idem* in place of *ibid*. Legal style reserves *ibid* for references in which there is no change in page or other part from the preceding reference.

vs., versus **(against)**   This is often just *v.* in legal documents and vs. in less formal situations—*Roe* v. *Wade* and the Cowboys vs. the Indians.

Sayings and Quotations About the Law

People have been commenting on the law since time began. Many Romans criticized the lawyers especially, as the *causidicii* were really trained to be persuaders, not champions of justice. Some of the ancient comments are still in use today, not as legal precedents but as maxims and words to live by. Here is a sampling of the more familiar ones:

Ius summum saepe summa est malitia. (Terence, second century B.C.E.)

Law at its most rigorous is often the worst evil.

Caveat emptor. Caveat vendor. Canem cave! (anon.)

Let the buyer beware. Let the seller beware. Beware the dog!

De minimis non curat lex. (anon.)

The law does not concern itself with trifles.

Iure naturae aequum est neminem cum alterius detrimento et iniuria fieri locupletiorem. (Publius Celsus, circa 77 C.E.)

Cave! _____

Remember that the future passive participle, the *-endum* form, when used with *est*, denotes obligation.

By the law of nature, it is only fair that no one should become richer through damages and injuries suffered by another.

Nemo est supra leges. (anon.)

No one is above the law.

Ancient Roman Law

During the fifth century B.C.E., the Romans formed a committee to review their laws and customs and to get them written down. After a year of work, the committee, *mirabile dictu*, published the Twelve Tables of Laws. Written on 12 bronze tablets, they were set up in the Forum for all to see and obey. They served as the basis for Roman law for most of the republican era. In Justinian's time, 528 C.E., the laws were organized again (there were lots more) and written into the *Corpus Iuris Civile*, a work still in use today.

Part of the whole text of the Twelve Tables has survived. Here are some excerpts:

◆ Interest on a loan should not exceed one-twelfth part of the principal per year.

◆ Anyone will be punished who by enchantments causes another's crops to fail.

◆ Anyone committing a robbery by night may be lawfully killed by the owner of the premises.

◆ A father can imprison, beat, keep at hard labor, sell, or even slay his son.

◆ Useless and extravagant funerals are forbidden. No gold ornaments (except gold fillings in teeth), can be buried with the body. The buried or burned body cannot have more than 3 purple stripes, and no more than 10 flute players can attend the funeral.

◆ Anyone can go into another's property and pick up the fruit that has fallen from his own tree.

If a Roman noticed that his neighbor buried his uncle with 4 purple stripes accompanied by 14 flute players, he could sue. The man would simply drag the other guy into court and ask for a day. When granted, the two would again appear and argue their own cases.

In the early days of the republic, there were no lawyers. In fact, there were no lawyers at all before the Romans. Judges, priests, courts, and kings meted out justice, and no one argued. In fifth-century B.C.E. Athens, the Greeks made oratory a part of the curriculum, and thus began rhetoric and the art of persuasion.

During Roman times, the orators and rhetoricians were *iuris prudentes* (wise men of the law). Many were impartial interpreters of the law. The *iuris prudentes* were not like our lawyers today. They did not appear in court to plead cases. During the early days of Rome, private citizens were still pleading their own cases. But soon helpers appeared, *advocati* (literally, called to), who provided expert advice. Somewhere in the second century B.C.E., the *advocati*, also known as *causidicii*, were allowed to speak for their clients. The rest is history.

Rules of evidence were a little looser than today. Lawyers were known to bring in weeping widows and hearsay evidence to persuade the court. While the *iuris prudens* remained respected for his learning and impartiality, the *advocati* became famous for their theatrics and susceptibility to bribes.

One of the greatest contributions to the field of law was the Roman concept of *ius gentium*, "the law of nations." This provided for all those within the Roman Empire who were not citizens. It came to be seen as a universal law and proper for all peoples. In fact, the Roman citizens themselves preferred that their cases be tried by it rather than their own civil law. Here is how it read:

> Ius gentium, autem, omni humano genere commune est; nam, usu exigente, et humanis necessitatibus, gentes humanae iura quaedam sibi constituerunt. Bella etenim orta sunt, et captivitates sequtae, et servitutes, quae sunt naturali iuri contrariae. (Corpus Iuris Civilis, Institutiones, II, 1, 2. circa 588 C.E.)

> The law of nations is the law common to all mankind: for nations have settled certain things for themselves as occasion and necessities of human life required. For instance, wars arose, and then followed captivity and slavery, which are contrary to the law of nature.

The Least You Need to Know

- *Ius* means "law," "right," "justice," or "juice"—all of which are necessary for a good life.

- If you have to write a paper, abbreviate—sparingly.

- Roman courts were like high theater.

Chapter 21

Medical and Scientific Latin

In This Chapter

- ◆ Roots of medical terms
- ◆ Reading prescriptions
- ◆ Flora and fauna
- ◆ The medical and scientific world of the Romans

Doctors use Latin for many reasons. For one, they can stand at the foot of your hospital bed and pretend to be discussing the upcoming surgery, all the while saying things like, "Wow! She's really having a bad hair day."

Doctors like to use Latin because their patients won't question their authority. If your doctor said, "You have a stuffy nose," you yourself might suggest a couple aspirin. But if he diagnoses your condition as *chronic sinusitis*, you would probably nod your head miserably and get the prescription.

Seriously, one reason Latin is used in the sciences is that it is an unchanging, dead language. Scientists the world over can correspond and refer to anything with the same, reliable words. Also, many early medical and scientific writings were in Latin; why reinvent the wheel?

Rx for Understanding Your Doctor

Anatomy, the science of the structure of animals and plants, is originally a Greek word meaning "to cut up." When the early anatomists cut up their specimens, they found that almost everything is connected: the ankle bone's connected to the shin bone, the shin bone's connected to the knee bone ... well, you know the song. This accounts for the popularity of prepositional prefixes, which show relationships. All those easy compound words reduce the number of original words doctors have to learn. So we have the nose, *nasal*; the back of the nose, *postnasal*; over the nose, *supranasal*; under the nose, *subnasal*; and *ad infinitum*.

> **Cave!**
>
> Be careful not to confuse words that begin with the prefix *ped-*, meaning "child," from the Greek *paedeia* with words that begin with *ped-*, meaning "foot," from the latin *pedi*. A *pedophile* is *not* someone who likes feet.

Here is a list of common prefixes, suffixes, and root words that will help you understand what your doctor is talking about:

ante (before)   Your pouting daughter can be referred to as having a prominent *antelabium*. *Anterior lingual gland* is the tip of the tongue. The *antebracchium* is your forearm.

arthro (joint)   An *arthropod* has jointed limbs, and *arthritis* is the inflammation of joints.

ectomy (the Greek tome, to cut, ex, out)   This is a popular suffix: *hysterectomy, appendectomy, mastectomy.*

itis (inflammation)   *Mediastinitis*, for example, is the inflammation of the cavity that separates the lungs and contains the heart. *Appendicitis* is an inflamed appendix; *arthritis* is an inflamed joint.

ocul (eye)   The *oculauditory* system includes sight and hearing.

musole, ule, le (small)   A *muscle* is from the Latin *mus* (mouse). Rippling muscles are reminiscent of a mouse under the skin.

osteo, oss (bone)   There are literally more than 50 words with this prefix, most common *osteoporosis*, a disorder in which the bones become porous.

ovum (egg)   There is an *oviduct*, the *ovaries*, and an *ovule*, a little egg.

pedi (foot)   The spider has a *pedipalpus*, a foot that palpates or feels. A *pedicoccus* is some kind of micrococcus that grows in beer and causes cloudiness and acid.

post (behind)   Beyond *postnatal*, *postnasal*, and *postbracchium*, we have *postabdomen*, where the sting of the scorpion lies.

sub (under)   *Subcaudal* is under the tail. *Submuscular* is under the muscle. Hundreds of compounds use this prefix, including *subungual* (under the claw).

supra (above)   A *supranumerary* anything is an extra, more than is usual. A supranumerary tooth causes many trips to the orthodontist. There is such a thing as a supranumerary placenta and supranumerary digit. This last would be a mother's nightmare; as soon as the newborn is brought to her hospital bed, she cautiously peeks under the blanket and starts counting fingers and toes … 11? Supranumerary!

vas (vessel)   *Vascular* is pertaining to ducts or vessels that convey fluids.

virus (venom, slime, stench)   A virus is that infectious agent that brings about all of the above.

Reading Those Prescriptions

In ancient times, there were no prescriptions. The doctor would just say, "Drink a little wild boar's manure mixed with vinegar," or he'd mix up a cocktail of ashes of deer's antlers and blood of a donkey mixed with wine. Today, we have that little piece of paper covered with chicken scratches. Your pharmacist can read it, and now you can, too. The following table is your prescription key.

Abbreviation	Latin	Meaning
a.c.	ante cibos	before meals
ad lib	ad libitum	freely
agit	agita	shake
aq	aqua	water
b.	bis	twice
c̄	cum	with
f.	fac	make
gtt.	guttae	drops
h.s.	hora somni	at the hour of sleep
i.d.	in die	a day
m.	mane	in the morning

continues

continued

Abbreviation	Latin	Meaning
n.	nocte	at night
omn	omni	every
p.c.	post cibos	after meals
p.o.	per os	by mouth
q.	quater	four times
Rx	recipe	take
s	sine	without
SA	secundum artem	according to your judgment
s.o.s.	si opus sit	if it is necessary
stat	statim	immediately
t.	ter	three times

There's another Latin word similar to *gutta* (drop). *Guttur, gutturis,* n., means "throat," and the English derivative is *guttural. Guttation* happens to your houseplants when they ooze drops of water.

Hysteria's Herstory

Our friend Pliny mentions a method of contraception for women. You cut open the head of a hairy spider, retract two small worms, and tie them on a woman with a strip of deerhide, and she will not get pregnant for one year. That's *your* story, Pliny.

Practice Makes Perfect 1

Write the following prescriptions in Latin and then translate:

1. Rx q.i.d. p.o.   _____
2. n. 3 gtt. p.o.   _____
3. c. aq. ad. lib.   _____
4. a.c. s. aq.   _____
5. h.s. 25 gtt.   _____

At the Zoo

It walks like a duck and it quacks like a duck, but the little sign at the zoo says *Anas platrhynchos*. Here's Latin again, making things complicated.

Actually, the Latin names for all plants (*flora*) and animals (*fauna*) make things less complicated. Scientists love to classify, sort, list, and categorize, and they have been trying to make the ultimate list since Aristotle. Finally, in the eighteenth century C.E., Linnaeus, using Latin, came up with the mother of all lists, dividing the world of living things into kingdoms, phyla, classes, orders, families, genera, and species.

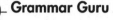 **Grammar Guru**

Genus, generis, n., is a regular third declension noun and, therefore, the plural is *genera*.

At the zoo, the signs designate the genus with the capital letter and the species with a lower case letter. The basic unit for all this classification is the species, a group of organisms that are more closely related than any other and capable of mating to produce offspring. The genus represents a group of species that are closely related, and so it goes.

Genus and species names are usually descriptive and often originate from a Latin or Greek source. Here are a few examples:

- *Arachnida* is a class of arthropods that includes scorpions, spiders, and mites. Arachne was a woman of Colophon, the daughter of Idmon, a dyer. A skillful weaver, she had the audacity to challenge Athena to a weaving contest. Of course, she lost, and in disgrace hanged herself. Athena changed her into a spider so she could go on spinning and weaving *ad infinitum*.

- *Canidae* is the dog family. *Canis latrans,* the barking dog, is a coyote. *Canis lupus,* the wolf dog, is the gray wolf. *Canis familiaris* is the family dog.

- *Lupinus perennis*, the wild lupine, is named for the lupus, the wolf, because the lupine robs the soil of its nutrients just as the wolf robs the shepherd of his sheep. Actually, it does just the opposite, but who's to contradict a good story?

- *Turdus migratorius*, the American robin, is actually a migratory thrush.

- *Nastursium officinale*, watercress, has the same name as the popular garden flower because they both have leaves that are bitter to the taste and make your *nasus torquet*, or "nose twist."

Flower Stories

Some common wildflowers not only have their Latin names, but are also connected to Greek and Roman mythology. The next time you pick a violet, for example, you can recall the story of poor, unfortunate Io and her bullish experience.

The story goes that Zeus, that king of all philanderers, was enamored with Io, a lovely but unfortunate nymph. To hide her from his wife, the ever-jealous Hera, he changed Io into a white heifer. Now, being a cow isn't much fun, and Io began to cry. Feeling sorry for her, Zeus changed her tears into sweet-smelling flowers that were called violets (in Greek: Io).

The anemone is named for the Greek god of the winds, and the little spring flower is supposed to have originated on Mt. Olympus, home of the gods. One story has Venus crying for her lost lover, Adonis, and her tears becoming anemones. Another has Adonis, who was unfortunate enough to be gored by a wild boar, dying in her arms and the drops of blood turning into the blood-red anemone.

The Medical World of the Romans

The most famous Greek doctor, Hippocrates (490 B.C.E.), enjoyed an excellent repu-tation, and, of course, left us his famous oath. In Roman times, medical practitioners were not so well esteemed. Many were Greeks of questionable education or Romans who simply followed another doctor around, picking up the art.

Martial, a first-century C.E. writer of epigrams, complains of being attended by a doc-tor who is accompanied by 100 medical students, all of whom have ice-cold hands. He writes the following:

> Languebam: sed tu comitatus protinus ad me venisti centum, Symmache, discip-ulis. Centum me tetigere manus Aquilone gelatae non habui febrem, Symmache, nunc habeo. (*Epigrams*, V.9)

> I was languishing. But you came to me, closely accompanied by 100 pupils, Symmachus. One hundred cold-as-ice hands touched me. I didn't have a fever, Symmachus, but now I do.

Many medical practices of Roman times reflect the lack of scientific knowledge that so enhances our lives today. For fractures of the ribs, for example, Pliny recommends goat's manure mixed in wine. For jaundice, he suggests the ashes of a deer's antlers or the blood of a donkey mixed with wine. Cure is guaranteed within 3 days. Onions were used for stomach trouble, snake sting, and dog bite. For ordinary bruises, crushed cabbage was applied.

On the other hand, Roman doctors used cures that have since been verified: burnt sponge for goiter (ashes of sponge contain iodine), a red-hot stone held against a wound (cauterization), chewing and swallowing of the berries of the castor oil plant as a purgative, and chewing sage for ulcers. The Romans thought that malaria came from bad night air, *malus aer*, not realizing mosquitoes brought on the feverish disease.

Finally, the Roman doctors used the same psychology modern doctors use today. They often used Greek, as we use Latin, to confound, confuse, and appear authoritative.

> Immo vero auctoritas aliter quam Graece eam tractantibus etiam apud inperitos expertesque linguae non est, ac minus credunt quae ad salutem suam pertinent, si intellegant. (*Natural History*, 29.8, 16–18)

> Truly medical treatises written in a language other than Greek have no prestige even among the unlearned men ignorant of Greek, and people tend to trust less any advice about their health if they understand the language.

The Least You Need to Know

- If you hear -*ectomy* from your doctor, it's probably not a good thing.
- If you hear -*scopy*, it's better. He's just looking.
- Prescriptions *can* be deciphered (poor handwriting, not so much).
- There are a million and a half named species of flora and fauna in the world. That's a lot of Latin.
- Roman doctors did not attend medical school.

Chapter 22

Late Latin and Church Latin

In This Chapter

- The church fathers and their works
- St. Augustine's *Confessions*
- The church litany
- Biblical Latin
- Medieval Music and holiday songs

There's no doubt that the Roman Empire fell around 500 C.E., gradually leading to the Dark Ages. The reasons why such an empire would disintegrate range from too many undefended boundaries to lead poisoning in the drinking water. Nevertheless, just as Rome was being overrun by Goths and Visigoths, the Christian church was beginning to come into its own. Cathedrals and monasteries were popping up all over Europe and were soon filled with holy brothers, all with not much to do but pray and copy manuscripts. Luckily for posterity, the monks occasionally copied a Latin manuscript from outside the church canon, thus preserving for us the works of Cicero, Vergil, Livy, and many others.

These monks also preserved Latin itself as a language. All the written works and church litany were exclusively in Latin or Greek. The Latin of the Christian church was basically the same language Cicero used, except new words were added or adapted to suit the needs of Christians. Medieval Latin differs slightly in spellings, forms, and syntax.

Verba Sancta: **Words of the Church Fathers**

The Christian church fathers were writers of Christian antiquity and, thus, the coiners of words that would eventually become Medieval Latin. These were men who lived from New Testament times to the eighth century. To be an official church father, one had to be in constant communion with the church, lead a holy life of exemplary conduct, achieve ecclesiastical approval, and be darned old. Among the most famous are St. Jerome, who wrote the first history of patristic literature; St. Ambrose, who helped transmit Eastern theology to the West; St. Augustine; and the last father, just getting in under the wire, St. Isidore of Seville.

Hysteria's Herstory

According to St. Jerome, a noblewoman named Fabiola founded a large, free, public hospital at Ostia. She recruited other women to work as nurses and contribute funds. Jerome called her "the glory of the Church, the astonishment of the Gentiles, the mother of the poor, and the consolation of the saints." She was a saint.

St. Augustine (354–430) was born and educated in the Roman province of Africa. He went to Milan, where he studied and wrote letters, essays, sermons, commentaries, and philosophical treatises. He converted to Christianity in 387 and became bishop of Hippo in Africa. In the following adapted selection from *The Confessions*, St. Augustine describes his moment of conversion.

The following vocabulary will help you read the selection from St. Augustine. Note that the forms are still very classical.

Latin	Form	Meaning	Derivative
aemulatio (*eye-moo-LAH-tee-oh*)	onis, f.	rivalry	emulate
amarus	a, um	bitter	
an		or	
codex	codicis, m.	book	codicil
commissatio	onis, f.	drinking party	—
concitus	a, um	excited	—

Latin	Form	Meaning	Derivative
confestim		immediately, suddenly	—
crebro	adverb	frequently	
diffugo	ere, fugi, fusus	flee, are dispersed	diffuse
ebrietas (eh-bree-AY-tahs)	tatis, f.	drunkeness	inebriated
impetus	us, m.	impulse, attack	impetus
impudicitia	ae, f.	immodesty	impudence
infusus	a, um	diffused, permeating	infuse
ovum	ovi, n.	egg	ovary
pauper	eris	poor	pauper
tenebrae	arum, f. pl.	shades, night	tenebrism
thesaurus	i, m.	treasure	treasure
tollo	ere, sustuli, sublatus	raise up	sublation
vado	ere, vasi	go, advance	invade

Sublation is the act of taking away. *Tenebrism* is a sixteenth-century school of art that uses a lot of dark background with the main subject illuminated by a streak of light.

Latin Today!

Words to take to the chapel: Everyone knows when to say:

mea culpa (*MAY-ah KOOL-pah*)

St. Augustine's *Confessions*

St. Augustine is torn between worldly pleasures and a life of renunciation. He leaves his companion, Alypius, and goes out to the garden and weeps. He hears a voice that says, "Take, read." He does and is converted. Here's the story in the original:

Dicebam haec et flebam, amarissima contritione cordis mei. Et ecce audio vocem de vicina domo cum cantu dicentis et crebro repetentis, quasi pueri and puellae, nescio: "Tolle, lege, tolle, lege." … Repressoque impetu lacrimarum, surrexi ut aperirem codicem et legerem quod primum caput invenissem. Audieram enim de Antonio tamquam sibi diceretur quod legebatur: "Vade, vende omnia, quae habes, da pauperibus et habebis thesaurum in caelis: et veni sequere me," et tali oraculo confestim ad te esse conversum.

I was saying these things and weeping, with the most bitter contrition in my heart. And behold, I hear a voice from a neighboring house of a person saying with a song and repeating over and over as if boys and girls, I do not know: "Take, read, take, read." … After holding back my tears I got up in order to open the book and read what chapter I came upon first. For I had heard about Antony and what he is said to have read: "Go, sell everything that you have, give to the poor and you will have a treasure in heaven; and come, follow me," and with such a sign immediately he was converted to you.

Verba Sancta: Words of the Church

When you hear Church Latin, you notice immediately some changes in pronunciation. The following guide to ecclesiastical pronunciation should help you speak or sing your Latin appropriately.

Letter	Example
a	father
e	met
e (at end of syllable)	they
i	machine
o	note
oo	boot
y	machine
Before ae, e, oe, i, y …	
c	chain
cc	catchy
sc	sheep
g	gentle

Letter	Example
Otherwise …	
c	candy
cc	accord
sc	Tabasco
g	good
v	very

Dipthong and Combinations	Example
ae	ay
ti	tsee
ei	ay-ee
eo	ay-oh

The Roman Catholic Church used Latin in its liturgy from the second century to 1969, when the Vatican Council permitted vernacular languages. The Mass is a celebration of the sacrament of the Eucharist, the ritual instituted by Jesus Christ at the Last Supper. The two parts of the Mass are the Liturgy of the Word and the Liturgy of the Eucharist. The first consists of readings and prayers. The second is the breaking of bread and communion.

The following table lists the most important terms of Church Latin.

Latin	Forms	Meaning	Derivative
adoro (*ah-DOH-roh*)	are, avi atus	worship	adore
aes (*ays*)	aeris, n.	bronze	—
agnus (*AH-nyoos*)	i, m.	lamb	—
ardeo (*AR-deh-oh*)	ere, ardui	burn	ardent
benedico (*be-ne-DEE-koh*)	ere, dixi, dictus	praise	benediction

continues

continued

Latin	Forms	Meaning	Derivative
benedictus (*be-ne-DEEK-toos*)	a, um	blessed	benediction
benignus (*be-nihg-noos*)	a, um	kind	benign
caritas (*KAHR-ee-tas*)	caritatis, f.	love, affection	charity
communicatio (*koh-moon-ih-KAH-tsee-oh*)	onis, f.	fellowship	communication
ex parte (*ehks PAHR-tay*)		in part	
facultas (*FAH-kool-tahs*)	facultatis, f.	goods	
glorifico (*gloh-ree-FEE-koh*)	are, avi, tus	glorify	glorification
gratia (*GRA-tsee-ah*)	ae, f.	grace	grace
miseror (*MEE-sehr-ohr*)	miserere	have pity	commiserate
pax (*PAHKS*)	pacis, f.	peace	pacify
peccatum (*pek-KAH-toom*)	i, n.	sin	peccadillo
perperam (*PEHR-pehr-ahm*)	wrongly	incorrectly,	—
sanctus (*SANHK-toos*)	a, um	holy	sanctify
sive ... sive (*SEE-veh*)		whether ... whether	—
spiritus (*SPIH-ree-toos*)	spiritus, m.	spirit	spirit
tinniens (*TIHN-ee-ehns*)	entis	clanging	tintinnabulation
unigenitus (*ooh-nee-JEN-ee-toos*)		only begotten son	—

The following is the greeting:

Priest: In nomine Patris, et Filii, et Spiritus Sancti.

Congregation: Amen.

Priest: Gratia Domini nostri Jesu Christi, et caritas Dei, et communicatio Sancti Spiritus sit cum omnibus vobis.

Congregation: Et cum spiritu tuo.

Here is the gloria (in part):

Gloria in excelsis Deo
et in terra pax hominibus bonae voluntatis.
… Quoniam tu solus Sanctus,
Tu solus Dominus,
Tu solus Altissimus,
Jesu Christe,
cum Sancto spiritu
in gloria Dei Patris.
Amen.

Glory to God in the highest,
and peace to his people on Earth.
… For you alone are the Holy One,
you alone are the Lord,
you alone are the Most High,
Jesus Christ,
with the Holy spirit,
in the glory of God the Father.
Amen.

Notice the vocative case, *Christe,* when using direct address. *Cum* is still followed by the ablative case.

Biblical Latin

Eusebius Hieronymus (*yoo-SEH-bee-uhs hee-eh-ROH-nee-mus*), St. Jerome to most people, translated the Bible from the Hebrew into the language of the common people who were called, in Latin, *vulgus.* Thus, he became the author of the Vulgate Bible. Vulgate Latin remains very classical in most of its constructions with the exception of clauses for indirect statement and an indifference to the subjunctive. You will notice that word order is a little more reasonable. Yeah!

The following excerpts are from 1 Corinthians 13:

1. Si linguis hominum loquar et angelorum, caritatem autem non habeam, factus sum velut aes sonans aut cymbalum tinniens.

11. Cum essem parvulus, loquebar ut parvulus, sapiebam ut parvulus, cogitabam ut parvulus. Quando factus sum vir evacuavi quae erant parvuli.

12. Videmus nunc per speculum in enigmate, nunc autem facie ad faciem. Nunc cognosco ex parte, tunc autem cognoscam sicut et cognitus sum.

13. Nunc autem manent fides, spes, caritas, tria haec: maior autem his est caritas.

1. If I speak with the tongues of men and of angels, but do not have love, I have become a noisy gong or a clanging cymbal.

11. When I was a child, I used to speak as a child, think as a child, reason as a child; when I became a man, I did away with childish things.

12. For now we see in a glass darkly, but then face to face; now I know in part, but then I shall know fully just as I also have been fully known.

13. But now abide faith, hope, and love, these three; but the greatest of these is love.

From the Gospel according to St. Luke 23:33–46, we have a description of the crucifixion:

33. Et postquam venerunt in locum, qui vocatur Calvariae, ibi crucifixerunt eum, et latrones unum a dextris, et alterum a sinistris.

> **Grammar Guru**
>
> Medieval Latin writers were a little less particular about grammar. They often used the indicative mood when classical Latin mandated the subjunctive. The present participle is used to indicate past tense—*profiscens* (having set out).

34. Iesus autem dicebat: "Pater, dimitte illis; non enim sciunt quid faciunt." Dividentes vero vestimenta eius, miserunt sortes.

44. Erat autem fere hora sexta, et tenebrae factae sunt in universa terra usque in nonam horam.

45. Et obscuratus est sol: et velum templi scissum est medium.

46. Et clamans voce magna Iesus ait: "Pater, in manus tuas commendo spiritum meum." Et haec dicens, expiravit.

33. And when they came to the place which is called Calvary, there they crucified Him and the criminals, one on the right and the other on the left.

34. But Jesus was saying, "Father, forgive them; for they know not what they do." And they cast lots, dividing up His garments.

44. And it was now about the sixth hour and darkness fell over the whole land until the ninth hour.

45. The sun being obscured; and the veil of the temple was torn in two.

46. And Jesus, crying out with a loud voice, said, "Father into Thy hands I commit My spirit." And saying this, He breathed His last.

Music Sacred and Profane

The Mass was originally set to plainchant, a single melodic line sung by one person, but over the years, the music has developed into an art form itself. Masses have been composed by musicians since the fifteenth century and include Haydn, Mozart, Beethoven, Berlioz, Dvorak, Verdi, Brahms, and Stravinsky.

Many hymns and choral pieces for the Christian church are also sung in Latin, the words taken from the liturgy.

"Ave Maria" by Giuseppe Verdi

Ave Maria, gratia plena, Dominus tecum benedicta tu in mulieribus et benedictus fructus ventris tui, Iesus.

Sancta Maria, Mater Dei, ora pro nobis peccatoribus nunc et in hora mortis nostrae.

Classical Latin poetry and verse had a metrical system with its own rules; a quantitative system of long and short syllables. Medieval and Late Latin verse resembles the English meters, which are accentual. This came about thanks to a bunch of wandering young men, perhaps connected to the church, called the Goliards. They traveled from town to town, spending as much time in taverns as in churches, and wrote drinking songs, satirical verses, and love songs. Collected in the thirteenth-century anthology *Carmina Burana*, these songs and verses are amusing and fairly easy to read.

From "Amatoria, Potatoria, Lusoria," extr. 60

Bibit hera, bibit herus
bibit miles, bibit clerus

bibit ille, bibit illa
bibit servus, cum ancilla
bibit velox, bibit piger
bibit albus, bibit niger
bibit constans, bibit vagus
bibit rudis, bibit magus
bibit pauper et aegrotus

Cave!

Note that the lines rhyme—something classical Latin poetry did not do—and the accents form a regular meter.

Hera, herus are equal to *domina, dominus. Canus* is Late Latin for *senex* (old man). *Presul* and *decanus* are leader and deacon.

From the "Carmina Burana"

The mistress drinks, the master drinks,
the soldier drinks, the cleric drinks,
that man drinks, that woman drinks,
the servant drinks with the maid,
the active man drinks, the lazy man drinks,
the white man drinks, the black man drinks,
the settled man drinks, the wanderer drinks,
the ignorant man drinks, the scholar drinks,
the poor man and the sick man drink.

Finally, Christmas Latin! It wouldn't be the holiday season without *"In Dulci Iubilo"* or *"Pax in Terra."* For all those carol fests and sing-a-longs, here are some Latin versions of more modern-day songs.

"Tintinnabula" ("Jingle Bells")

Tinc, tinc, tonc, tinc, tinc, tonc
Tintinnabula!
Quam iucundum vehere in raeda festiva!

Tinc, tinc, tonc, tinc, tinc, tonc
Tintinnabula!
Quam iucundum vehere, Io Saturnalia!
Per nivem currimus
In raeda festiva
Per montes eximus

Tene Memoria

Note the comparative form of the adjectives, *ior*, and the ablative of comparison, *lilio* and *rosa*.

Ridens omnia
In equis sonora
In animis soles
In mundo omnia rident
Pro Tintinnabulis! Euge!

"Nicolaus Venit ad Nos" ("Santa Claus Is Coming to Town")

Attende ad te, noli flere
Noli plorare ausculta me
Nicolaus venit ad nos.
Te videt dormientem
Novit vigilantem.
Novit agentem ben et non
Igitur ne malus sis! Ergo!

"Rudolphus" ("Rudolph, the Red-Nosed Reindeer")

Rudolphus cervus nasum
rubicundum habebat
Quem si videre possis
elucere referas.
Lucificare cervi deridentes solebant
Neque sinebant eum comminus colludere.
Ecce dixit Nicholaus pride festum
"O, Rudolphe, nocte hac
visne Traham ducere?"
Quam tunc iucundus fuit
cervis iubilantibus!
"Rudolphe," nunc dicebant,
"Notus eris posteris."

The Least You Need to Know

- The Christian church is a treasure house of Latin.

- St. Augustine was converted in Latin.

- Church Latin is timeless.

- Goliards were the party people of the Middle Ages.

Chapter 23

Live! From Ancient Rome!

In This Chapter

- Our country's Latin
- Institutional mottoes
- Quotations through the ages
- Advice from the past
- Latin expressions in English
- Repartee for every occasion

Romans quoted Romans. The church fathers quoted Romans. The Renaissance writers quoted Romans. The Reformation writers and the Romantic writers quoted Romans. And so it went until we had books and books of Roman quotations.

We quote Roman writers for several reasons. First, what they said is often wise and useful. If we lived our lives according to all the precepts thought up by the Romans, we would all attain sainthood.

Second, we repeat what the Romans wrote because it reaffirms the frailty of mankind and makes us more sympathetic to our own failings.

When we see that 2,000 years ago jealousy, greed, and insincerity were problems, we can look upon today's society with a little more sympathy.

On the opposite side of the coin, when we read of men and women who value honesty, education, love, and family, isn't it heartening to think that we can still honor those ideals? If they've lasted 2,000 years, doesn't that give us hope that they will survive the next 2,000, too?

Finally, we can use these quotes for family, university, or doghouse seals. *Cave Canem!* would go very nicely over the doghouse door and will give Fido elevated status.

Latin in the Federal Government

Our founding fathers were steeped in Latin. The traditional education brought over from England required a working knowledge of the classics. The early patriots admired the Roman republic and its venerable Senate. So it's no wonder that many of our federal seals contain Latin words.

The Great Seal of the United States features an eagle grasping a gravity-defying ribbon emblazoned with *E pluribus unum* (one from many), meaning "one country from many states." The origins of this slogan are detailed in an article by Margaret A. Brucia in *The Classical Outlook* (1997), which notes that the phrase was originally in a Latin poem describing a poor farmer making a *moretum*, a pesto that combines green garlic and white cheese into one color. This phrase is also on the presidential seal, the seals of the Senate, the State Department, and the Supreme Court.

> **Latin Today!**
>
> *Words to take to Washington:*
> senator (*SEHN-ah-tor*)
> pro tempore (*proh-TEM-poh-re*)
> in absentia (*in ab-SEN-tee-ah;*
> *in ab-SEN-sheh* in English)

The Air Force seal says *Caelum ad proelium elige* (Choose the sky for battle); the Navy declares *acta, non verba* (actions, not words). The National Archive seal aptly says *Littera scripta manet* (The written word remains).

Finally, on the lowly dollar bill we find on the other side of the Great Seal, *Annuit coeptis* (He nods approval of beginnings) and *novus ordo seclorum* (a new order of the ages).

State Mottoes

Most state mottoes are self-explanatory and can be found in any library reference section. Here's a selection:

Arizona: *Diat Deus* (God enriches). Another word for Pluto, god of the Underword, is *Dis*. This word also means "rich" (presumably there is a connection with going underground and getting rich).

Connecticut: *Qui transtulit sustinet* (He who came across, holds up).

District of Columbia: *Iustitia omnibus* (Justice for all).

Kansas: *Ad astra per aspera* (Through the rough spots to the stars).

Maine: *Dirigo* (I direct).

Mississippi: *Virtute et armis* (By courage and arms).

Missouri: *Salus populi suprema lex est* (The welfare of the people is the supreme law).

New York: *Excelsior* (Higher)!

North Carolina: *Esse quam videri* (To be rather than to seem).

Oregon: *Alis volat propriis* (He flies with his own wings).

Virginia: *Sic semper tyrannis* (Thus always to tyrants).

West Virginia: *Montani semper liberi* (Mountain men are always free).

Wyoming: *Cedant arma togae* (Arms yield to the toga).

University Mottoes

More than you'll ever want to know about the Latin mottoes and seal inscriptions used by institutions of higher education can be found in *U.S. Colleges and Universities*, written by Harry J. Farnon and published in the February/March 1989 issue of *The Classical Journal*. Here are just a few:

Amherst College: *Terras irradient* (Let them illumine the earth).

Brown University: *In Deo speramus* (In God we trust).

Columbia University: *In lumine tuo videbimus lumen* (In thy light we shall see light).

Dartmouth College: *Vox clamantis in deserto* (A voice of one crying in the wilderness).

Harvard University: *Veritas* (Truth).

Hunter College: *Mihi cura futuri* (My anxiety is for the future).

Miami University: *Prodesse quam conspici* (To be productive, rather than to be ornamental).

Trinity College: *Pro ecclesia et patria* (For church and country).

Tulane University: *Non sibi, sed suis* (Not for herself, but for her own).

University of Chicago: *Crescat scientia, vita excolatur* (Let the knowledge grow, let life be enriched).

Grammar Guru

Remember that with the ablative case, the English preposition sometimes must be provided.

University of Florida: *Civium in moribus rei publicae salus* (In the character of its citizens lies the welfare of the state).

University of Michigan: *Artes, scientia, veritas* (The arts, knowledge, truth).

University of Washington: *Lux sit* (Let there be light).

Quotations on Human Failings

No one is perfect, and so it has been since Caesar. All the vices possible then—greed, hate, making false statements, and excessive spending—are still with us, perhaps even multiplied and enhanced by modern technology.

Nemo liber est qui corpori servit.
No one is free who is a slave to his body.

Parva leves capiunt animas.
Small things capture small (light) minds.

Pessimum genus inimicorum laudantes.
Flatterers are the worst kind of enemies.

Proprium humani ingenii est odisse quem laeseris.
It is human nature to hate a person whom you have injured.

Quotations on Human Virtues

Luckily, all the virtues of mankind—goodness, wisdom, sympathy, and honor—are still with us, too. It's a wonderful testimony to mankind that these ideas have survived.

Amicus humani generis.
A friend of the human race.

Ars longa, vita brevis.
Art is long; life, short.

Cogito, ergo sum.
I think, therefore I am.

Curae leves loquuntur ingentes stupent.
Slight griefs talk, great ones are speechless.

Words to Live By

Following the tenets of the Romans, goodness and mercy will continue, and our children and grandchildren will inherit a better world.

Cave!

Don't confuse *aestas* (summer) with *aetas* (age) or *aestimatio* (estimate).

Veritas vos liberabit.
The truth will set you free.

Si finis bonus est, totum bonum erit.
If the end is good, everything will be good.

Non semper erit aestas.
It will not always be summer.

Snappy Comebacks

There's nothing more satisfying than a snappy comeback in Latin. For one, your audience won't have the foggiest idea what you've said. You will have to expose their ignorance, "Oh, that's Latin. Don't you know Latin?" and further humiliate them by translating for them.

A snappy comeback in Latin will drop mouths, raise eyebrows, and favorably impress your superiors. Here are some scenarios with the appropriate remark:

> **Hysteria's Herstory**
>
> We have precious few words direct from Roman women. In the largest collection of quotations published, Sappho is the only woman quoted from all of Greek and Roman times. Many women are quoted by men, however, and we know that Sempronia, wife of the consul in 77 B.C.E., did publish poetry.

When the Dow plunges: *Sic transit gloria mundi* (Thus passes the glory of the world). This saying has been attributed to Thomas à Kempis in the fifteenth century and used in the crowning of the pope.

To critics of your work space: *Imperium in imperio* (An empire within an empire). This was the original motto of the state of Ohio.

On seeing the most pitiful comb-over ever: *Calvo turpius est nihil comato* (Worse than baldness is nothing with hair).

In defense of your own most pitiful comb-over: *Etiam capillus unus habet umbram* (Even one hair has a shadow).

On making a colossal mistake: *Experientia docet* (Experience teaches).

Behind your brother-in-law's back, pointing to his head: *Supellex curta* (Scanty furniture).

The Least You Need to Know

- Human nature hasn't changed in 2,000 years.
- There's a Latin saying for every occasion.
- Insults are safer in Latin.

Part 6

Grammar Workbook

When you learn how to play basketball, the coach doesn't recite all the regulations, hand you a rulebook, and send you out in the first game of the season. You have to practice, memorize the plays, and get acquainted with the game. So it is with learning a language. Consider this workbook section preseason practice. It helps you remember the rules, get used to the vocabulary, and practice translating. Welcome to *The Complete Idiot's Summer Training Camp for Grammar*.

The workbook is divided into sections according to the parts of speech, the basic categories of words according to their function in a sentence. Nouns and pronouns name things; verbs show action or a state of being; adjectives modify nouns or pronouns; and adverbs modify verbs, adjectives, or other adverbs. Prepositions relate a noun or pronoun that appears with it to another word in the sentence; conjunctions connect words and interjections express feeling or emotion. These are the same in both English and Latin, so it'll be helpful if you remember the definitions.

24

Workbook I: Working With Nouns and Verbs

Nouns (person, place, or thing) and verbs (what they do) are the basic building blocks of a sentence. This workbook chapter helps you work with the nouns you've met as well as review verbals. Each section reviews the grammar, gives you some vocabulary practice, and ends with sentences and selections to translate. The answers can be found in Appendix D.

Working With Nouns and Pronouns

Review Chapters 3 and 4 for nouns and Chapter 8 for pronouns. For the complete noun forms and how to use them, see Appendix B.

Grammar Review

Fill in the blanks:

A noun is a _____, _____, or _____. The _____ ending tells how the noun is used in the sentence. Nouns are grouped in _____s. The first declension is characterized by the letter _____, the second by the letter _____, and the third by the letter _____. The genitive case is translated by _____ or apostrophe _____.

Nouns come in three genders, _____, _____, and _____. Most first declension nouns are _____. Second declension nouns are either _____ or _____. Third declension has all three genders.

A pronoun takes the place of a _____. Personal pronouns take the place of _____. Third person pronouns sometimes take the place of _____. In English, the reflexive pronouns have the suffix _____.

Vocabulary Review

1. List five Latin words that designate people:

   _____   _____

   _____   _____

   _____

2. List five nouns that end in -*a* in the singular and their meanings:

   _____   _____

   _____   _____

   _____

   What gender are they? _____

3. List five nouns that end in -*us* and their meanings:

   _____   _____

   _____   _____

   _____

   What gender are they? _____

 Cave! _____

Some third declension nouns end in -*us* in the nominative. Look at the genitive form to find the declension.

4. What gender are *aedificium, aurum, consilium,* and *dictum?*

    _____

    Give their nominative plural forms:

    _____   _____

    _____   _____

    _____

5. Give the Latin word for the following:

    a. flip-flops   _____

    b. chicken   _____

    c. dog   _____

    d. wine   _____

6. Translate:

    a. professor   _____

    b. gladiator   _____

    c. discipulus   _____

    d. dictator   _____

7. Give the Latin pronoun for the following:

    a. I   _____

    b. you   _____

    c. we   _____

    d. you (plural)   _____

8. Translate:

    a. hic discipulus   _____

    b. illae soleae   _____

    c. eius vinum   _____

Translation Practice

1. Translate:

    a. illa, ea, haec   _____

    b. hic, is, ille   _____

    c. meus frater   _____

    d. Te amo.   _____

    e. Me appellate Ishmael.   _____

Tene Memoria

Nouns ending in -_us_ are usually masculine; nouns ending in -_a_ are usually feminine; nouns ending in -_um_ are usually neuter. But there are exceptions to every rule.

Working With Verbs and Verbals

Review Chapters 5 and 6 for verbs and verbals. For all the verb forms, see Appendix B.

Grammar Review

1. Match the verb ending with the English personal pronoun:

mus	I
o	they
tis	we
ntur	you s.
s	you pl.
tur	she

2. Answer the following questions in English:

    a. What is a verbal? _____

    b. Give an example of an infinitive in English. _____

    How about in Latin? _____

c. The present participle in English ends in _____.

d. Participles can be used as what two parts of speech? _____

e. The *-nd* form of a verb must be translated _____.

Grammar Guru _____

Many of our grammatical terms come from Latin: case/*casus*, conjugation/
coniugatio, gender/*genus*, noun/*nomina*, letter/*littera*, and syllables/*syllaba*.

Vocabulary Practice

1. Change to the singular form and translate:

    a. sudant   _____

    b. referunt   _____

    c. consumunt   _____

2. Translate the following. Provide your own subject, either a noun or pronoun.

    a. admonent   _____

    b. convolant   _____

    c. exsistit   _____

3. Translate the following:

    a. Pecunia exigitur   _____

    b. Villa ornatur   _____

    c. Troglodytae desliliunt _____

Translation Practice

1. Translate these verbals:

    a. Vult dormire.   _____

    b. Videtur agere.   _____

    c. Necesse est sublevare. _____

2. And now translate the following into Latin, nominative case:

a. The listeners _____

b. The active man _____

c. The suffering women _____

Latin Today!

Words to take to the altar:

Amor omnia vincit (*AH-mohr OHM-nee-ah WIHN-kit*)

Semper fidelis (*SEHM-per fee-DEL-is; SEHM-per feye-day-lis* in English)

---

3. Translate the following familiar phrases:

a. Esse aut non esse. _____

b. Carthago delenda est. _____

c. Modus operandi _____

4. Translate the following selection from Cicero's *Orations:*

Improbi cives populum Romanum vita privare, imperium delere, populi Romani nomen exstinguere volunt.

_____

_____

Workbook II: Adjective, Adverb, and Advanced Verb Work

In Workbook II, we review adjectives and adverbs, along with a continuation of verb forms and tenses. Grammar exercises and vocabulary practice will prepare you for translating sentences and selections from classical authors. Answers are in Appendix D.

Working With Adjectives, Adverbs, and Verb Tenses

This workbook is practice for Chapters 7, 9, and 10 and reviews all you need to know about adjective, adverb, and verb tenses. Complete forms are in Appendix B.

Adjectives and Adverbs Grammar Review

Fill in the blanks:

Adjectives agree with the noun they modify in _____, _____, and _____. Some adjectives are used as _____, such as "blues" and _____. Adjectives can show comparisons by using their comparative and superlative endings. An example of a comparative adjective in Latin is _____, and an example of a superlative adjective in Latin is _____. The comparative degree is translated _____ and the superlative, _____.

Grammar Guru

Latin grammar developed relatively late, around the second century B.C.E., and was modeled on the Greek. By the second century C.E. Romans were going full steam ahead, developing parts of speech, tenses, and all the rules and exceptions that lead to the grammatical nightmare we face in school today.

The accusative case is used for the _____ of a verb.

Questions in Latin are shown by the use of an _____ word, the adding of _____ to the first word, or by beginning the sentence with _____ or _____.

Adverbs in English usually end in _____ and modify verbs, adjectives, or other adverbs. Latin adverbs often end in _____ or _____.

The dative case is used for the _____ object, and the ablative case is used often. Two of the most common ablatives are _____ and _____.

Vocabulary Review

1. Translate the following adverbs:

    a. whence   _____

    b. in such a way   _____

    c. always   _____

    d. for the first time   _____

    e. meanwhile   _____

2. Match the terms in Column A with those in Column B. Use your common sense and have the adjective agree in number, gender, and case with the noun.

Column A	Column B
1. poplites	a. medias
2. dei	b. publicis
3. cibum	c. praeacutum
4. res	d. alterius
5. aedificiis	e. nullum
6. cornu	f. immortales
7. corporis	g. mutili

3. From the pool of words at the end of the list, choose the adjective that agrees in number, gender, case, and common sense:

a. opus _____

b. lex _____

c. homo _____

d. arbores _____

e. balineas _____

f. cura _____

g. apes _____

h. Graecia _____

i. Romani _____

publicum, populi, vetusta, tota, singuli, alienus, propinquas, magna, pensiles

Cave! _____

The adjective *Graecus, a, um* (Greek) is also used for the noun "a Greek" (*Graecus*), or "the Greeks" (*Graeci*). The country of Greece is in the first declension: *Graecia, ae, f.*

4. Translate the following sentences. Underline the nouns in the accusative case.

a. Belgae unam partem incolunt.

_____

b. Aquitani aliam partem incolunt.

_____

c. Galli tertiam partem incolunt.

_____

Working With Tenses of Verbs

All Latin verbs have principal parts—forms from which all the tenses are created. All verbs have the present, imperfect, and future tenses, and most have the present, past, and future perfect tenses as well. Review Chapter 10 and Appendix B.

Verb Tense Grammar Review

Fill in the blanks:

The first principal part of *amo* is _____ and is translated _____. The second principal part is _____ and is translated _____. The third principal part is _____ and is translated _____. The fourth principal part is _____ and is translated _____.

The sign of the imperfect tense is _____ and is translated _____. The sign of the future tense in the first and second conjugations is _____ or _____. In the third and fourth conjugation it's _____ in the first person and _____ in all the rest.

The present perfect tense has endings with a lot of _____'s. The past perfect tense has endings with _____, and the future perfect tense has endings that resemble the future tense of the verb _____.

The imperative form is used to give a command and is often the second principal part without the _____.

Vocabulary Practice

1. Translate the following:

    a. exercuimus   _____

    b. poterat   _____

    c. iaciebam   _____

    d. capiebas   _____

    e. sudabant   _____

Tene Memoria

Remember that the subjunctive mood is also used for a more gentle command like *Fiat lux!* (Let there be light!).

---

2. Practice yelling these commands and then translate:

    a. Dicite! (*DEE-kih-tay*)   _____

    b. Vendite! (*WEHN-dee-tay*)   _____

    c. Urina! (*OO-ree-nah*)   _____

3. Fill in the blanks with the correct form:

First PP	Second PP	Third PP	Fourth PP
a. invado	_____	invadi	invasus
b. moveo	movere	_____	motus
c. _____	venire	veni	_____
d. video	videre	_____	_____

Latin Today!

Words to take through the security line at the airport:
   Quid novi? (*KWID NOH-whee*) What's new?
   O tempora, o mores! (*Oh TEM-poh-rah, oh MOH-rays*)

Translation Work

1. Translate the following:

   a. In taberna otior. _____

   b. Tigres Princetoni in arena ludunt. _____

   c. Lauti sunt _____

   d. Iecerunt _____

2. The following verbs are selected from the writings of Cicero and Caesar. Translate, watching for the tense.

   a. arbitrabantur _____

   b. fecit _____

   c. persuasit _____

   d. iusserunt _____

   e. movet _____

3. Spot the seven! In the following sentences, find the seven verbs in the perfect tenses and then translate:

   a. Consulem vidi. _____

   b. Viros invitavero. _____

   c. Ipsa sum hospita. _____

   d. Multa praeterivi. _____

   e. Homo canem deportavit. _____

   f. Fungos et helvellas condiunt. _____

   g. Quaesivi diligenter. _____

   h. Femina fabulam narravit. _____

   i. Nuclei margaritae sunt. _____

   j. Unum cornu exstetit. _____

26

Workbook III: Working With the Remaining Parts of Speech and Other Complexities

Here we review more parts of speech, the use of clauses, the subjunctive mood, and more complex sentences.

Working With Phrases and Clauses

Review the prepositional phrase in Chapter 11, temporal and causal clauses and the ablative absolute in Chapter 12, and relative clauses in Chapter 13.

Phrases and Clauses Grammar Review

Choose the correct answer to fill in the blank:

1. Some prepositions are used as _____.

   a. propositions

   b. suffixes

   c. prefixes

   d. conjunctions

2. Deponent verbs are _____.

   a. active in form, passive in meaning

   b. not all there

   c. passive in form, active in meaning

   d. all of the above

3. The ablative absolute often uses the phrase _____.

   a. Has been _____ed

   b. Had been _____ed

   c. Having been _____ed

   d. Out there

4. Relative clauses begin with a _____.

   a. relative pronoun

   b. indefinite pronoun

   c. relative noun

   d. personal pronoun

5. The verb in a purpose clause is always in _____.

   a. trouble

   b. the indicative

   c. the subjunctive

   d. the infinitive

6. A temporal clause is introduced by a word denoting _____.

   a. temper

   b. weather

   c. time

   d. temporary insanity

 Grammar Guru _____

Sigismund, Holy Roman Emperor of 1414, said to an underling who objected to his grammar, "*Ego sum rex Romanus et supra grammaticam*" (I am the Roman king and am above grammar).

Phrases and Clauses Vocabulary Review

1. Translate these prepositional phrases:

   a. Contra violentiam   _____

   b. Ad spectandum   _____

   c. Ad me   _____

2. Unscramble the following words from Chapters 11, 12, and 13 and then give the meaning:

a. mustra	b. eanpemgor	c. ogle
d. shortu	e. ropal	f. reecl
g. sam	h. lasel	i. rupe

3. Match the opposites:

a. sub	regredior
b. ante	vah
c. parvus	vivus
d. puer	supra
e. eugepae	post
f. mortuus	doleo
g. rideo	magnus
h. progredior	puella

Translation Practice

1. Translate these clauses from Caesar and Cicero and other Latin writers:

   a. Murenae quas ille amabat   _____

   b. "Hecyram" quam mihi in silentio numquam agere licuit   _____

   c. Membra inter quae manus, os, dentes sunt   _____

   d. Bos cuius unum cornu exsistit   _____

2. Translate the following ablative absolutes:

   a. Concilio convocato   _____

   b. C. Mario et L. Valerio consulibus, Graecus non iucundus erat.   _____

   c. Convivium coepit, mensa allata.   _____

   d. His rebus dictis, Caesar rostrum relinquit.   _____

3. Translate the deponent verbs:

   a. Mortuus est.   _____

   b. Egrediens puer clamat.   _____

   c Pollicitus sum.   _____

   d. Deus prolocutus est.   _____

Cave!

Although the deponent verbs have passive endings, they are always translated with an active meaning.

Working With the Subjunctive and More Clauses

Review the clauses in Chapter 14 and the subjunctive mood in Chapters 15 and 16. The subjunctive verb forms are in Appendix B.

Grammar Review

Fill in the blank:

The _____ mood of a verb gives a command. The _____ mood of a verb indicates something is happening. The _____ mood of a verb shows an action that might happen. An example of the subjunctive mood in Latin is _____. In English the helping verbs _____ or _____ are used to show the subjunctive. The subordinate conjunctions _____ and _____ are used to introduce clauses that usually have the verb in the subjunctive. Purpose clauses begin in English with the words _____. _____ clauses usually follow a phrase such as "in such a way," "so that," or "with the result that."

A _____ sentence is a simple sentence with a subordinate clause. Indirect statements come after verbs of stating, such as _____. The subject in Latin will be in the _____ case and the verb in the _____ mood.

Tene Memoria

Subjunctive forms look different from the indicative in contradictory ways. The first conjugation has *e* before the personal ending instead of *a*, the imperfect is the infinitive with an ending, the verb *esse* will have *i*'s instead of *e*'s. If it's weird, it's subjunctive.

Vocabulary Review for Chapters 14 Through 16

1. Give the Latin word from which the following English words derive:

   a. ponderous   _____

   b. ciborium   _____

   c. dulcimer   _____

   d. ambulatory   _____

2. Translate the following:

   a. The weight of duty   _____

   b. The sight of land   _____

   c. The root of the tree   _____

3. From the following list, identify the five verbs in the subjunctive and then translate:

   a. praestarent   _____

   b. fuit   _____

   c. exirent   _____

   d. exspectare   _____

   e. petissent   _____

   f. pervenit   _____

   g. fiat   _____

   h. eamus   _____

   i. proficisci   _____

Translation Practice

1. Translate the following sentences taken from the Latin selections:

   a. Ita clamorem fecit ut exire
      necesse esset.   _____

   b. Amabat murenam adeo ut in
      piscina sederet.   _____

   c. Ipsa sum hospita.   _____

   d. Cotidie patior.   _____

Latin Today!

Words to take to the cemetery:
   requiescat in pace (*RES-kwee ESS-kaht in PAH-keh*)
   in memoriam (*in meh-MOH-ree-ahm*)
And don't forget the flowers.

---

2. More sentences from Latin authors to translate:

   a. Gaudeamus.   _____

   b. Frigida cubila sunt.   _____

   c. Ego, qui a ostreis et murenis
      abstinebam, a beta et malva
      deceptus sum.   _____

   d. Rosa carne omni, nuclei corporum,
      qui margaritae sunt, in ima decidunt. _____

Vocabulary Lists

Latin-to-English Vocabulary

The chapter in which the word first appears is in parentheses.

a/ab (11)   by, away from

abeo, abire, abii, abitus (8)   go away

abhorreo, ere, ui (5)   to shrink back, abhor

absolutus, a, um (6)   perfected, complete

abstineo, ere, stinui (6)   to abstain

absum, abesse, abfui (15)   to be absent

absurdus, a, um (7)   absurd

accido, ere, cidi (11)   to happen, fall

accido, ere, cidi, cisus (5)   to cut down

accipio, accipere, accepi, acceptus (6)   to accept

acerbus, a, um (19)   sour, sharp

actus, us, m. (4)   act

ad (1)   to, toward, near

addo, addere, addidi, additus (11)   to add

adduco, ere, duxi, ductus (6)   to bring

adeo (9)   to such a degree

adicio, ere, ieci, iectus (6) to add on

adiutrix, icis, f. (4) helper

adiuvo, are, avi, atus help, aid

admoneo, ere, monui, monitus (5) to admonish, warn

aedificium, i, n. (3) building

aestas, aestatis, f. (4) summer

aestimatio, aestimationis, f. (4) estimate

affero, afferre, attuli, allatus (12) to bring toward

affligo, ere, flixi, flictus (5) to damage, knock down

ager, agri, m. (15) field, land

agmen, inis, n. (4) line

ago, agere, egi, actus (6) to do, drive, discuss, live

agricola, ae, m. (11) farmer

alces, alcis, m./f. (11) elk

alienus, a, um (7) foreign

aliquis, aliquid (13) someone, anyone

alius, a, um (14) another, other

alo, alere, alui, alitus (12) to feed

alter, era, erum (7) the one, the other

altus, a, um (19) high, deep

ambulo, are, avi, atus (15) to walk

amica, ae, f. (3) friend

amicus, i, m. (3) friend

amo, are, avi, atus (6) to love

amplus, a, um (7) large, ample

animadverto, ere, verti, versus (11) to notice

animus, i, m. (3) mind, soul, disposition

anser, anseris, m./f. (4) goose

ante (11) before

antecedo, ere, cessi, cessus (5) to surpass

antequam (14) before

apis, apis, f. (4) bee

appello, are, avi, atus (5) to call, name

appendo, ere, pendi, pensus to pay out, to weigh

applico, are, avi, atus (5) to apply, attach

apprehendo, ere, hendi, hensus (5) to grab

apud (13) at the home of

aqua, ae, f. (3) water

arbor, arboris, f. (4) tree

architectus, i, m. (2) architect

Arpinas, Arpinatis, n. (17) villa at Arpinum

articulus, i, m. (1) joint

ascendo, ere, scendi, scensus (10) to climb

asper, aspera, asperum (7) sharp, harsh

astrum, i, n. (12) star

at (3) but

audio, ire, audivi, auditus (6) to listen

auris, auris, f. (12) ear

aurum, i, n. (3) gold

aut (3) or

aut ... aut (3) either ... or

autem (3) moreover

auxilium, i, n. (11) aid

balineum, balinei, n. (3) bath

bellum, i, n. (15) war

beta, ae, f. (3) beet

bibo, ere, bibi (9) to drink

bipennis, is, f. (4) axe

bonus, a, um (7) good

bos, bovis, m./f. (13) ox, cow

brevis, breve (15) short

cado, cadere, cecidi, casus (5) to fall

caedo, ere, cecidi, caesus (5) to kill, cut

caelum, i, n. (19) sky

Caesar, Caesaris, m. (4) Caesar

calamitas, calamitatis, f. (1) calamity

calidus, a, um (9) warm

canis, canis, m./f. (14) dog

canto, are, avi, atus (12) to sing

capella, ae, f. (3) nanny goat

caper, capri, m. (15) goat

capillus, i, m. hair

capio, capere, cepi, captus (5) to capture, make (plan)

caput, capitis, n. (15) head

caro, carnis, or carnis, f. (4) meat

casus, us, m. (13) chance, accident

cauda, ae, f. (3) tail

causa, ae, f. (1) cause, sake

cautus, a, um (17) cautious

caveo, ere, cavi, cautus (6) to beware

cedo, cedere, cessi, cessus (11) to move, yield

celer, eris, ere (13) swift

cena, ae, f. (3) dinner

centum (9) one hundred

cerevisia, ae, f. (3) beer

certe (11) definitely

cervus, i, m. (13) deer

ceterus, a, um (7) other, remaining, the rest

cibus, i, m. (14) food

civis, civis, m./f. (14) citizen

civitas, civitatis, f. (4) city, state

clamo, are, avi, atus (5) to shout

clamor, clamoris, m. (1) noise

clunis, clunis, m. (4) buttock

comes, comitis, m./f. (4) companion

committo, ere, misi, missus (14) to begin

commoveo, ere, movi, motus (11) to upset, bother

communis, e (7) common

concha, conchae, f. (3) shell

concido, ere, cidi (5) to fall, kill

concilium, i, n. (14) council

condicio, onis, f. (4) condition

condio, condire, ivi, itus (5) to season

condo, ere, condidi, conditus (5) to found, build

consilium, consilii, n. (3) plan, counsel

consisto, ere, constiti (6) to stop, become solid

conspicio, ere, spexi, spectus (14) to see, catch sight of

constituo, ere, stitui, stitutus (12) to decide, be made

consuetudo, tudinis, f. (12) custom

consul, consulis, m. (2) consul

consumo, ere, sumpsi, sumptus (5) to consume, use up

contra (11) against

conventus, us, m. (4) coming together

convivium, i, n. (3) party

convolo, are, avi, atus (5) to fly about

coquo, coquere, coxi, coctus (5) to cook

coquus, coqui, m. (3) cook

cornu, us, n. (12) horn

corpus, corporis, n. (15) body

cotidie (14) daily

credo, ere, credidi, creditus (15) to believe

credulus, a, um (7) gullible

creor, ari, atus, sum (12) to create

crus, cruris, n. (4) leg

crux, crucis, f. (13) cross

cubile, cubilis, n. (15) bed

culpa, ae, f. (15) blame

cum (11) when, since, although, with

cur (7) why

cura, ae, f. (12) cure, care

curia, ae, f. (20) senate house, court

curo, are, avi, atus (14) to care for

de (11) down, about, concerning

dea, ae, f. (3) goddess

decem (9) ten

deceptus, a, um (15) taken down

decido, ere, cidi (5) to fall down, cut down

decretum, i, n. (3) decree

defessus, a, um (19) tired

deinde (14) then, next

deleo, ere, delevi, deletus (6) to destroy

delictum, i, n. (20) fault

delinquo, ere, deliqui, delictus (15) to be short of established standards, be derelict

dens, dentis, m. (4) tooth

deporto, are, avi, atus (11) to deport, carry away

derectus, a, um (15) straight

desilio, ire, ui, itus (5) to jump down

deus, dei, m. (3) god

dexter, destra, dextrum (7) right

diarroia (Greek) (17) diarrhea

dico, ere, dixi, dictus (5) to say

dictator, dictatoris, m. (4) dictator

dictum, i, n. (3) contract

dies, diei, m. (4) day

diffundo, ere, fudi, fusus (5) to pour out, scatter

dis, ditis (19) rich

discipulus, i, m. (3) student

discordia, ae, f. (1) discord

dissimulo, are, avi, atus (10) to pretend

diu (15) for a long time

do, dare, dedi, datus (6) to give

doleo, ere, ui (6) to be sad

domus, us, f. (15) home, house

donec (14) until

dormio, ire, ivi, itus (6)   to sleep

duco, ducere, duxi, ductum (6)   to lead

dulcis, is, e (15)   sweet

dum (14)   while

duo (9)   two

durus, a, um (7)   hard, harsh

dux, ducis, m. (4)   leader

e, ex (11)   out of

edo, edere (19)   to eat

ego (8)   I

eius (8)   his, her

elephantus, i, m. (1)   elephant

eo, ire, ii, itus (8)   to go

Ephesus, i, m. (2)   Ephesus

epistula, ae, f. (3)   letter

equus, equi, m. (11)   horse

erigo, ere, rexi, rectus (6)   to straighten out

esse (5)   to be

est (1)   is

et (3)   and

et … et (3)   both … and

etiam (3)   even, also

Europa, ae, f. (1)   Europe

exanimo, are, avi, atus (12)   to die

excelsus, a, um (14)   high, lofty, tall

excipio, ere, cepi, ceptus (15)   to make exceptions, take out

excogito, are, avi, atus (12)   to think up, devise

exeo, exire, exii, exitus (8)   to go out

exigo, ere, exegi, exactus (5)   to take out, demand

exsisto, ere, stiti, stitus (5)   to stand out

exspectatio, onis, f. (14)   anticipation

exterus, a, um (7)   outer

extremus, a, um (7)   hindmost, last

fabula, ae, f. (14)   story

facies, ei, f. (20)   face, appearance

facilis, e (7)   easy

facio, ere, feci, factus (10)   to do, make

factum, i, n. (20)   fact, deed

femina, ae, f. (3)   woman

femur, femoris, *or* feminis, n. (4)   thigh

fero, ferre, tuli, latus (6)   to bear, carry

ferrum, i, n. (3)   iron

fictilis, e (14)   clay, earthenware

figura, ae, f. (14)   shape

filia, ae, f. (3)   daughter

filius, filii, m. (3)   son

fio, fieri, factus sum (16)   to become

flagrans, flagrantis (20)   flaming

fleo, flere, flevi, fletus (13)   to weep

flumen, fluminis, n. (19)   river

fluo, fluere, fluxi, fluxus (19)   to flow

foras (9)   outside

forma, ae, f. (1)   form

fortasse (19)   perhaps

fortis, forte (9)   brave, strong

frater, ris, m. (4)   brother

fraus, fraudis, f. (4)   mischief

frigidus, a, um (15)   cold

frons, frontis, f. (14) forehead, brow

fructus, us, m. (20) fruit

funambulus, i, m. (3) tightrope walker

fundus, i, m. (3) estate, farm

fungosus, a, um (7) spongy

fungus, i, m. (1) mushroom

gaudeo, ere, gavisus sum (15) to rejoice

gero, ere, gessi, gestus (12) to wear, wage

glaber, glabra, glabrum (19) bald

gladiator, oris, m. (4) gladiator

gloria, ae, f. (1) glory

gradior, gradi, gressus sum (12) to step, walk, go

Graecus, i, m. (3) Greek

gratia, ae, f. (18) thanks

habeo, ere, habui, habitus (10) to have

habito, are, avi, atus (10) to live

harena, ae, f. (19) sand

hecyra, ae, f. (3) mother-in-law

heluella, ae, f. (17) potherbs, boiled greens

herba, ae, f. (3) greens, grass

herbosus, a, um (7) grassy

hic (9) here

hic, haec, hoc (8) this, these

hiems, hiemis, f. (4) winter

hippopotamus, i, m. (1) hippopotamus

hircus, i, m. (3) billy goat

hodie (9) today

homo, hominis, m./f. (4) man, human being

honor, oris, m. (4) honor

hora, ae, f. (3) hour

hortus, i, m. (12) garden

hospita, ae, f. (3) guest

humanus, a, um (2) kind, gentle, humane

humilis, e (9) humble

iacio, ere, ieci, iactus (10) to throw, hurl

iam (15) now

idem, eadem, idem (8) the same

igitur (15) therefore

ille, illa, illud (8) that, that one

immortalis, e (7) immortal

impar, imparis (18) unequal

impensa, ae, f. (3) cost

imus, a, um (14) deepest

in (11) in, on

inaures, inaurium, f. pl. (4) earrings

incido, ere, cidi, cisus (15) to cut into

includo, ere, clusi, clusus (5) to include

industria, ae, f. (1) work

inferus, a, um (7) lower

infirmus, a, um (7) weakened

iniquus, a, um (14) unfair

inquit (5) he/she said

insula, ae, f. (3) island

intellegentia, ae, f. (1) knowledge

intellego, ere, intellexi, intellectus (11) to know

inter (11) between, among

interea (9) meanwhile

invado, ere, vadi, vasus (10) to attack, invade

invenio, invenire, inveni, inventus (10) to invent

invito, are, avi, atus (10) to invite

ipse, ipsa, ipsum (13) self, very

iratus, a, um (9) angry

is, ea, id (8) he, she, it

istuc (14) there, to that place

ita (9) in such a way

ita! (11) yes!

Italia, ae, f. (1) Italy

itaque (9) and so

item (9) likewise, similarly

iter, itineris, n. (11) way, journey

iubeo, ere, iussi, iussus (15) to order

iucundus, a, um (15) pleasant

ius, iuris, n. (4) right

laboro, are, avi, atus (10) to work

lacrimo, are, avi, atus (15) to cry

laetus, a, um (9) happy

lana, ae, f. (12) wool

lapis, lapidis, m. (19) stone

latus, a, um (7) wide

lautus, lauti, m. (3) gourmet, gentleman

lavo, lavare, lavi, lautus (19) to wash

lectus, i, m. (3) bed, couch

lego, ere, legi, lectus (12) to read, choose

lenis, is, e (14) gentle, kind

lex, legis, f. (4) law

liber, era, erum (7) free

liber, libri, m. (3) book

libero, are, avi, atus (14) to free

licet, ere, licuit (6) it is/was allowed

litoteta (Greek) (17) the simple life

locus, i, m. (3) place

longus, a, um (12) long

loquor, loqui, locutus sum (12) to speak

ludo, ere, lusi, lusus (6) to play

ludus, i, m. (14) school, game

luna, ae, f. (15) moon

lupus, i, m. (15) wolf

magis (14) more

magister, stri, m. (11) teacher

magistratus, us, m. (2) magistrate

magnitudo, magnitudinis, m. (4) size

magnopere (13) greatly

magnus, a, um (7) great

maiores, maiorum, m. pl. (4) ancestors, forefathers

malus, a, um (11) bad

malva, ae, f. (3) mallow

mando, are, avi, atus (6) to demand, command

mando, mandere, mandi, mansus (6) to chew

mane (7) in the morning

maneo, ere, mansi, mansus (6) to remain

mangonico, are, avi, atus (6) to improve appearance for a sale

manus, manus, f. (12) hand, band

margarita, ae, f. (3) pearl

mare, maris, n. (19) sea

mas, maris, m. (12) a male

mater, matris, f. (4) mother

matrimonium, i, n. (20) marriage

maturus, a, um (12) ripe, mature

maximus, a, um (11) greatest

medius, a, um (7) middle of

membrum, membri, n. (18) member

mensa, ae, f. (3) table

merx, mercis, f. (4) merchandise

metus, us, m. (12) fear

meus, mea, meum (8) my

mihi (9) to me

miles, militis, m. (12) soldier

mille (indecl) (9) thousand

minime! (11) not at all!

miror, mirari, miratus (15) to wonder

mirus, a, um (14) wonderful

miser, misera, miserum (9) wretched, miserable

mitis, mitis, mite (17) sweet, gentle, kind

mitto, ere, misi, missus (10) to send

modus, i, m. (3) way

moneo, ere, ui, monitus (10) to warn

morior, moriri, mortuus sum (12) to die

mors, mortis, f. (4) death

mortuus, a, um (12) dead

moveo, ere, movi, motus (10) to move

mox (15) soon

mulier, eris, f. (4) woman

multus, a, um (7) much, many

mundus, i, m. (3) world

muraena, ae, f. (3) moray eel

musso, are, avi, atus (19) to mutter

mutilus, a, um (7) broken

mutuus, mutua, mutuum (14) borrowed

nam (13) for

narro, are, avi, atus (11) to tell, narrate

nascor, nasci, natus sum (12) to be born

nasus, i, m. (3) nose

nasutus, a, um (7) long-nosed

navis, navis, f. (19) ship

necesse (6) necessary

nemo (15) no one

nervus, nervi, m. (3) nerve

nihil (14) nothing

nimbus, i, m. (19) cloud

nobilis, e (1) noble

nodus, i, m. (3) knot, node

noli, nolite (16) don't (+ inf.)

nolo, nolere, nolui (16) to not want

nomen, inis, n. (13) name

non (9) not

nos (8) we, us

noster, nostra, nostrum (8) our

nosti (19) you know

notus, a, um (7)   known

novem (9)   nine

novissimus, a, um (12)   last, latest

novus, a, um (13)   new

nox, noctis, f. (15)   night

nucleus, nuclei, m. (3)   kernel

nullus, a, um (7)   none

numquam (9)   never

nunc (9)   now

obligo, are, avi, atus (5)   to obligate, earmark

obruo, ere, i, itus (5)   to bury, hide

obtineo, ere, tinui, tentus (13)
to occupy

octo (9)   eight

oculus, i, m. (19)   eye

officium, i, n. (14)   duty, office

olim (9)   once upon a time

omnis, e (7)   every, all

onus, oneris, n. (15)   load, burden

operor, ari, atus sum (20)   to work hard

opprimo, ere, pressi, pressus (11)
to put down, press, crush

opus, operis, n. (4)   work

orator, oratoris, m. (2)   orator

orbis, orbis, m. (20)   circle

orno, are, avi, atus (5)   to decorate

os, oris, n. (14)   mouth

ossum, i, n. (19)   bone

ostrea, ostreae, f. (3)   oyster

otiosus, a, um (17)   at leisure

otium, i, n. (3)   leisure

ovum, i, n. (22)   egg

palla, ae, f. (15)   stole

palma, ae, f. (1)   palm

palor, palari, palatus sum (12)
to wander

pando, pandere, passus sum (20)
to spread out

par, paris (20)   equal

paro, are, avi, atus (19)   to prepare

pars, partis, f. (4)   part

parvus, a, um (11)   small

pater, patris, m. (4)   father

patior, pati, passus sum (12)   to suffer

patria, ae, f. (14)   fatherland

paulo (9)   a little

pax, pacis, f. (4)   peace

pecunia, ae, f. (3)   money

pellis, is, f. (14)   skin, hide

pendo, pendere, di, sus (6)   to hang

pensilis, pensile (7)   hanging

per (11)   through

perago, ere, egi, actus (6)   to complete, accomplish

perficio, ere, feci, fectus (12)   to finish

permuto, are, avi, atus (6)   to exchange

perna, ae, f. (3)   ham, thigh

pernicitas, atis, f. (4)   agility

pes, pedis, m. (4)   foot

peto, ere, ivi itus (5)   to seek, attack

pila, ae, f. (3)   ball

pisces, piscis, m./f. (4) fish

piscina, ae, f. (3) fishpond

placo, are, avi, atus (12) to calm, quiet, appease

placeo, ere, placui, placitus (5) to please, satisfy

plebs, plebis, f. (12) common people

pluit, pluere, pluit (19) it rains

poculum, i, n. (3) cup, mug

poena, ae, f. (3) penalty

polliceor, polliceri, pollicitus (12) to promise

pondus, ponderis, n. (14) weight

pono, ere, posui, positus (11) to put, place

poples, poplitis, m. (4) behind the knee

populus, i, m. (1) people

porto, are, avi, atus (10) to carry

possum, posse, potui (5) to be able

post (11) after, behind

postquam (9) after

praeacutus, a, um (7) sharp

praeceler, celeris, e (14) very swift

praecipuus, a, um (14) special

praesto, are, steti, status (5) to take charge of

praeter (11) except

praetereo, ire, ii, itus (10) to omit, pass over

prandeo, ere, prandi, pransus (10) to eat breakfast, lunch

prandium, i, n. (3) breakfast, lunch

pretium, i, n. (3) price

primum (9) for the first time

primus, a, um (20) first

privatim (9) privately, at home

privatus, a, um (2) private

pro + the ablative (11) for, on behalf of, in place of

procumbo, ere, cubui, cubitus (5) to fall down

professor, oris, m. (1) teacher, professor

proficiscor, proficisci, profectus sum (12) to leave

prope (11) near

propinquus, a, um (7) near

propter (11) on account of

publicus, a, um (2) public

puella, ae, f. (3) girl

puer, eri, m. (12) boy

pugil, pugilis, m. (4) boxer

pugno, are, avi, atus (5) to fight

pullus, i, m. (3) chicken

quaero, quaerere, quaesivi, quaesitus (10) to look for, search

quaeso, ere, quaesivi, quaesitus (5) to ask for, request

qualis, e (7) what kind of

quam (7) than

quamquam (16) although

quando (7) when

quantus, a, um (14) how much

quartus, a, um (9) fourth

quattuor (9) four

-que (enclitic) (3) and

qui, quae, quod (13)   who, which

quidam, quaedam, quiddam or quoddam (13)   a certain

quies, quietis, f. (13)   quiet, rest

quinam, quinam, quidnam (13)   who, pray?, what?

quinque (9)   five

quis? quid? (13)   who? what?

quisque (13)   each, every

quisquis (13)   whoever

quisvis (13)   whomever you want

quo (14)   where

quo modo (7)   how

quoque (15)   also

quot? (7)   how many?

radix, radicis, f. (14)   root

ramus, i, m. (14)   branch

recipio, ere, cepi, ceptus (12)   to take on, receive

recipio, ere, cepi, ceptus (se) (12)   to retreat

reclino, are, avi, atus (5)   to recline

refero, ferre, tuli, latus (5)   to bring back

regina, ae, f. (11)   queen

reicio, ere, ieci, iectus (11)   to reject

relinquo, ere, liqui, ictus (5)   to leave behind

reliquus, reliqua, reliquum (7)   the rest of

remaneo, ere, mansi, mansus (11)   to remain

res, rei, f. (4)   thing, matter

respondeo, ere, spondi, sponsus (10)   to respond

rete, retis, n. (4)   net

rex, regis, m. (11)   king

rideo, ere, risi, risus (12)   to laugh

rodo, ere, rosi, rosus (12)   to gnaw at, wear down

Roma, ae, f. (1)   Rome

Romanus, a, um (7)   Roman

rumor, oris, m. (4)   rumor

sacerdos, dotis, m. (11)   priest

saepe (15)   often

sal, salis, m. (4)   salt (noun)

salio, ire, salui *or* salii, salitus (11)   to jump

salveo, ere (14)   to be well

sapiens, sapientis (12)   wise

scelus, sceleris, n. (19)   crime

scio, ire, scivi, scitus (12)   to know

scribo, ere, scripsi, scriptus (13)   to write

se (8)   self (third person reflexive pronoun)

sed (3)   but

sedeo, ere, sedi, sessus (14)   to sit

sedo, are, avi, atus (11)   to soothe, refresh

sella, ae, f. (13)   chair

semper (9)   always

senator, senatoris, m. (1)   senator

senatus, us, m. (2)   senate

septem (9)   seven

sequor, sequi, secutus sum (12) to follow

servus, i, m. (15); serva, ae, f. (15) slave

sex (9) six

si (14) if

sic (14) thus

sicut (3) as, just as

silentium, silentii, n. (2) silence

silva, ae, f. (19) woods

similis, e (7) similar

simul (9) at the same time

sine (with abl.) (11) without

singulus, a, um (7) single

sinister, sinistra, sinistrum (7) left

solea, ae, f. (3) sandal

soleo, ere, solui, solitus (15) to be accustomed

sollertius, a, um (14) skilled

solus, a, um (7) alone

somnus, i, m. (19) sleep

soror, sororis, f. (4) sister

species, ei, f. (14) sight, appearance

specto, are, avi, atus (12) to look at

spero, are, avi, atus (12) to hope

statim (15) immediately

statuo, statuere, statui, statutus (11) to decide

stipo, are, avi, atus (5) to plant, press

sto, stare, steti, status (10) to stand

stola, ae, f. (12) dress

strepitus, us, m. (4) noise

stupeo, ere, stupui, stupitus (19) to be stupified

suavis, suave (7) delicious, pleasing

sub (11) under

subinde (14) immediately afterward

subito (14) suddenly

sublevo, are, avi, atus (6) to get up

subruo, ere, rui, rutus (5) to uproot

sudo, are, avi, atus (5) to sweat

sum, esse, fui, futurus (5) to be

summus, a, um (7) top of

sumptuarius, a, um (7) sumptuary, having to do with excessive spending

sumptus, us, m. (4) cost

super/supra (11) above

superior, superius, superior (2) higher

supero, are, avi, atum (6) to surpass

superus, a, um (7) above

suus, a, um (8) his/her/their own

taberna, ae, f. (11) shop, bar

taceo, ere, tacui, tacitus (15) to be quiet

tam (14) so

tamen (9) nevertheless

tango, ere, tetigi, tactus (19) to touch

tantus, a, um (14) so great

tardo, are, avi, atus (12) to slow down

tempus, temporis, n. (4) time

teneo, ere, ui, tentus (13) to hold

tergum, i, n. (19) back

terra, ae, f. (3) land

terreo, ere, ui, territus (14) to frighten

toga, ae, f. (2) toga

tot (9) so many

totus, a, um (7) whole

trado, ere, tradidi, traditus (14) to hand over

traho, ere, traxi, tractus (15) to draw, drag

trans (with acc.) (11) across

transversus, a, um (12) lying crosswise

tres, tria (9) three

tristis, triste (19) sad

triumphalis, e (7) triumphal, of a triumph

troglodyta, ae, m./f. (2) caveman/-woman

tu (8) you

tum (9) then

turba, ae, f. (3) crowd

turpis, turpe (19) disgusting, awful, base

tutor, ari (15) to keep safe

tuus, tua, tuum (8) your (sing.)

ubi (15) where, when

ubique (19) everywhere

ullus, a, um (7) any

umquam (9) ever

unda, ae, f. (19) wave

unde (9) from when, whence

universitas, tatis, f. (2) university

unus, a, um (9) one

urbs, urbis, f. (12) city

urinator, is, m. (4) diver

urino, are, avi, atus (6) to dive

ursus, i, m.; ursa, ae, f. (11) bear

usus, usus, m. (11) use

ut (20) in order that

utinam (15) would that

uva, ae, f. (19) grapes

uxor, uxoris, f. (4) wife

vado, vadere, vasi (20) to go, advance

valeo, ere, valui, valiturus (15) to be strong, well

varietas, varietatis, f. (14) variety

vasum, i, n. (2) vase

velo, are, avi, atus (19) to cover, wear a veil

veluti (14) as, just as

venatus, us, m. (4) hunting

vendo, vendere, vendidi, venditus (6) to sell

venio, ire, veni, ventus (10) to come

venter, ventris, m. (14) stomach

verbosus, a, um (7) wordy

verbum, i, n. (3) word

vereor, eri, veritus sum (14) to fear

vero (9) truly

versiculus, i, m. (3) a single line

verto, ere, verti, versus (19) to turn

vester, vestra, vestrum (8) your (pl.)

vetustas, vetustatis, f. (4) old age

vetustus, a, um (14) old

via, ae, f. (12) road

victoria, ae, f. (1) victory

video, ere, vidi, visus (10)   to see

villa, villae, f. (1)   house

vinco, ere, vici, victus (10)   to conquer

vinculum, i, n. (20)   chain

vinea, ae, f. (19)   vine, vineyard

vinum, i, n. (3)   wine

violentia, ae, f. (1)   violence

vir, viri, m. (3)   man

virtus, virtutis, f. (18)   strength, good-ness

vita, vitae, f. (3)   life

vivarium, vivarii, n. (18)   fishpond

vivo, vivere, vixi, victus (14)   to live

vix (19)   scarcely

volo, velle, volui (5)   to want

vos (8)   you (pl.)

vox, vocis, f. (4)   voice

vulpes, vulpis, f. (19)   fox

vultus, us, m. (4)   countenance, face

English-to-Latin Vocabulary

Words whose meaning come directly to English are omitted.

abhor   abhorreo, ere, ui

about   de + ablative

above   super, supra, superus, a, um

abstain   abstineo, ere, ui

absurd   absurdus, a, um

accept   accipio, ere, cepi, ceptus

across   trans + accusative

act   actus, us, m.

add   addo, ere, addidi, additus

after   post + accusative (a preposition)

after (conj.)   postquam

against   contra + accusative

agility   pernicitas, tatis, f.

aid   auxilium, i, n.

all   omnis, e

allow   licet, ere, licuit

alone   solus, a, um

also, even   etiam

also   quoque

although   cum

although   quamquam

always   semper

ancestors   maiores, maiorum, m. pl.

and   et

and   -que (enclitic)

and so   itaque

angry   iratus, a, um

another   alius, a, um

anticipation   exspectatio, onis, f.

any   ullus, a, um

anyone   aliquis, aliquid

apply   applico, are, avi, atus

as, just as   veluti, sicut

ask   quaero, ere, quaesivi, quaesitus

at the home of   apud + accusative

at the same time, together   simul

at leisure   otiosus, a, um

attach   applico, are, avi, atus

attack   invado, ere, vadi, vasus

away from   ab + ablative

axe   bipennis, e

back   tergum, i, n.

bad   malus, a, um

bald   glaber, bra, brum

ball   pila, ae, f.

band   manus, us, f.

bath   balineum, i, n.

be   esse

be able   possum, posse, potui

be absent   absum, abesse, abfui

be accustomed   soleo, ere, solui, solitus

be born   nascor, nasci, natus sum

be derelict   delinquo, ere, deliqui, delictus

be dumbfounded   stupeo, ere, stupui, stupitus

be quiet   taceo, ere, tacui, tacitus

be sad   doleo, ere, dolui

be upset   commoveo, ere, movi, motus

be well, be strong   valeo, ere, valui, valiturus

be well, healthy   salveo, ere

bear (n.)   ursus, i, m.; ursa, ae, f.

bear, carry   fero, ferre, tuli, latus

become   fio, fieri, factus sum

bed   cubile, is, n.

bee   apis, is, m./f.

beer   cerevisia, ae, f.

beet   beta, ae, f.

before   ante, antequam

best   optimus, a, um

begin   committo, ere, misi, missus

behind the knee   poples, poplitis, m.

believe   credo, ere, credidi, creditus

between   inter

beware   caveo, ere, cavi, cautus

blame   culpa, ae, f.

body   corpus, corporis, n.

bone   ossum, i, n.

book   liber, libri, m.

borrowed   mutuus, a, um

both ... and   et ... et

boxer   pugil, pugilis, m.

boy   puer, eri, m.

branch   ramus, i, m.

brave   fortis, is, e

breakfast   prandium, i, n.

breathe   spiro, are, avi, atus

bring back   refero, ferre, tuli, latus

bring to   adduco, ere, duxi, ductus

bring toward   affero, afferre, attuli, allatus

broken   mutilus, a, um

brother   frater, fratris, m.

building   aedificium, i, n.

bury   obruo, ere, obrui, obritus

but   at

but   sed

buttock   clunis, is, m.

by   a, ab + ablative

calamity   calamitas, tatis, f.

call   appello, are, avi, atus

calm (v.)   placo, are, avi, atus

capture   capio, ere, cepi, captus

care cura, ae, f.

care for curo, are, avi, atus

carry porto, are, avi, atus

carry away deporto, are, avi, atus

catch hold of arripio, ere, ripui, reptus

cause causa, ae, f.

cautious cautus, a, um

caveman/-woman trogodyta, ae, m./f.

certain quidam

chain vinculum, i, n.

chair sella, ae, f.

chance casus, us, m.

chew mando, ere, mandi, mansus

chicken pullus, i, m.

choose lego, ere, legi, lectus

circle orbis, is, m.

citizen civis, is, m.

city urbs, is, f.

clay fictilis, e

climb up ascendo, ere, scendi, scensus

cloud nimbus, i, m.

cold frigidus, a, um

come venio, ire, veni, ventus

come upon, invent invenio, ire, veni, ventus

coming together conventus, us, m.

common communis, e

common people plebs, bis, f.

companion comes, itis, m.

complete absolutus, a, um

complete (v.) perago, ere, egi, actus

concerning de + ablative

condition condicio, onis, f.

conquer vinco, ere, vici, victus

consume consumo, ere, sumpsi, sumptus

contract dictum, i, n.

cook (v.) coquo, ere, coxi, coctus

cook (noun) coquus, i, m.

cost sumptus, us, m.; impensa, ae, f.

couch lectus, i, m.

council concilium, i, n.

countenance, face vultus, us, m.

cow bos, bovis, f.

create creor, creari, creatus sum

crime scelus, sceleris, n.

cross crux, crucis, f.

crowd turba, ae, f.

cry lacrimo, are, avi, atus

cup poculum, i, n.

custom consuetudo, tudinis, f.

cut caedo, ere, cecidi, caesus

cut down accido, ere, cidi

cut into incido, ere, cidi, cissus

daily cotidie

daughter filia, ae, f.

day dies, diei, m.

death mors, mortis, f.

decide constituo, ere, stitui, stitutus

decide statuo, ere, statui, statutes

decorate orno, are, avi, atus

decree decretum, i, n.

deep altus, a, um

deepest imus, a, um

deer   cervus, i, m.

definitely   certe

delicious, pleasing   suavis, e

demand   exigo, ere, egi, actus

demand   mando, are, avi, atus

destroy   deleo, ere, delevi, deletus

diarrhea   diarroia, ae, f.

die   exanimo, are, avi, atus

die   morior, moriri, mortuus sum

dinner   cena, ae, f.

discord   discordia, ae, f.

discuss   ago, agere, egi, actus

disgusting   turpis, e

dive   urino, are, avi, atus

diver   urinator, oris, m.

do, drive, discuss, live, spend   ago, agere, egi, actus

do, make   facio, facere, feci, factus

do not   noli (sing.), nolite (pl.) + infinitive

dog   canis, is, m.

down from   de + ablative

draw, drag   traho, ere, traxi, tractus

dress   stola, ae, f.

drink   bibo, bibere, bibi

drive   ago, agere, egi, actus

duty   officium, i, n.

each, every   quisque

ear   auris, auris, f.

earrings   inaures, ium, f. pl.

easy   facilis, e

eat breakfast, lunch   prandeo, ere, prandi, pransus

eat   edo, ere

egg   ovum, i, n.

eight   octo

either ... or   aut ... aut

elk   alces, alcis, m./f.

equal   par, paris

estate   fundus, i, m.

estimate   aestimatio, onis, f.

even   etiam

ever   umquam

everywhere   ubique

except   praeter + accusative

except, make exception   excipio, ere, cepi, ceptus

exchange   permuto, are, avi, atus

eye   oculus, i, m.

face   facies, ei, f.

fact   factum, i, n.

fall   accido, ere, cidi

fall   cado, ere, cecidi, casus

fall   concido, ere, cidi

fall down   decido, ere, cidi

fall down   procumbo, ere, cubui, cubitus

farmer   agricola, ae, m.

father   pater, ris, m.

fatherland   patria, ae, f.

fault   delictum, i, n.

fear   metus, us, m.

fear   vereor, eri, veritus sum

feed   alo, ere, alui, alitus

field   ager, ri, m.

fight   pugno, are, avi, atus

finish   perficio, ere, feci, fectus

first   primus, a, um

fish   pisces, piscis, m./f.

fish pond, game preserve   vivarium, i, n.

fish pond, swimming pool   piscina, ae, f.

five   quinque

flaming   flagrans, antis

flow   fluo, ere, fluxi, fluxus

fly about   convolo, are, avi, atus

follow   sequor, sequi, secutus sum

food   cibus, i, m.

foot   pes, pedis, m.

for   nam

for a long time   diu

for, on behalf of   pro + the ablative

forehead   frons, frontis, f.

foreign   alienus, a, um

form   forma, ae, f.

found   condo, ere, condidi, conditus

four   quattuor

fourth   quartus, a, um

fox   vulpes, vulpis, f.

free   liber, era, erum

free   libero, are, avi, atus

friend   amicus, i, m.

frighten   terreo, ere, ui, itus

fruit   fructus, us, m.

garden   hortus, i, m.

gentle   lenis, e

get up   sublevo, are, avi, atus

girl   puella, ae, f.

give   do, dare, dedi, datus

gnaw at, wear away   rodo, ere, rosi, rosus

go   eo, ire, ii, itus

go out   exeo, ire, ii, itus

goat   caper, capri, m.

god   deus, i, m.

goddess   dea, ae, f.

gold   aurum, i, n.

good   bonus, a, um

goose   anser, anseris, m./f.

gentleman   lautus, i, m.

grab   apprehendo, ere, hendi, hensus

goat   hircus, i, m.; capella, ae, f.

grapes   uva, ae, f.

grass   herba, ae, f.

grassy   herbosus, a, um

great   magnus, a, um

greatly   magnopere

guest   hospita, ae, f.

gullible   credulus, a, um

hair   capillus, i, m.

hand   manus, i, m.

hand over   trado, ere, didi, ditus

hang   pendo, ere, pendi, pensus

hanging   pensilis, e

happen   accido, ere, cidi

happy   laetus, a, um

hard   durus, a, um

have   habeo, ere, ui, itus

he, she, it   is, ea, id

head   caput, capitis, n.

hear   audio, ire, ivi, itus

help (v.)   adiuvo, are, avi, atus

helper   adiutrix, tricis, f.

herbs, grasses   helvella, ae, f.

here   hic

high, deep   altus, a, um

high   excelsus, a, um

higher   superior, superius

his, her, its   eius

hold   teneo, ere, nui, ntus

hope   spero, are, avi, atus

horn   cornu, us, n.

horse   equus, i, m.

hour   hora, ae, f.

house   domus, us, f.

house   villa, ae, f.

how   quo modo

how many   quot

how much   quantus, a, um

humble   humilis, e

hundred   centum, i, n.

hunting   venatus, us, m.

I   ego

if   si

immediately   statim

immediately afterward   subinde

improve appearance   mangonico, are, avi, atus

in order that   ut

in such a way   ita

in, on   in + ablative

include   includo, ere, si, sus

invite   invito, are, avi, atus

iron   ferrum, i, n.

island   insula, ae, f.

joint   articulus, i, m.

jump   salio, ire, salii *or* salui, salitus

jump down   desilio, ire, ui, itus

just as, as   sicut, veluti

keep safe   tutor, ari

kernel   nucleus, i, m.

kill   caedo, ere, cecidi, caesus

kill   concido, ere, cidi

kind, humane   humanus, a, um

king   rex, regis, m.

knock down   affligo, ere, flixi, flictus

knot   nodus, i, m.

know   intellego, ere, lexi, lectus

know   scio, ire, ivi, itus

knowledge   intellegentia, ae, f.

known   notus, a, um

land   terra, ae, f.

large   amplus, a, um

last   extremus, a, um

latest   novissimus, a, um

laugh   rideo, ere, risi, risus

law   lex, legis, f.

lead   duco, ere, duxi, ductus

leader   dux, ducis, m.

leave behind   relinquo, ere, liqui, lictus

leave, set out proficiscor, proficisci, profectus sum

left sinister, sinistra, sinistrum

leg crus, cruris, n.

leisure otium, i, n.

letter epistula, ae, f.

life vita, ae, f.

line agmen, agminis, n.

listen audio, ire, ivi, itus

little paulo

live, dwell habito, are, avi, atus

live vivo, ere, vivi, vitus, ago, ere, egi, actus

load, burden onus, oneris, n.

long longus, a, um

long-nosed nasutus, a, um

look at specto, are, avi, atus, conspicio, ere, spexi, spectus

look for quaero, ere, quaesivi, itus

love amo, are, avi, atus

lower inferus, a, um

lunch prandium, i, n.

lying across transversus, a, um

make facio, ere, feci, factus

make a plan consilium capio, ere, cepi, captus

male mas, maris, m.

mallow malva, ae, f.

man homo, hominis, m./f.

man vir, viri, m.

marriage matrimonium, i, n.

meanwhile interea

meat caro, carnis, or caronis, f.

member membrum, i, n.

merchandise merx, mercis, f.

middle of medius, a, um

mind animus, i, m.

mischief fraus, fraudis, f.

money pecunia, ae, f.

moon luna, ae, f.

moray eel muraena, ae, f.

more magis

moreover autem

morning mane

mother mater, matris, f.

mother-in-law hecyra, ae, f.

mouth os, oris, n.

move, yield cedo, ere, cessi, cessus

move moveo, ere, movi, motus

much, many multus, a, um

mushroom fungus, i, m.

my, mine meus, a, um

name (v.) appello, are, avi, atus

name nomen, inis, n.

near (prep.) ad + acc.

near (adv., prep.) prope

near (adj.) propinquus, a, um

necessary necesse

nerve nervus, i, m.

net rete, retis, n.

never numquam

nevertheless tamen

new novus, a, um

next to propinquus, a, um

night nox, noctis, f.

nine novem

no one nemo

noble nobilis, e

noise clamor, oris, m.

noise strepitus, us, m.

none nullus, a, um

nose nasus, i, m.

not non

not at all! minime!

not want nolo, nolere, nolui

nothing nihil

notice animadverto, ere, verti, versus

now, already iam

now nunc

obligate obligo, are, avi, atus

occupy obtineo, ere, tinui, tentus

often saepe

old vetustus, a, um

old age vetustas, vetustatis, f.

omit, pass over praetereo, ire, ii, itus

on account of propter + accusative

once upon a time olim

one unus, a, um

only modo

order iubeo, ere, iussi, iussus

other ceterus, a, um

our noster, nostra, nostrum

out of e, ex + ablative

outer exterus, a, um

outside foras

own suus, a, um

ox bos, bovis, m./f.

oyster ostrea, ae, f.

palm palma, ae, f.

part pars, partis, f.

party convivium, i, n.

pay out appendo, ere, pendi, pensus

peace pax, pacis, f.

pearl margarita, ae, f.

penalty poena, ae, f.

people populus, i, m.

perhaps fortasse

place locus, i, m.

plan consilium, i, n.

plant, press stipo, are, avi, atus

play ludo, ere, lusi, lusus

pleasant iucundus, a, um

please placeo, ere, placui, placitus or placo, are, avi, atus

pour out diffundo, ere, fudi, fusus

prepare paro, are, avi, atus

pretend dissimulo, are, avi, atus

price pretium, i, n.

priest sacerdos, dotis, m.

private privatus, a, um

privately privatim

professor professor, oris, m.

promise polliceor, polliceri, pollicitus

public publicus, a, um

put down opprimo, ere, pressi, pressus

put, place pono, ere, posui, positus

queen   regina, ae, f.

quiet   quies, quietis, f.

rains (v.)   pluit

read   lego, ere, legi, lectus

receive   recipio, ere, cepi, ceptus

recline   reclino, are, avi, atus

reject   reicio, ere, ieci, iectus

rejoice   gaudeo, ere, gavisus sum

remain   maneo, ere, mansi, mansus

remain   remaneo, ere, mansi, mansus

respond   respondeo, ere, spondi, sponsus

rest of   reliquus, a, um

retreat   se recipio, ere, cepi, ceptus

rich   dis, ditis

rich life   litota, ae, f.

right   ius, iuris, n.

right (hand)   dexter, dextra, dextrum

river   flumen, fluminis, n.

road   via, ae, f.

root   radix, radicis, f.

sad   tristis, e

said   inquit

salt   sal, salis, m.

same   idem, eadem, idem

sand   harena, ae, f.

sandal   solea, ae, f.

say   dico, ere, dixi, dictus

scarcely   vix

school, game   ludus, i, m.

sea   mare, maris, n.

season (v.)   condio, ire, ivi, itus

see   video, ere, vidi, visus

seek, beg, attack   peto, ere, ivi, itus

seems   videtur

self   ipse, ipsa, ipsum

self (reflexive)   se

sell   vendo, ere, vendidi, venditus

senate   senatus, us, m.

senate house   curia, ae, f.

send   mitto, ere, misi, missus

seven   septem

shape   figura, ae, f.

sharp   asper, aspera, asperum

sharp   praeacutus, a, um

shell   concha, ae, f.

ship   navis, is, f.

shop, bar   taberna, ae, f.

short   brevis, e

shout   clamo, are, avi, atus

shrink back   abhorreo, ere, ui

sight, appearance   species, speciei, f.

silence   silentium, i, n.

similar   similis, e

since   cum

sing   canto, are, avi, atus

single   singulus, a, um

single line   versiculus, i, m.

sister   soror, sororis, f.

sit   sedeo, ere, sedi, sessus

six   sex

size   magnitudo, tudinis, m.

skilled   sollertius, a, um

skin, hide   pellis, is, f.

sky   caelum, i, n.

slave   servus, i, m.

sleep (v.)   dormio, ire, ivi, itus

sleep (n.)   somnus, i, m.

slow down   tardo, are, avi, atus

small   parvus, a, um

so   tam

so great   tantus, a, um

so many   tot

soldier   miles, militis, m.

someone   aliquis, aliquid

son   filius, i, m.

soon   mox

soothe   sedo, are, avi, atus

soul   animus, i, m.

speak   loquor, loqui, locutus sum

special   praecipuus, a, um

spongy   fungosus, a, um

spread out   pando, ere, passussum

stand   sto, stare, steti, status

stand out   exsisto, ere, stiti, stitus

star   astrum, i, n.

state   civitas, tatis, f.

step   gradior, gradi, gressus sum

stole, cloak   palla, ae, f.

stomach   venter, ventris, m.

stone   lapis, lapidis, m.

stop   consisto, ere, stiti

story   fabula, ae, f.

straight   derectus, a, um

straighten out   erigo, ere, erexi, erectus

strength   virtus, tutis, f.

strong   fortis, e

student   discipulus, i, m.

suddenly   subito

suffer   patior, pati, passus sum

summer   aestas, aestatis, f.

sumptuary, excessive spending   sumptu-arius, a, um

surpass   antecedo, ere, cessi, cessus

surpass   supero, are, avi, atus

sweat   sudo, are, avi, atus

sweet   dulcis, e

sweet, gentle   mitis, e

swift   celer, eris, ere

swift   praeceler, eris, ere

table   mensa, ae, f.

tail   cauda, ae, f.

take charge of   praesto, are, steti, status

take on   recipio, ere, cepi, ceptus

take out   excipio, ere, cepi, ceptus

taken down   deceptus, a, um

teacher   magister, magistri, m.

tell, narrate   narro, are, avi, atus

ten   decem

than   quam

thanks   gratia, ae, f.

that   ille, illa, illud

the other   alter, altera, alterum

then   deinde

then   tum

therefore   igitur

thigh femur, femoris *or* feminis, f.

thing res, rei, f.

think up excogito, are, avi, atus

this hic, haec, hoc

thousand mille

three tres, tria

through per + accusative

throw iacio, ere, ieci, iactus

thus sic

tightrope walker funambulus, i, m.

time tempus, oris, n.

tired defessus, a, um

to me mihi

to such a degree adeo

to that place istuc

today hodie

tooth dens, dentis, m.

top of summus, a, um

touch tango, ere, tetigi, tactus

toward ad + accusative

tree arbor, oris, f.

truly vero

turn verto, ere, verti, versus

two duo, duae, duo

under sub + ablative *or* accusative

unfair iniquus, a, um

university universitas, tatis, f.

until donec

uproot subruo, ere, rui, rutus

use (n.) usus, us, m.

variety varietas, tatis, f.

very ipse, ipsa, ipsum

victory victoria, ae, f.

violence violentia, ae, f.

voice vox, vocis, f.

wage (v.) gero, ere, gessi, gestus

walk ambulo, are, avi, atus

wander palor, palari, palatus sum

want volo, velle, volui

war bellum, i, n.

warm calidus, a, um

warn, admonish admoneo, ere, monui, monitus

warn moneo, ere, monui, monitus

wash lavo, are, lavi, lautus

water aqua, ae, f.

wave unda, ae, f.

way modus, i, m.

way, journey iter, itineris, n.

we nos

weakened infirmus, a, um

wear gero, ere, gessi, gestus

wear a veil velo, are, avi, atus

weep fleo, ere, flevi, fletus

weigh out appendo, ere, pendi, pensus

weight pondus, ponderis, n.

what? quid?

what kind of quails, e

when (c.) cum

when (c. or i.) quando

when ubi

whence unde

where ubi, quo

while dum

who, which qui, quis, quid

who, pray? quinam?

who? quis?

whoever quisquis

whomever you want quisvis

whole totus, a, um

why cur

wide latus, a, um

wife uxor, uxoris, f.

wine vinum, i, n.

winter hiems, hiemis, f.

wise sapiens, ientis

with cum + ablative

without sine + ablative

wolf lupus, i, m.

woman femina, ae, f.

woman mulier, ieris, f.

wonder miror, ari, miratus sum

wonderful mirus, a, um

wool lana, ae, f.

word verbum, i, n.

wordy verbosus, a, um

work industria, ae, f.

work (v.) laboro, are, avi, atus

work (n.) opus, operis, n.

work hard operor, ari, atus sum

world mundus, i, m.

would that utinam

wretched, miserable miser, misera, miserum

write scribo, ere, scripsi, scriptus

yield cedo, ere, cessi, cessus

yes ita

you (pl.) vos

you (sing.) tu

your (pl.) vester, vestra, vestrum

your (sing.) tuus, a, um

Grammar Summary

This appendix provides all the forms you will encounter in translating Latin. The "Brief Summary of Syntax" section shows you how to use them to form sentences.

Forms

When you see an unfamiliar form of a Latin word, you can refer to this section for the case and number of a noun; or person, number, tense, voice, or mood of a verb.

Nouns

Let's start with nouns.

First Declension Nouns

Nouns of the first declension are feminine except for nouns denoting men. Some dative and ablative plurals are *abus*. For example: *filiabus* and *deabus*.

aqua, ae, f. (water)

Case	Singular	Plural
Nominative	aqua	aquae
Genitive	aquae	aquarum
Dative	aquae	aquis
Accusative	aquam	aquas
Ablative	aqua	aquis
Vocative	aqua	aquae

Second Declension Nouns

Most nouns of the second declension that end in *-us*, *-er*, or *-r* are masculine. Those ending in *-um* are neuter.

lectus, i, m. (bed)

Case	Singular	Plural
Nominative	lectus	lecti
Genitive	lecti	lectorum
Dative	lecto	lectis
Accusative	lectum	lectos
Ablative	lecto	lectis
Vocative	lecte	lecti

filius, i, m. (son)

Case	Singular	Plural
Nominative	filius	filii
Genitive	fili	filiorum
Dative	filio	filiis
Accusative	filium	filios
Ablative	filio	filiis
Vocative	fili	filii

Irregular

After the first century, Latin used the double *i* for the genitive singular of *–ius* nouns such as *filius*. Generally, before Cicero, the genitive had one *i*.

The vocative of a noun ending in *-ius* is *i*.

deus, i, m. (god)

Case	Singular	Plural
Nominative	deus	dei, dii, di
Genitive	dei	deorum, deum
Dative	deo	deis, diis, dis
Accusative	deum	deos
Ablative	deo	deis, diis, dis

dictum, i, n. (saying)

Case	Singular	Plural
Nominative	dictum	dicta
Genitive	dicti	dictorum
Dative	dicto	dictis
Accusative	dictum	dicta
Ablative	dicto	dictis

Third Declension Nouns

Some third declension nouns have *i* before the genitive plural, and some have neuter endings. These are called *i stems*.

mater, matris, f. (mother)

Case	Singular	Plural
Nominative	mater	matres
Genitive	matris	matrum
Dative	matri	matribus
Accusative	matrem	matres
Ablative	matre	matribus

corpus, corporis, n. (body)

Case	Singular	Plural
Nominative	corpus	corpora
Genitive	corporis	corporum
Dative	corpori	corporibus
Accusative	corpus	corpora
Ablative	copore	corporibus

Note: The nominative and accusative neuter forms are always the same.

Third Declension *i* Stems, Masculine and Feminine

urbs, urbis, f. (city)

Case	Singular	Plural
Nominative	urbs	urbes
Genitive	urbis	urbium
Dative	urbi	urbibus
Accusative	urbem	urbes(is)
Ablative	urbe	urbibus

Third Declension *i* Stems, Neuter

mare, maris, n. (sea)

Case	Singular	Plural
Nominative	mare	maria
Genitive	maris	marium
Dative	mari	maribus
Accusative	mare	maria
Ablative	mari	maribus

Fourth Declension Nouns

In the fourth declension, nouns ending in *-us* are masculine and those ending in *-u* are neuter except for *manus* and *domus*, which are feminine.

senatus, us, m. (senate)

Case	Singular	Plural
Nominative	senatus	senatus
Genitive	senatus	senatuum
Dative	senatui	senatibus
Accusative	senatum	senatus
Ablative	senatu	senatibus

cornu, cornus, n. (horn)

Case	Singular	Plural
Nominative	cornu	cornua
Genitive	cornus	cornuum
Dative	cornu	cornibus
Accusative	cornu	cornua
Ablative	cornu	cornibus

Irregular Nouns

domus, us, f. (house)

Case	Singular	Plural
Nominative	domus	domus
Genitive	domus (i)	domuum (orum)
Dative	domui (o)	domibus
Accusative	domum	domos (us)
Ablative	domo (u)	domibus

Fifth Declension Nouns

Fifth declension nouns are feminine except for *dies*, which is masculine.

res, rei, f. (thing)

Case	Singular	Plural
Nominative	res	res
Genitive	rei	rerum
Dative	rei	rebus
Accusative	rem	res
Ablative	re	rebus

Adjectives

And now here are the adjectives to describe the nouns.

First and Second Declension Adjectives

These adjective endings are similar to the nouns of the first and second declension.

altus, a, um (high, deep)

	Singular			Plural		
	Masc.	Fem.	Neut.	Masc.	Fem.	Neut.
Nominative	altus	alta	altum	alti	altae	alta
Genitive	alti	altae	alti	altorum	altarum	altorum
Dative	alto	altae	alto	altis	altis	altis
Accusative	altum	altam	altum	altos	altas	alta
Ablative	alto	alta	alto	altis	altis	altis

Third Declension Adjectives (Three Endings)

Third declension adjectives are similar to the third declension *i* stem noun, with one exception: the ablative singular.

acer, ris, re (sharp)

	Singular			Plural		
	Masc.	Fem.	Neut.	Masc.	Fem.	Neut.
Nominative	acer	acris	acre	acres	acres	acria
Genitive	acris	acris	acris	acrium	acrium	acrium
Dative	acri	acri	acri	acribus	acribus	acribus
Accusative	acrem	acrem	acre	acres	acres	acria
Ablative	acri	acri	acri	acribus	acribus	acribus

Third Declension Adjectives (Two Endings)

For these adjectives, the nominative and feminine singular are the same.

omnis, omne (all)

	Singular			Plural		
	Masc.	Fem.	Neut.	Masc.	Fem.	Neut.
Nominative	omnis	omnis	omne	omnes	omnes	omnia
Genitive	omnis	omnis	omnis	omnium	omnium	omnium
Dative	omni	omni	omni	omnibus	omnibus	omnibus
Accusative	omnem	omnem	omne	omnes	omnes	omnia
Ablative	omni	omni	omni	omnibus	omnibus	omnibus

Third Declension Adjectives (One Ending)

For these adjectives, there is only one nominative singular form.

potens, potentis (powerful)

	Singular			Plural		
	Masc.	Fem.	Neut.	Masc.	Fem.	Neut.
Nominative	potens	potens	potens	potentes	potentes	potentia
Genitive	potentis	potentis	potentis	potentium	potentium	potentium
Dative	potenti	potenti	potentibus	potentibus	potentibus	potentibus
Accusative	potentem	potentem	potens	potentes	potentes	potentia
Ablative	potenti	potenti	potenti	potentibus	potentibus	potentibus

Note: The present participle is declined like *potens* but has the ablative singular *e*.

Irregular Adjectives

ullus, a, um (any)

	Singular			Plural		
	Masc.	**Fem.**	**Neut.**	**Masc.**	**Fem.**	**Neut.**
Nominative	ullus	ulla	ullum	ulli	ullae	ulla
Genitive	ullius	ullius	ullius	ullorum	ullarum	ullorum
Dative	ulli	ulli	ulli	ullis	ullis	ullis
Accusative	ullum	ullam	ullum	ullos	ullas	ulla
Ablative	ullo	ulla	ullo	ullis	ullis	ullis

Note: Other irregular adjectives similarly declined are *alius, alter, neuter, nullus, totus, uter,* and *uterque.*

Comparison of Adjectives

The comparative forms are declined like third declension nouns. Superlative forms are declined like first and second declension adjectives.

Regular

Positive	Comparative	Superlative
altus, a, um	altior, altius	altissimus, a, um
turpis, e	turpior, turpius	turpissimus, a,um
miser, era, erum	miserior, miserius	miserrimus, a, um
acer, ris, re	acrior, acrius	acerrimus, a, um
facilis, e	facilior, facilius	facillimus, a, um

Note: Adjectives ending in *-er* have *errimus* in the superlative.

Five adjectives ending in *-lis* have *limus* in the superlative: *facilis, difficilis, similis, dissimilis,* and *humilis.*

Irregular

Positive	Comparative	Superlative
bonus (good)	melior (better)	optimus (best)
malus (bad)	peior (worse)	pessimus (worst)
magnus (great)	maior (greater)	maximus (greatest)
parvus (small)	minor (smaller)	minimus (smallest)
multus (much)	plus (more)	plurimus (most)

Declension of Comparatives

	Singular Masc. and Fem.	Neut.	Plural Masc. and Fem.	Neut.
Nominative	peior	peius	peiores	peiora
Genitive	peioris	peioris	peiorum	peiorum
Dative	peiori	peiori	peioribus	peioribus
Accusative	peiorem	peius	peiores	peiora
Ablative	peiore	peiore	peioribus	peioribus

Adverbs

And now adverbs to describe the adjectives and verbs.

Comparison of Adverbs

Positive	Comparative	Superlative
alte	altius	altissime
misere	miserius	miserrime
fortiter	fortius	fortissime
facile	facilius	facillime

Numerals

Only *unus*, *duo*, *tres*, and *mille* are declined. All other numbers have only one form.

Declension of Numerals

unus, a, um (one)

	Masc.	Fem.	Neut.
Nominative	unus	una	unum
Genitive	unius	unius	unius
Dative	uni	uni	uni
Accusative	unum	unam	unum
Ablative	uno	una	uno

duo (two)

	Masc.	Fem.	Neut.
Nominative	duo	duae	duo
Genitive	duorum	duarum	duorum
Dative	duobus	duabus	duobus
Accusative	duos, duo	duas	duo
Ablative	duobus	duabus	duobus

tres (three)

	Masc.	Fem.	Neut.
Nominative	tres	tres	tria
Genitive	trium	trium	trium
Dative	tribus	tribus	tribus
Accusative	tres	tres	tria
Ablative	tribus	tribus	tribus

mille (one thousand)

	Singular (Adjective)	Plural (Noun)
Nominative	mille	milia
Genitive	mille	milium
Dative	mille	milibus
Accusative	mille	milia
Ablative	mille	milibus

Personal Pronouns

Remember that pronouns do not modify. Personal pronouns take the place of a person.

	First Person Singular	First Person Plural
Nominative	ego (I)	nos (we)
Genitive	mei (of me)	nostrum or nostri (of us)
Dative	mihi (to me)	nobis (to us)
Accusative	me (me)	nos (us)
Ablative	me (by me)	nobis (by us)

	Second Person Singular	Second Person Plural
Nominative	tu	vos
Genitive	tui	vestrum, vestri
Dative	tibi	vobis
Accusative	te	vos
Ablative	te	vobis

	Third Person Singular (Reflexive)	Third Person Plural (Reflexive)
Nominative	—	—
Genitive	sui	sui
Dative	sibi	sibi
Accusative	se *or* sese	se *or* sese
Ablative	se *or* sese	se *or* sese

Demonstrative Pronouns/Adjectives

When a demonstrative modifies another word, it is an adjective: this. When it stands alone, it is a pronoun: he, she, or it.

hic, haec, hoc (this)

	Singular Masc.	Fem.	Neut.	Plural Masc.	Fem.	Neut.
Nominative	hic	haec	hoc	hi	hae	haec
Genitive	huius	huius	huius	horum	harum	horum
Dative	huic	huic	huic	his	his	his
Accusative	hunc	hanc	hoc	hos	has	haec
Ablative	hoc	hac	hoc	his	his	his

ille, illa, illud (that)

	Singular Masc.	Fem.	Neut.	Plural Masc.	Fem.	Neut.
Nominative	ille	illa	illud	illi	illae	illa
Genitive	illius	illius	illius	illorum	illarum	illorum
Dative	illi	illi	illi	illis	illis	illis
Accusative	illum	illam	illud	illos	illas	illa
Ablative	illo	illa	illo	illis	illis	illis

is, ea, id (this, that)

	Singular Masc.	Fem.	Neut.	Plural Masc.	Fem.	Neut.
Nominative	is	ea	id	ei	eae	ea
Genitive	eius	eius	eius	eorum	earum	eorum
Dative	ei	ei	ei	eis	eis	eis
Accusative	eum	eam	id	eos	eas	ea
Ablative	eo	ea	eo	eis	eis	eis

Relative Pronouns

The interrogative adjective is exactly like the relative pronoun. For example, *qui deus?* (what god?).

qui, quae, quod (who, which, what)

	Singular Masc.	Fem.	Neut.	Plural Masc.	Fem.	Neut.
Nominative	qui	quae	quod	qui	quae	quae
Genitive	cuius	cuius	cuius	quorum	quarum	quorum
Dative	cui	cui	cui	quibus	quibus	quibus
Accusative	quem	quam	quod	quos	quas	quae
Ablative	quo	qua	quo	quibus	quibus	quibus

Interrogative Pronouns

The plural of the interrogative pronoun is like the plural of the relative pronoun.

quis, quid (who, what?)

	Singular Masc.	Fem.	Neut.	Plural Masc.	Fem.	Neut.
Nominative	quis	quis	quid	qui	quae	quae
Genitive	cuius	cuius	cuius	quorum	quarum	quorum
Dative	cui	cui	cui	quibus	quibus	quibus
Accusative	quem	quem	quid	quos	quas	quae
Ablative	quo	quo	quo	quibus	quibus	quibus

Regular Verbs

First Conjugation

Principal parts: *amo, amare, amavi, amatus*

Stems: *ama, amav, amat*

Indicative

Tense	Active Voice Singular	Plural	Passive Voice Singular	Plural
Present	amo (I love)	amamus	amor (I am loved)	amamur
	amas	amatis	amaris	amamini
	amat	amant	amatur	amantur
Imperfect	amabam (I was loving)	amabamus	amabar (I was being loved)	amabamur
	amabas	amabatis	amabaris	amabamini
	amabat	amabant	amabatur	amabantur
Future	amabo (I will love)	amabimus	amabor (I will be loved)	amabimur
	amabis	amabitis	amaberis	amabimini
	amabit	amabunt	amabitur	amabuntur
Present Perfect	amavi (I loved)	amavimus	amatus sum (I have been loved)	amati sumus
	amavisti	amavistis	amatus es	amati estis
	amavit	amaverunt	amatus est	amati sunt

continues

Indicative (continued)

Tense	Active Voice Singular	Plural	Passive Voice Singular	Plural
Past Perfect (Pluperfect)	amaveram (I had loved)	amaveramus	amatus eram (I had been loved)	amati eramus
	amaveras	amaveratis	amatus eras	amati eratis
	amaverat	amaverant	amatus erat	amati erant

Tense	Active Voice Singular	Plural	Passive Voice Singular	Plural
Future Perfect	amavero (I will have loved)	amaverimus	amatus ero (I will have been loved)	amati erimus
	amaveris	amaveritis	amatus eris	amati eritis
	amaverit	amaverint	amatus erit	amati erunt

Note: The participle will agree with the subject in number and gender. Alternate endings are *-i, -ae, -a, -us, -a,* and *-um.*

Subjunctive

Tense	Active Voice Singular	Plural	Passive Voice Singular	Plural
Present	amem	amemus	amer	amemur
	ames	ametis	ameris	amemini
	amet	ament	ametur	amentur
Imperfect	amarem	amaremus	amarer	amaremur
	amares	amaretis	amareris	amaremini
	amaret	amarent	amaretur	amarentur
Present Perfect	amaverim	amaverimus	amatus sim	amati simus
	amaveris	amaveritis	amatus sis	amati sitis
	amaverit	amaverint	amatus sit	amati sint

Tense	Active Voice Singular	Plural	Passive Voice Singular	Plural
Past Perfect	amavissem	amavissemus	amatus essem	amati essemus
(Pluperfect)	amavisses	amavissetis	amatus esses	amati essetis
	amavisset	amavissent	amatus esset	amati essent

Imperative

Present: *ama! amate! amare! amamini!* (Love! Be loved!)

Future: *amato! amatote!*

Infinitive

Tense	Active	Passive
Present	amare (to love)	amari (to be loved)
Perfect	amavisse (to have loved)	amatus esse (to have been loved)
Future	amaturus esse (to be about to love)	amatum iri (to be about to be loved)

Participles

Tense	Active	Passive
Present	amans (loving)	—
Perfect	—	amatus (having been loved)
Future	amaturus (about to love)	amandus, a, um (about to be loved)

Second Conjugation

Principal parts: *moneo, ere, monui, monitum* (to warn)

Stems: *mone, monu, monit*

Indicative

Tense	Active Voice Singular	Plural	Passive Voice Singular	Plural
Present	moneo	monemus	moneor	monemur
	mones	monetis	moneris	monemini
	monet	monent	monetur	monentur
Imperfect	monebam	monebamus	monebar	monebamur
	monebas	monebatis	monebaris	monebamini
	monebat	monebant	monebatur	monebantur
Future	monebo	monebimus	monebor	monebimur
	monebis	monebitis	moneberis	monebimini
	monebit	monebunt	monebitur	monebuntur
Present Perfect	monui	monuimus	monitus sum	moniti sumus
	monuisti	monuistis	monitus es	moniti estis
	monuit	monuerunt	monitus est	moniti sunt
Past Perfect	monueram	monueramus	monitus eram	moniti eramus
(Pluperfect)	monueras	monueratis	monitus eras	moniti eratis
	monuerat	monuerant	monitus erat	moniti erant
Future Perfect	monuero	monuerimus	monitus ero	moniti erimus
	monueris	monueritis	monitus eris	moniti eritis
	monuerit	monuerint	monitus erit	moniti erunt

Subjunctive

Tense	Active Voice Singular	Plural	Passive Voice Singular	Plural
Present	moneam	moneamus	monear	moneamur
	moneas	moneatis	monearis	moneamini
	moneat	moneant	moneatur	moneantur

Tense	Active Voice		Passive Voice	
	Singular	Plural	Singular	Plural
Imperfect	monerem	moneremus	monerer	moneremur
	moneres	moneretis	monereris	moneremini
	moneret	monerent	moneretur	monerentur
Present Perfect	monuerim	monuerimus	monitus sim	moniti simus
	monueris	monueritis	monitus sis	moniti sitis
	monuerit	monuerint	monitus sit	moniti sint
Past Perfect	monuissem	monuissemus	monitus essem	moniti essemus
(Pluperfect)	monuisses	monuissetis	monitus esses	moniti essetis
	monuisset	monuissent	monitus esset	moniti essent

Imperative

Tense	Active Voice		Passive Voice	
	Singular	Plural	Singular	Plural
Present	mone	monete	monere	monemini

Infinitive

Tense	Active	Passive
Present	monere	moneri
Perfect	monuisse	monitus esse
Future	moniturus esse	monitum iri

Participles

Tense	Active	Passive
Present	monens	—
Perfect	moniturus	monendus
Future	—	monitus

Third Conjugation

Principal parts: *mitto, mittere, misi, missus*

Stems: *mitt-, mis-, miss-*

Indicative

Tense	Active Voice Singular	Plural	Passive Voice Singular	Plural
Present	mitto	mittimus	mittor	mittimur
	mittis	mittitis	mitteris, mittere	mittimini
	mittit	mittunt	mittitur	mittuntur
Imperfect	mittebam	mittebamus	mittebar	mittebamur
	mittebas	mittebatis	mittebaris	mittebamini
	mittebat	mittebant	mittebatur	mittebantur
Future	mittam	mittemus	mittar	mittemur
	mittes	mittetis	mitteris	mittemini
	mittet	mittent	mittetur	mittentur
Present Perfect	misi	misimus	missus sum	missi sumus
	misisti	misistis	missus es	missi estis
	misit	miserunt	missus est	missi sunt
Past Perfect (Pluperfect)	miseram	miseramus	missus eram	missi eramus
	miseras	miseratis	missus eras	missi eratis
	miserat	miserant	missus erat	missi erant
Future Perfect	misero	miserimus	missus ero	missi erimus
	miseris	miseritis	missus eris	missi eritis
	miserit	miserint	missus erit	missi erunt

Subjunctive

Tense	Active Voice Singular	Plural	Passive Voice Singular	Plural
Present	mittam	mittamus	mittar	mittamur
	mittas	mittatis	mittaris	mittamini
	mittat	mittant	mittatur	mittantur
Imperfect	mitterem	mitteremus	mitterer	mitteremur
	mitteres	mitteretis	mittereris	mitteremini
	mitteret	mitterent	mitteretur	mitterentur
Present Perfect	miserim	miserimus	missus sim	missi simus
	miseris	miseritis	missus sis	missi sitis
	miserit	miserint	missus sit	missi sint
Past Perfect (Pluperfect)	misissem	misissemus	missus essem	missi essemus
	misisses	misissetis	missus esses	missi essetis
	misisset	misissent	missus esset	missi essent

Imperative

Tense	Active Voice Singular	Plural	Passive Voice Singular	Plural
Present	mitte	mittite	mittere	mittimini

Infinitive

Tense	Active	Passive
Present	mittere	mitti
Perfect	misisse	missus esse
Future	missurus esse	missum iri

Participles

Tense	Active	Passive
Present	mittens	—
Perfect	missurus	missus
Future	—	mittendus

Third Conjugation -*io* and Fourth Conjugation

Principal parts: *capio, capere, cepi, captus*

Stems: *capi-, cep-, capt-*

Indicative

Tense	Active Voice Singular	Plural	Passive Voice Singular	Plural
Present	capio	capimus	capior	capimur
	capis	capitis	caperis, capere	capimini
	capit	capiunt	capitur	capiuntur
Imperfect	capiebam	capiebamus	capiebar	capiebamur
	capiebas	capiebatis	capiebaris	capiebamini
	capiebat	capiebant	capiebatur	capiebantur
Future	capiam	capiemus	capiar	capiemur
	capies	capietis	capieris	capiemini
	capiet	capient	capietur	capientur
Present Perfect	cepi	cepimus	captus sum	capti sumus
	cepisti	cepistis	captus es	capti estis
	cepit	ceperunt	captus est	capti sunt

Tense	Active Voice Singular	Plural	Passive Voice Singular	Plural
Past Perfect	ceperam	ceperamus	captus eram	capti eramus
(Pluperfect)	ceperas	ceperatis	captus eras	capti eratis
	ceperat	ceperant	captus erat	capti erant
Future Perfect	cepero	ceperimus	captus ero	capti erimus
	ceperis	ceperitis	captus eris	capti eritis
	ceperit	ceperint	captus erit	capti erunt

Subjunctive

Tense	Active Voice Singular	Plural	Passive Voice Singular	Plural
Present	capiam	capiamus	capiar	capiamur
	capias	capiatis	capiaris	capiamini
	capiat	capiant	capiatur	capiantur
Imperfect	caperem	caperemus	caperer	caperemur
	caperes	caperetis	capereris	caperemini
	caperet	caperent	caperetur	caperentur
Present Perfect	ceperim	ceperimus	captus sim	capti simus
	ceperis	ceperitis	captus sis	capti sitis
	ceperit	ceperint	captus sit	capti sint
Past Perfect	cepissem	cepissemus	captus essem	capti essemus
(Pluperfect)	cepisses	cepissetis	captus esses	capti essetis
	cepisset	cepissent	captus esset	capti essent

Imperative

Tense	Active Voice Singular	Plural	Passive Voice Singular	Plural
Present	cape	capite	capere	capimini

Note: The fourth conjugation present passive infinitive is *-iri*. For example: *muniri* (to be fortified).

Infinitive

Tense	Active	Passive
Present	capere	capi
Perfect	cepisse	captus esse
Future	capturus esse	captum iri

Irregular Verbs

Irregular verbs are often different in the present and imperfect tenses.

Principal parts: *sum, esse, fui, futurus* (to be)

Indicative

Present Singular	Plural	Imperfect Singular	Plural	Future Singular	Plural
sum	sumus	eram	eramus	ero	erimus
es	estis	eras	eratis	eris	eritis
est	sunt	erat	erant	erit	erunt

Note: Other tenses are formed regularly. For example:

Perfect Singular	Plural
fui	fuimus
fuisti	fuistis
fuit	fuerunt

Subjunctive

Present

Singular	Plural
sim	simus
sis	sitis
sit	sint

Note: All other tenses are formed regularly. For example:

Imperfect

Singular	Plural
essem	essemus
esses	essetis
esset	essent

Imperative

Present: *es, este*

Future: *esto, estote*

Principal parts: *possum, posse, potui* (to be able)

Present Indicative		Present Subjunctive	
Singular	**Plural**	**Singular**	**Plural**
possum	possumus	possim	possimus
potes	potestis	possis	possitis
potest	possunt	possit	possint

Note: All other forms are regular.

Principal parts: *fero, ferre, tuli, latus* (to carry)

Indicative

Indicative–Present Tense

Active Voice		Passive Voice	
Singular	**Plural**	**Singular**	**Plural**
fero	ferimus	feror	ferimur
fers	fertis	ferris	ferimini
fert	ferunt	fertur	feruntur

Note: All other forms are regular.

Principal parts: *eo*, *ire*, *ivi* or *ii*, *iturus* (to go)

Indicative–Present

Indicative		Subjunctive	
Singular	**Plural**	**Singular**	**Plural**
eo	imus	eam	eamus
is	itis	eas	eatis
it	eunt	eat	eant

Imperfect: ibam, etc.

Future: *ibo*, *ibis*, etc.

Note: All other forms are regular.

Principal parts: *fio*, *fiere*, *factus sum* (be made)

Indicative–Present Active

Present	**Indicative**
fio	fimus
fis	fitis
fit	fiunt

Note: All other forms are regular.

Volo

Volo, Nolo, Malo

Principle parts: *volo, velle, volui* (be willing); *nolo, nolle, nolui* (be unwilling); *malo, malle, malui* (prefer)

Indicative—Present

volo	nolo	malo
vis	non vis	mavis
vult	non vult	mavult
volumus	nolumus	malumus
vultis	non vultis	mavultis
volunt	nolunt	malunt

Future: *volam, nolam malam*, etc.

Note: All other forms are regular.

Brief Summary of Syntax

Nouns

- An appositive is in the same case as the noun it describes.
- An adjective agrees with the noun it modifies in number, gender, and case.
- An adjective can be used as a noun.
- The relative pronoun agrees with its antecedent in number and gender but takes its case from its use in its own clause.
- A relative pronoun can be used at the beginning of a sentence as a conjunction.
- The reflexive pronoun usually refers to the subject of the clause in which it appears.
- The subject of a verb is in the nominative case.
- A predicate noun or adjective is in the nominative case.

- The person or thing directly addressed is in the vocative case.

- The genitive case is used to show possession.

- The genitive case is translated "of."

- The genitive case is used to designate the object toward which a feeling or action is directed.

- The dative case is used for the indirect object.

- The dative case is used with the verbs *favor, help, please, trust, believe, persuade, command, obey,* and so on.

- The dative case is used with *sum* to show possession.

- The accusative case is used for the direct object.

- The subject of the infinitive in an indirect statement is in the accusative case.

- The accusative case shows duration of time or extent of space.

- The accusative is used as the object of many prepositions.

- The accusative is used with *ad* and *in* to show motion toward.

- Exclamations use the accusative case.

- The ablative case is used to show from, with, when, or where.

- The ablative case is used with the passive voice and *ab* to show personal agent.

- The ablative case without a preposition shows the means or instrument by which something is done.

- The ablative is used to show cause.

- The ablative is used with many prepositions.

- The ablative absolute construction is in the ablative case. Duh!

- With names of towns, *domus* and *rus*, the locative case shows where. This is the singular of the first and second declension genitive. Elsewhere, it is like the ablative.

Verbs

- The present tense represents an action going on in the present.

- The imperfect tense denotes continued or repeated action in the past.

- The future tense represents an action in the future.

- The present perfect tense represents action that has been completed or is completed at the time of speaking.

- The past perfect tense denotes an act completed in the past before another had begun.

- The future perfect tense denotes action as completed in the future.

- The indicative mood is used to express a fact.

- The subjunctive mood can be used to represent an idea as willed. The present subjunctive is used, and the negative is *ne*.

- Purpose clauses introduced by *ut* take the subjunctive. The negative is *ne*.

- Verbs of fearing are followed by the subjunctive introduced by *ne* (that) or by *lest* or *ut* (that not).

- Result clauses introduced by *ut* take the subjunctive. The negative is *ut non*.

- *Cum* (when, since, although) is followed by the subjunctive.

- Noun clauses in indirect statements, indirect questions, causal clauses, or conditional clauses are all in the subjunctive.

- The infinitive can be used as the subject of a verb.

- The infinitive is used after the verbs *say*, *know*, *think*, *tell*, *perceive*, and so on.

- The imperative mood is used to give commands.

- A participle is a verbal adjective and must agree with the noun it modifies in number, gender, and case.

- The future passive participle and the verb *to be* are used to show obligation.

- A gerund is a verbal noun of the second declension and is found only in the singular.

- A supine is a verbal noun of the fourth declension used only in the accusative and ablative.

Selections from Latin Authors Often Used in Traditional Curriculum

This appendix contains selections from Latin authors that are often included in a traditional curriculum. The translations are here, as well, to give an overall picture of the content, to save time in looking up every word, and to help you over that impossible sentence. Your translation, of course, will be yours alone, unique and reflecting your own vocabulary choice, tone, and interpretation.

The Latin is timeless, and you'll find many people have memorized the first lines. Surprise your boss, your seatmate on the subway, or your English professor by reciting offhandedly the first line of Cicero's "Oration." Heads will turn.

From *Commentaries on the Gallic War* by Julius Caesar

A Geography Lesson I.1

Gallia est omnis divisa in partes tres, quarum unam incolunt Belgae, aliam Aquitani, tertiam qui ipsorum lingua Celtae, nostra Galli appellantur. Hi omnes lingua, institutis, legibus inter se differunt. Gallos ab Aquitanis Garumna flumen, a Belgis Matrona et Sequana dividit.

Gaul is all divided into three parts, one of which the Belgians inhabit, another the Aquitanians, and a third those who are called Celts in their own language, Gauls in our language. These all differ between themselves in language, institutions, and laws. The Garonne River divides the Gauls from the Aquitanians; the Marne and Seine divide the Gauls from the Belgians.

Horum omnium fortissimi sunt Belgae, propterea quod a cultu atque humanitate provinciae longissime absunt, minimeque ad eos mercatores saepe commeant atque ea quae ad effeminandos animos pertinent important, proximique sunt Germanis, qui trans Rhenum incolunt, quibuscum continenter bellum gerunt.

Of all these the bravest are the Belgians, because they are farthest from the culture and civilization of the province and least often visited by merchants who bring in those things that pertain to weakening spirits; and also because they are nearest to the Germans who live across the Rhine, with whom they are continually at war.

Qua de causa Helvetii quoque reliquos Gallos virtute praecedunt, quod fere cotidianis proeliis cum Germanis contendunt, cum aut suis finibus eos prohibent, aut ipsi in eorum finibus bellum gerunt.

For this reason the Helvetians also surpass the rest of the Gauls in courage, because they are struggling in almost daily fights with the Germans, either trying to keep them out of Gallic territory or waging war with them in German lands.

Eorum una pars, quam Gallos obtinere dictum est, initium capit a flumine Rhodano; continetur Garumna flumine, Oceano, finibus Belgarum; attingit etiam ab Sequanis et Helvetiis flumen Rhenum; vergit ad septentriones. Belgae ab extremis Galliae finibus oriuntur; pertinent ad inferiorem partem fluminis Rheni; spectant in septentrionem et orientem solem. Aquitania a Garumna flumine ad Pyrenaeos montes et eam partem Oceani quae est ad Hispaniam pertinet; spectat inter occasum solis et septentriones.

One part of these, which is said to be occupied by the Gauls, starts from the river Rhone and is contained by the Garonne River, the ocean and the territory of the

Belgians; moreover it touches the Rhine River by the Sequani and the Helvetians; and it turns toward the north. The Belgians, beginning from the edge of the Gallic territory, reach to the lower part of the river Rhine; they look towards the north and east. Aquitania, starting from the Garonne, reaches to the Pyrenees mountains and to that part of the ocean which is near Spain; it looks between the west and north.

The Helvetians Surrender I.27

Helvetii omnium rerum inopia adducti legatos de deditione ad eum miserunt. Qui cum eum in itinere convenissent seque ad pedes proiecissent suppliciterque locuti flentes pacem petissent, atque eos in eo loco quo tum essent suum adventum exspectare iussisset, paruerunt. Eo postquam Caesar pervenit, obsides, arma, servos qui ad eos perfugissent poposcit.

The Helvetians, influenced by the lack of all things, sent deputies to him concerning surrender. When they found him on the march, they threw themselves crying at his feet, plaintively spoke, and asked for peace. And he ordered them to wait his arrival in that place where they were then and they obeyed. After Caesar got there, he demanded hostages, arms, and the slaves which had fled with them.

(Dizzied by success, Caesar went on to 7 years of victories, conquering village after town after tribe. By 51 B.C.E., he had finished off the last hope of the Gauls, the famous Vercingetorix, and claimed all of Gaul for the Roman people.)

Vercingetorix VII.89

Postero die Vercingetorix concilio convocato id bellum se suscepisse non suarum necessitatium, sed communis libertatis causa demonstrat, et quoniam sit fortunae cedendum, ad utramque rem se illis offerre, seu morte sua Romanis satisfacere, seu vivum tradere velint. Mittuntur de his rebus ad Caesarem legati. Iubet arma tradi, principes produci. Ipse in munitione pro castris consedit; eo duces producuntur; Vercingetorix deditur, arma proiciuntur.

On the next day Vercingetorix, when a council had been called together, pointed out that he had undertaken that war, not for his own sake, but for the sake of everyone's liberty; and since they must yield to fortune, he offered himself to them for whichever course they pleased; either to give satisfaction to the Romans by his death, or to hand him over alive. Ambassadors were sent concerning these things to Caesar. He ordered them to hand over their arms and to produce the leaders. He himself sat on the entrenchments in front of the camp. The leaders were brought before him there. Vercingetorix was surrendered and his arms thrown down.

From *The First Speech Against Catiline* by Marcus Tullius Cicero

The First Catilinian Oration accuses Catiline of masterminding the conspiracy to seize the capital and the consulship. Cicero recounts the sordid past of the failed politician and urges Catiline to leave Rome. He ends the First Oration with comparing Catiline and his followers to a disease and finishes with a classic periodic sentence: long, full of clauses, well balanced, and ending with the most important word, a verb, a plea to Jupiter to sacrifice Catiline to eternal damnation—*mactabis.*

1.1-2 Introduction

Quo usque tandem abutere, Catilina, patientia nostra? quam diu etiam furor iste tuus nos eludet? quem ad finem sese effrenata iactabit audacia? Nihilne te nocturnum praesidium Palati, nihil urbis vigiliae, nihil timor populi, nihil concursus bonorum omnium, nihil hic munitissimus habendi senatus locus, nihil horum ora voltusque moverunt?

For how long, Catiline, will you abuse our patience? How long, still, will that madness of yours make fun of us? When will that unbridled audacity stop throwing itself around? Does nothing move you? Not the nightly garrison on the Palatine, the watches of the city, the fear of the people, the meeting of all good men, the Senate meeting in this most fortified place, the faces and expressions of these people?

Patere tua consilia non sentis, constrictam iam horum omnium scientia teneri coniurationem tuam non vides? Quid proxima, quid superiore nocte egeris, ubi fueris, quos convocaveris, quid consili ceperis quem nostrum ignorare arbitraris?

Do you not know that your plans lie exposed? Do you not see that your conspiracy is held fast by the knowledge of all these men? Do you think that there is a man among us who does not know what you did last night or the night before that, where you were, whom you called together, what plan you made?

O tempora, o mores! Senatus haec intellegit, consul videt; hic tamen vivit. Vivit? immo vero etiam, in senatum venit, fit publici consili particeps, notat et designat oculis ad caedem unum quemque nostrum. Nos autem fortes viri satis facere rei publicae videmur, si istius furorem ac tela vitamus.

Oh the times, oh the ways! The Senate knows these things, the consul sees; yet this man lives. He lives? Indeed, truly still, he comes into the Senate, takes part in the public debate, notes and designates with his eyes each and every one of us for slaughter. We, however, brave men that we are, seem to do enough for the republic if we avoid the anger and weapons of that man.

Good-Bye, Catiline I. 33

Hisce ominibus, Catilina, cum summa rei publicae salute, cum tua peste ac pernicie cumque eorum exitio qui se tecum omni scelere parricidioque iunxerunt, proficiscere ad impium bellum ac nefarium. Tu, Iuppiter, qui isdem quibus haec urbs auspiciis a Romulo es constitutus, quem Statorem huius urbis atque imperi vere nominamus, hunc et huius socios a tuis ceterisque templis, a tectis urbis ac moenibus, a vita fortunisque civium omnium arcebis et homines bonorum inimicos, hostis patriae, latrones Italiae scelerum foedere inter se ac nefaria societate coniunctos aeternis suppliciis vivos mortuosque mactabis.

With these omens, Catiline, go out to your impious and nefarious war, with highest safety of the republic, with your own disaster and ruin, and with the destruction of those who joined themselves with you in every crime and act of treason. You, Jupiter, who by Romulus was established under the same auspices under which this city was established, whom we justly call the founder of this city and empire, you will keep him and his confederates from your temple and those of the other gods, from the houses and walls of the city, from the lives and fortunes of all her citizens. And these men, the enemies of good men, public enemies of their own country, robbers of Italy, men who are joined together in an evil confederacy and companionship in crime, these men, alive and dead, you will sacrifice to eternal punishment.

(On the next day, Cicero makes a speech, the Second Oration, before the people of Rome, describing the now departed Catiline and his conspiracy. Three weeks later he spoke before the people again.)

From *The Third Speech Against Catiline*

Delivered before the people, Cicero explains his methods.

I Saved You All! I.1

Rem publicam, Quirites, vitamque omnium vestrum, bona, fortunas, coniuges liberosque vestros atque hoc domicilium clarissimi imperi, fortunatissimam pulcherrimamque urbem, hodierno die deorum immortalium summo ergo vos amore, laboribus, consiliis, periculis meis e flamma atque ferro ac paene ex faucibus fati ereptam et vobis conservatam ac restitutam videtis.

The republic, citizens, the life of all of you, your goods, fortunes, your wives and children, and this residence of our most famous empire, this most blessed and beautiful city, on this very day because of the great love of the immortal gods and by my work, plans and dangers as you see, have been snatched from fire and sword, almost from the jaws of fate and preserved and restored for you.

Answer Keys

These answer keys include answers to all the Practice Makes Perfect questions, as well as any exercises and translations within the chapters. Note that all translations from the Latin are the author's.

Chapter 1

Practice Makes Perfect

1. The senator is not a hippopotamus.
2. The mushroom is noble.
3. Rome is in Europe.
4. Rome is not in America.
5. Discord is a disaster.
6. Victory is glory.

Chapter 2

Practice Makes Perfect 1

1. inferior—superior
2. humanus—divinus
3. victoria—calamitas
4. publicus—privatus
5. clamor—silentium

Practice Makes Perfect 2

Ask questions to a friend or your boss:

Are you a consul?

Are you a hippopotamus?

Are you a cavewoman?

Are you an orator?

Are you a senator?

Chapter 3

Practice Makes Perfect 1

Translate from Latin into English:

1. Life of an oyster
2. The sandal of the girl
3. Water of Rome
4. Dinner of grass
5. Daughter of a goddess

Translate from English into Latin:

1. Herba Romae
2. Vita puellae
3. Mensa troglodytae
4. Margarita ostreae
5. Femina piscinae

Practice Makes Perfect 2

Translate from Latin into English:

1. The cup of the student
2. A man of silence
3. Nose of an elephant
4. Leisure of the people
5. Vase of iron
6. Way of the world
7. The woman's beer

Translate from English into Latin:

1. Pretium terrae
2. Verbum poenae
3. Filius lauti
4. Versiculus epistulae
5. Hospita Graeci

Practice Makes Perfect 3

Translate from Latin into English:

1. Houses of the Greeks
2. Nerves of steel
3. Kernels of oysters
4. Cups of beer
5. The baths of the students

Translate from English into Latin:

1. Vasa deae
2. Cenae virorum
3. Loci filiorum
4. Vita convivii
5. Lectus hospitae

Practice Makes Perfect 4

Translate from Latin into English:

1. Ham and eggs
2. Women and men
3. Public and private
4. Oysters but not elephants
5. Elephants but also hippos

Translate from English into Latin:

1. Sumptus universitatis (*SUMP-toos oo-nee-WEHR-see-tahs*)
2. Aestimationes architecti (*eyes-tim-ah-tee-OHN-ays ahr-kih-TEEHK-tee*)
3. Tempus vitae (*TEM-puhs WEE-teye*)
4. Arbores Romae (*ahr-BOH-rays ROH-meye*)
5. Clunes ferri (*KLOO-nays FEH-ree*)

Chapter 4

Practice Makes Perfect 1

Translate from Latin into English:

1. The convention of brothers
2. Line of elephants
3. Calamity of the state
4. Old age of the dictator
5. Friend of the woman

Practice Makes Perfect 2

Fill in the correct endings.

Declension	Nominative		Genitive	
	s.	*pl.*	*s.*	*pl.*
First	a	ae	ae	arum
Second	us	i	i	orum
Third	—	es	is	um
Fourth	us	us	us	uum
Fifth	—	es	ei	erum

Translate from Latin into English:

1. The thing of life
2. Feet of the boxers
3. Net of the gladiator
4. Vase of salt
5. Silence of the lambs

Translate from English into Latin:

1. Feminae domus (*FEH-mih-neye DOH-mus*)
2. Strepitum viarum (*STREH-pih-tum wee-AH-rum*)
3. Conventus comitum (*kohn-WEHN-tus KOH-mih-tum*)
4. Crus agni (*KROOS AHG-nee*)
5. Duces mundi (*DOO-kayss MOON-dee*)

Mark the correct column.

Latin	Nominative s.	Nominative pl.	Genitive s.	Genitive pl.
gloriae		X	X	
Caesaris			X	
alumni		X	X	
alumna	X			
ostreae		X	X	
pacis			X	
res	X	X		

Latin	Nominative s.	Nominative pl.	Genitive s.	Genitive pl.
rete	X			
uxor	X			
ferri			X	
strepitus	X	X	X	
sumptuum				X
comitium				X
viri		X	X	
silentii			X	
pacum				X

Chapter 5

Practice Makes Perfect 1

1. clamo (I shout)
2. pugnant (they fight)
3. coquit (cooks)
4. stipo (plant)
5. decidit (he falls)

Practice Makes Perfect 2

1. condiunt (they season)
2. exigit (it demands)
3. abhorrent (they shrink back)
4. relinquunt (they leave)
5. obruit (he buries)

Practice Makes Perfect 3

Translate from Latin into English:

1. They plant.
2. I cook.
3. The tightrope walkers surpass.
4. The table falls.
5. The brother leaves.

Practice Makes Perfect 4

Fill in the blanks:

1. Graecus (*GREYE-kus*)
2. Dux (*DOOKS*)
3. Coquus (*KOH-kwu*s)
4. Muraenae (*moo-REYE-neye*)
5. Dictatores (*dihk-tah-TOH-rayss*)
6. Trogodytae (*troh-goh-DIH-teye*)

7. Arbores (*ah-BOH-rayss*)

8. Apis (*AH-pis*)

9. Funambulus (*foo-NAHM-boo-lus*)

10. Ostreae (*OHS-treh-eye*)

Write in Latin:

1. Peto

2. Venit

3. Concidunt

4. Applicat

5. Subruunt

Practice Makes Perfect 5

Translate from Latin into English:

1. Mushrooms are scattered.

2. Caesar is called dictator.

3. He is left.

4. It is said.

5. Money obligates.

Translate from English into Latin:

1. Caro consumitur.

2. Labor includitur.

3. Ostrea tenetur.

4. Pedes stipantur.

5. Aurum obruitur.

Chapter 6

Practice Makes Perfect 1

Translate from Latin into English:

1. To sleep

2. To bring, carry

3. To change

4. To do

5. To overcome

Translate these into Latin:

1. Ferre (*FEH-reh*)

2. Erigere (*eh-RIH-geh-reh*)

3. Esse (*ESS-eh*)

4. Mandare (*mahn-DAH-reh*)

5. Sublevare (*sub-leh-WAH-reh*)

Ready to translate into Latin?

1. Potest mandare. (*POH-test mahn-DAH-reh*)

2. Permutare (*pehr-moo-TAH-reh*)

3. Dormire est superare. (*dohr-MEE-reh ehst soo-pehr-AH-reh*)

4. Videtur esse (*wee-day-tur ESS-eh*)

5. Necesse est erigere. (*neh-keh-seh ehst eh-RIH-geh-reh*)

Practice Makes Perfect 2

Translate from Latin into English:

1. The diving boys
2. The grieving woman
3. Hanging garden
4. Acting
5. Listening

Translate from English into Latin:

1. Audientes
2. Peragens
3. Dolentes feminae
4. Urinans
5. Pendentes

Practice Makes Perfect 3

Translate:

1. It must be changed.
2. It must be done.

Now some gerunds:

1. Selling
2. Leading
3. Being careful
4. Getting up

Translate English into Latin:

1. Dolentis.
2. Dormiendum.
3. Tempus est peragendi.
4. Permutat ad vendendum.

Reviewing Verbals

Gerund: *vendendo, agendi, perficiendum*

Passive periphrastic: *curandum est, adicienda est*

Infinitive: *dormire, consistere, agere, dare*

Present participle: *stantium*

Chapter 7

Practice Makes Perfect 1

Matching:

volens—wanting

volitans—flying about

florens—flourishing

cadens—falling

clamans—shouting

providens—prudent

languens—drooping

Practice Makes Perfect 2

Translate:

1. Noble woman
2. Triumphal dinner
3. In the middle of the tail
4. Weak building
5. Roman people

The Most Agreeable Words

senatoris—nervosi

vasis—Graecis

coquus—bonus

denti—longo

hospitam—suavem

hippopotamus—absurdus

Practice Makes Perfect 3

Translate:

1. More noble
2. Longer
3. Most angry
4. Weakest
5. More common

Practice Makes Perfect 4

Translate:

1. I capture the flag.
2. I catch the goose.
3. I seize the elephant.
4. I uproot the trees.
5. The cook cooks dinner.
6. Work consumes time.
7. I look for Caesar.

Practice Makes Perfect 5

Turn the phrases into questions and then translate them (answers will vary):

1. Num vexillum capio? "I'm not capturing the flag, am I?"
2. Apprehendone anserem? "Am I grabbing the goose?"
3. Elephantumne capio? "Am I capturing the elephant?"
4. Nonne arbores subruo? "I'm uprooting trees, aren't I?"
5. Coquusne cenam coquit? "Is the cook cooking?"
6. Laborne tempus consumit? "Does work take time?"
7. Caesaremne peto? "Am I attacking Caesar?"

Chapter 8

Practice Makes Perfect 1

Translate from Latin into English:

1. Our father
2. Your sister
3. I am a dictator.
4. We the people
5. Your letter

Practice Makes Perfect 2

Translate from Latin into English:

1. She/That woman says.
2. He was.
3. She/This woman lies down.
4. They/Those people walk.
5. Her/his house

Practice Makes Perfect 3

Translate from Latin into English:

1. She grabs her brother.
2. He decorates his house.
3. This calamity
4. That thing
5. This net

Practice Makes Perfect 4

Translate from Latin into English:

1. You are sad.
2. You stop.
3. You hear.
4. You destroy.
5. You add on.

Chapter 9

Practice Makes Perfect 1

Match the faces with the adverb:

Humiliter	
Laete	
Sane	
Innocenter	
Suaviter	
Absurde	
Calide	
Misere	
Irate	
Frigide	

Practice Makes Perfect 2

Translate:

1. Hodie, non mane

2. Numquam secunda hora

3. Irate

Now translate the Latin into English:

1. Two and two make four.

2. Now or never

3. Then and now

Chapter 10

Practice Makes Perfect 1

1. We were making.

2. They were carrying.

3. We were.

4. He was giving.

5. You were doing.

Practice Makes Perfect 2

1. You will say.

2. We will be.

3. I will love.

4. You will be able.

5. They will have.

Practice Makes Perfect 3

1. I have asked.

2. He has carried away.

3. He did not want.

4. He had surpassed.

5. She had moved.

Practice Makes Perfect 4

Try yelling these commands:

1. Eat!

2. Move!

3. Don't move!

4. Go!

5. Carry!

Practice Makes Perfect 5

1. **Fuimus:** 1st plural present perf. active. "We have been"

2. **Misit:** 3rd sing., present perf. active. "He has sent"

3. **Veni:** 1st sing,. present perf. active. "I came"

4. **Veniebant:** 3rd pl., imperfect, active. "They were coming"

5. **Potueram:** 1st sing., pluperfect active. "I had been able"

6. **Amavit:** 3rd sing., pres. perf. active. "He has loved"

7. **Factum est:** 3rd sing., pres. perf. passive. "It has been done"

8. **Data erant:** 3rd pl., pluperf. passive. "They had been given"

9. **Steti:** 1st sing, pres. perf. active. "I stood"

10. **Ceperint:** 3rd pl., future perf. active. "They will have taken"

Chapter 11

Practice Makes Perfect 1

Translate these prepositional phrases:

1. To the house

2. By the sister

3. From the number of shells

4. After dinner

5. By the priest

Practice Makes Perfect 2

1. He goes out.

2. He goes in.

3. I walk in.

4. He arrives.

5. He led away.

Practice Makes Perfect 3

Choose the proper interjection:

1. Hei

2. Oh

3. Eheu

4. Oi

5. Io

6. Minime

7. Io

8. Ohe

Respond in Latin:

1. Are you an architect? *Reader's choice*

2. Do you love asparagus? *Reader's choice*

3. Does the elephant climb a tree? *Minime.*

4. Do you live in a fishpond? *Reader's choice*

5. Do you love to read? *Reader's choice*

6. Is the farmer a good man? *Certe.*

7. Does the Queen of Sheba live in your house? *Reader's choice*

Chapter 12

Practice Makes Perfect 1

Translate these sentence fragments:

1. When you see a star
2. Before I read a book
3. After the soldier walks across the road
4. At the same time as they sing
5. Although the road is long

Practice Makes Perfect 2

1. The dog having been fed, we made the trip.
2. The farmer having been pleased, the horses were led from the city.
3. When the toga was put on, the senator walked out of the house.
4. The Lord having been born, we sing in church.
5. The republic having been saved, Cicero was praised.

Practice Makes Perfect 3

1. He was born.
2. I speak.
3. They were going forth.
4. I suffered.
5. Are you wandering?

Chapter 13

Practice Makes Perfect 1

Fill in the correct pronoun:

1. Which
2. Whom
3. Who
4. Whom
5. Whose

Practice Makes Perfect 2

1. cervus
2. femina
3. epistula
4. vir or Caesar
5. Bos
6. vir or Caesar

Practice Makes Perfect 3

Translate the following clauses:

1. The line in which you warn me
2. She to whom Quintus sent a table
3. I who abstained from oysters
4. The kernels which are pearls
5. He who first invented hanging baths

Practice Makes Perfect 4

Translate from Latin into English:

1. A certain deer has a red nose.

2. Which cow jumped over the moon?

3. Invite whomever you wish.

4. Caesar himself had a catapult.

Chapter 14

Practice Makes Perfect 1

1. Expectatio ludi

2. Pellis cervi

3. Cibus canis

4. Forma frontis

5. Quies otii

Practice Makes Perfect 2

1. Many praise some so that they may be praised by others.

2. Many were praising some so that they would be praised by others.

3. He sent slaves into the shop to seize the friend.

Clauses with a Result

1. He made such a noise that it was necessary to leave.

2. He loved the eel to such a degree that he sat in the fishpond.

Practice Makes Perfect 3

1. … because he was special. (d)

2. … when there is nothing to do. (e)

3. … in order to capture the deer. (c)

4. … when we hear a story. (b)

5. … if my dog was away. (a)

Translate from Latin into English:

1. When Caesar heard these things, he ordered the soldiers to retreat.

2. Since these things are so, I will go to Rome.

3. I did these things, while it was permitted.

4. While these things were being done, the slaves left.

5. Stay at home until I return.

6. If he stays, he lives.

Chapter 15

Practice Makes Perfect 1

1. I saw nothing.

2. I come to the line written across.

3. They grab the tail.

4. We left Arpinati.

5. He cut the nerves.

Practice Makes Perfect 2

1. The gourmets season mushrooms, boiled greens, and grasses.
2. The noble man carries away this statue.
3. Sergius Orata invented the fish-ponds.
4. The wife added earrings.
5. The cavemen climb trees.
6. I inquired diligently.
7. Some are single.
8. There is silence.
9. One horn stands out.
10. The kernels fall.

Practice Makes Perfect 3

1. I come to the line written across in which you warn me.
2. The day made it happen that Quintus remained in Arcanum.
3. She said, "I myself am a guest," because Statius had gone ahead to see to dinner for us.
4. We all reclined except her, to whom Quintus sent a table.
5. The gourmets want to add among the honored those things born from the earth which have been excluded from the law.

Chapter 16

Practice Makes Perfect 1

Translate the following compound sentence:

1. In the noble city of Ephesus, Greeks lived and it is said that an unfair law was enacted.
2. An architect receives a public job and sets his price.
3. The shape of an elk is similar to a goat but is a little bit bigger.
4. They lean themselves on trees and in such a way take a rest.
5. Either they uproot the trees by the roots or cut them.
6. They knock the weakened trees down with their weight and they themselves fall.
7. Cavemen of Ethiopia feed themselves by hunting alone and daily climb trees.
8. He plants his feet on the left thigh and cuts the hamstring with his right hand.
9. The elephant is slowed by his leg and in a short time is dead.
10. And so it had bothered me that she had spoken so sharply.

Practice Makes Perfect 2

1. If not more than a quarter of the cost is used up in the work, it is added to the estimate with no penalty.

2. They do not lie down to rest nor, if they fall down by accident, are they able to straighten out and get up.

Practice Makes Perfect 3

Statements by ancient authors:

1. Quintus told me that she did not want to sleep with him.

2. They say that he is most wise who knows himself what the work is.

3. Gullible hope encourages life and says that tomorrow will always be better.

4. For no one is so old as to think that he is not able to live for one more year.

Practice Makes Perfect 4

Some examples of indirect questions:

1. Do not wonder when this happened and how I am suffering.

2. He promises to say how much the cost will be.

3. To not know what happened before you were born is to always remain a child.

4. Now I know what love is.

5. Many doubt what would be best.

Practice Makes Perfect 5

1. Quintus remained in Arcanum.

2. The next morning he came to me in Aquinum.

3. He told me that she did not want to sleep with him.

4. When she had left, she was of the same mood as I had seen.

Chapter 19

Sentences You Can Read—Review of Cases

1. Romulus the king died.

2. The good king cried.

3. The books of the Holy Scriptures are read often.

4. He is in your province.

5. Marius freed Italy.

6. He went across the river.

7. They say that Plato came to Italy.

8. Romulus reigned for 37 years.

9. Oh, poor me!

10. He gave the signal to the soldiers.

11. I have never pleased myself.

12. He persuaded the Helvetians easily.

13. My name is Caesar.

14. The duty of the consul is to give commands.

15. The thigh of an elephant is large.

16. He sent a thousand soldiers.

17. The bravest of all these are the Belgians.

18. A pearl comes out of the shell.

19. He is loved by them.

20. Nothing is more pleasing than life.

21. Elks are protected by horns.

22. They live by hunting alone.

23. In that very year, Ennius was born.

24. The land captured, Caesar gave part to the soldiers.

25. It is bad to be sad.

26. To err is human.

27. These golden vases are on the table.

More Sentences You Can Read— Review of Verb Usage

1. Romulus founded a city.

2. Glory often follows work.

3. Wise men live happily.

4. In the city of Ephesus, a Greek king remained with the queen.

5. I shall write to you.

6. Castor and Pollux were seen fighting from their horses.

7. A man had been dragged by a boy from the water.

8. The noise was heard by the crowd.

9. It is a rare bird.

10. As many men there are, there are as many opinions.

11. Art is long, life, short.

12. What is this to me?

13. Free the republic from fear.

14. Do not wish what cannot be done.

15. Let him conquer.

16. In the world, God is he who reigns, who governs, who watches over the courses of the stars.

17. By God the world was built.

18. The king is loved greatly.

19. I was wondering at this.

20. Men believe what they want.

21. I hope that the memory of our friendship will be eternal.

More Hints for Translating

Even more sentences you can read:

1. If we conquer, all will be safe.

2. Fortune favors the brave.

3. Do not the nightly guard on the Palatine, the watchers of the city, the fear of the people, the meeting of all good men, the fortification of the senate's meeting place, the faces and expressions of these men move you?

Chapter 21

Practice Makes Perfect 1

1. Recipe quater in die per os. "Take four times a day by mouth."

2. Nocte tres guttae per os. "At night, three drops by mouth."

3. Cum aqua ad libitum. "With water, freely."

4. Ante cibos sine aqua. "Before meals, without water."

5. Hora somni viginti quinque guttae. "At bedtime, 25 drops."

Chapter 24

Grammar Review for Nouns

A noun is a **person, place,** or **thing.** The **case** ending tells how the noun is used in the sentence. Nouns are grouped in **declensions.** The first declension is characterized by the letter *a.* The second by the letter *o* the third by the letter *e.* The genitive case is translated by *of* or *'s.*

Nouns come in three genders, **masculine, feminine,** and **neuter.** Most first declension nouns are **feminine,** second declension nouns are either **masculine** or **neuter.** Third declension has all three genders.

A pronoun takes the place of a **noun.** Personal pronouns take the place of **persons.** Third person pronouns sometimes take the place of **things.** In English the reflexive pronouns have the suffix **self.**

Vocabulary Review

1. *Reader's choice;* some examples are amicus, lautus, filius, mater, pater.

2. *Reader's choice;* some examples are aqua (water), epistula (letter), piscina (fishpond), terra (land). All are feminine.

3. *Reader's choice*; some examples are populus (people), servus (slave), mundus (world), lectus (bed). All are masculine.

4. Neuter. aedificia, aura, consilia, dicta.

5.
   a. soleae
   b. pullus
   c. canis
   d. vinum

6.
   a. professor
   b. gladiator
   c. student
   d. dictator

7.
   a. ego
   b. tu
   c. nos
   d. vos

8.
   a. this student
   b. those flip-flops
   c. his/her wine

Translation Practice

1.
   a. she
   b. he
   c. my brother
   d. I love you.
   e. Call me Ishmael.

Grammar Talk (Review for Verbs)

1.
   mus—we
   o—I
   tis—you pl.
   ntur—they
   s—you sing.
   tur—he, she, it

2.
   a. A verbal is a verb form that can be used as a noun or adjective.
   b. *Reader's choice*; example: To look at. Spectare
   c. ing
   d. noun or adjective
   e. must be ———ed

Vocabulary Practice

1.

    a. sudat (she sweats)

    b. refert (he carries back)

    c. consumit (she uses up)

2. *Reader's choice of subject*

    a. They warn.

    b. Birds fly around.

    c. It stands out.

3.

    a. Money is taken out.

    b. The house is decorated.

    c. Cavemen jump down.

Translation Practice

1.

    a. He wants to sleep.

    b. He seems to drive.

    c. It is necessary to get up.

2.

    a. audientes

    b. peragens

    c. dolentes feminae

3.

    a. To be or not to be.

    b. Carthage must be destroyed.

    c. Way of working.

4. Wicked citizens want to deprive the Roman people of life, destroy the empire, and extinguish the name of the Roman people.

Chapter 25

Adjectives and Adverbs Grammar Review

Adjectives agree with the noun they modify in **number, gender,** and **case.** Some adjectives are used as **nouns,** such as the "blues" and *reader's choice* **"goods."** Adjectives can show comparisons by using their comparative and superlative endings. An example of a comparative adjective in Latin is *reader's choice* **"longior"** and an example of a superlative adjective in Latin is *reader's choice* **"longissimus."** The comparative degree is translated **"more"** and the superlative, **"most."**

The accusative case is used for the **direct object** of a verb.

Questions in Latin are shown by the use of an **interrogative word,** the adding of *-ne* to the first word or by beginning the sentence with *num* or *nonne.*

Adverbs in English usually end in *-ly* and modify verbs, adjectives or other adverbs. Latin adverbs often end in *-e* or *-iter.*

The dative case is used for the **indirect** object and the ablative case is used often. Two of the most common ablatives are *reader's choice* **agent, means, accompaniment.**

1.
   a. unde
   b. ita
   c. semper
   d. primum
   e. interea

2.
poplites/mutili

dei/immortales

cibum/nullum

res/medias

aedificiis/publicis

cornu/praeacutum

corporis/alterius

3.
   a. opus publicum
   b. lex vetusta
   c. homo alienus
   d. arbores propinquas
   e. balineas pensiles
   f. cura tota
   g. apes singuli
   h. Graecia magna
   i. Romani populi

4.
   a. The Belgians inhabit one part. unam partem
   b. The Aquitani inhabit another part. aliam partem
   c. The Gauls inhabit a third part. tertiam partem

Verb Tense Grammar Review

The first principal part of *amo* is *amo* and is translated **"I love."** The second principal part is *amare* and is translated **"to love."** The third principal part is *amavi* and is translated **"I have loved,"** and the fourth principal part is *amatus* and is translated **"having been loved."**

The sign of the imperfect tense is **ba** and is translated **was or were ——— ing.** The sign of the future tense in the first and second conjugations is **bi** or **bu.** In the third and fourth conjugation, it's **a** in the first person and **e** in all the rest.

The present perfect tense has endings with a lot of **i's.** The past perfect tense has endings with *-era,* and the future perfect tense has endings that resemble the future tense of the verb **to be.**

The imperative form is used to give a command and is often the second principal part without the *-re.*

Vocabulary Practice

1.
- a. We exercised.
- b. He was able.
- c. I was throwing.
- d. You were seizing.
- e. They was sweating.

2.
- a. Speak!
- b. Sell!
- c. Dive!

3.
- a. invadere
- b. movi
- c. venio, ventus
- d. vidi, visus

Translation Work

1.
- a. I hang out in the bar.
- b. The Princeton Tigers play in the arena.
- c. They have been washed.
- d. They threw.

2.
- a. They thought.
- b. He did.
- c. He persuaded.
- d. They ordered.
- e. He moves.

3.
- a. Consulem vidi. "I saw the consul."
- b. Viros invitavero. "I shall have invited the men."
- d. Multa praeterivi. "I have overlooked many things."
- e. Homo canem deportavit. "The man carried away the dog."
- g. Quaesivi diligenter. "I inquired diligently."
- h. Femina fabulam narravit. "The wife told the story."
- j. Unum cornu exstetit. "One horn stood out."

Chapter 26

Phrases and Clauses Grammar Review

1. c
2. c
3. c
4. a
5. c
6. c

Phrases and Clauses Vocabulary Review

1.
    a. against violence
    b. to watch (for the purpose of watching)
    c. toward me

2.
    a. astrum—star
    b. magnopere—greatly
    c. lego—I read
    d. hortus—garden
    e. palor—I wander
    f. celer—swift
    g. mas—male
    h. sella—chair
    i. puer—boy

3.
    a. sub/supra
    b. ante/post
    c. parvus/magnus
    d. puer/puella
    e. eugepae/vah
    f. mortuus/vivus
    g. rideo/doleo
    h. progredior/regredior

Translation Practice

1.
    a. The eels which he loved
    b. "Hecyra" which I was never allowed to present in silence
    c. Members among which are hands, mouth, teeth
    d. Cow whose one horn stands out

2.
    a. The council having been called together
    b. When C. Marius and L. Valerius were consuls, the Greek was not pleased.
    c. The dinner began, the table having been brought in
    d. These things having been said, Caesar left the rostrum.

3.
    a. He died.
    b. Going out, the boy shouts.
    c. I have promised.
    d. The god has spoken out.

Grammar Review of Subjunctive and More Clauses

The **imperative** mood of a verb gives a command. The **indicative** mood of a verb indicates something is happening. The **subjunctive** mood of a verb shows an action that might happen. An example of the subjunctive mood in Latin is *reader's choice* **fiat.** In English the helping verbs **let** or **may** are used to introduce clauses that usually have the verb in the subjunctive. The subordinate conjunctions **ut** and **ne** are used to introduce clauses that usually have the verb in the subjunctive. Purpose clauses begin in English with the words **in order to. Result** clauses usually follow words such as "in such a way," "so that," or "with the result that."

A **complex** sentence is a simple sentence with a subordinate clause. Indirect statements come after verbs of stating, such as *dico.* The subject in Latin is in the **accusative** case and the verb in the **infinitive** mood.

Vocabulary Review

1.
   a. pondus
   b. cibum
   c. dulcis
   d. ambulo

2.
   a. pondus officii
   b. species terrae
   c. radix arboris

3.
   a. praestarent—they took charge of
   b. fuit is indicative—he was
   c. exirent—they went out
   d.   exspectare is infinitive—to await
   e. petissent—they begged
   f. pervenit is indicative—either "he arrives," or "he arrived."
   g. fiat—let there be!
   h. eamus—let's go!
   i. proficisci is infinitive—to set out

Translation Practice

1.
   a. He made such a noise it was necessary to leave.
   b. He loved the eel to such a degree that he sat in the fishpond.
   c. I am a guest myself.
   d. I suffer daily.

2.

    a. Let us rejoice

    b. The beds are cold.

    c. I, who abstained from oysters and eels, was brought down by a beet and marrow.

    d. When all the flesh has been worn down, the centers of the bodies, which are pearls, fall to the bottom.

Index

M

Q

T

W–X–Y–Z

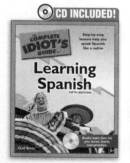

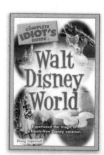